Indian foreign policy

MANCHESTER
1824

Manchester University Press

Indian foreign policy

An overview

Harsh V. Pant

Manchester University Press

Published by Manchester University Press
Altrincham Street, Manchester M1 7JA
www.manchesteruniversitypress.co.uk

British Library Cataloguing-in-Publication Data
A catalogue record for this book is available from the British Library

Library of Congress Cataloging-in-Publication Data applied for

ISBN 978 1 7849 9335 1 hardback
ISBN 978 1 7849 9336 8 paperback

First published 2016

Typeset by Out of House Publishing
Printed in Great Britain by Bell and Bain Ltd, Glasgow

To the loving memory of Ija

Contents

Preface

Indian foreign policy has been rapidly evolving over the last two decades. As India has risen economically and militarily in recent years, its political clout on the global stage has also seen a commensurate increase. From the peripheries of international affairs, India is now at the center of major power politics. It is viewed as a major balancer in the Asia-Pacific, a major democracy that can be a major ally of the West in countering China even as India continues to challenge the West on a whole range of issues – non-proliferation, global trade and climate change.

Indian foreign policy was largely driven by a sense of idealism since its independence in 1947. India viewed global norms as important as it kept a leash on the interests of great powers and gave New Delhi "strategic autonomy" to pursue its interests. But as India itself has emerged as a major global power, its foreign policy has moved towards greater "strategic realism."

This book is an overview of Indian foreign policy as it has evolved in recent times. The focus of the book is on the 21st century with historical context provided as appropriate. It is an introductory book on Indian foreign policy and is not intended to be a detailed examination of any of its particular aspects. It examines India's relationships with major powers, with its neighbors and other regions, as well as India's stand on major global issues. With a gradual accretion in its powers, India has become more aggressive in the pursuit of its interests, thereby emerging as an important player in the shaping of the global order in the new millennium. Since all issues, regions, and countries cannot be covered in a single volume, small snapshots of important issues have been provided in each section.

This project has taken a few years to materialize and I am thankful to Manchester University Press and Orient BlackSwan for helping me in the process. A number of individuals helped me with various parts of the book. Special thanks to Frank O'Donnell, Yogesh Joshi, Kundan Singh, and Deeksha Tewari for their assistance! My wife, Tuhina, and daughter, Vaidehi, remain very patient with me despite my occasional negligence. There is no way to fully acknowledge their roles nor would I want to try it. This book is dedicated to the memory of my grandmother, Ija, who passed away while I was working on this project. I will always cherish the time I got to spend with her and the sheer joie de vivre which she brought to my life and to everyone else's she managed to touch. For that and for everything else, I will always be grateful.

1

Introduction

In November 2008, the financial capital of India, Mumbai, was struck by terrorists who the Indian (as well as the American and the British) intelligence later confirmed had received extensive training from the Pakistan-based group, Lashkar-e-Toiba, or Army of the Pure. Given the sophistication of planning and execution involved, it soon became apparent that this was a commando-style operation that possibly had the involvement of a state actor. As physical evidence mounted in terms of satellite phone calls, equipment and boats used for the attack, Pakistan's hand was seen as smeared all over the operation. Though India conceded that probably the newly installed civilian administration in Islamabad of Asif Ali Zardari was not behind the attacks, the army and the Inter Services Intelligence (ISI) were seen as the main culprit.[1]

The public outcry after the Mumbai attacks was strong enough for the Indian government to consider using the military option vis-à-vis Pakistan. But it soon turned out that India no longer had the capability of imposing quick and effective retribution on Pakistan and that it no longer enjoyed the kind of conventional superiority vis-à-vis its regional adversary that it had enjoyed for the past five decades.[2] This was a surprising conclusion for a nation that the international community regarded as a major global economic and military power, pursuing a defense modernization program estimated to be over US$50 billion over the next five years.

A year earlier, in another incident that confounded observers, India's Cabinet Secretary sent a note to all the ministers of his government advising them against attending a function organized by the Gandhi Peace Foundation on behalf of the Dalai Lama.[3] A number of reasons were alluded to for such an action. Perhaps the Prime Minister wished to assuage the concerns of the Indian communist parties, then part of the ruling coalition, that the Indian foreign policy was tilting toward Washington in order to send the message that India desired to preserve the upward trajectory in Sino-Indian ties. Yet outside observers remained perplexed about the goals of the Indian government, since it contravened India's long-held position that the Dalai Lama is a not a mere political dissident but a spiritual leader widely revered in India. Indeed some argued that India's genuflection to Chinese concerns about the Dalai Lama were probably not even in India's national interest. The Indian government's position neither lived up to the ideals that India often claims it stands for nor clearly enhanced India's strategic interests vis-à-vis China. When the Chinese authorities subsequently cracked down on the Tibetan protests in Lhasa and elsewhere during the Olympic torch relay, the Indian government could not even bring itself to forcefully condemn the Chinese behavior.[4] For the Indian government, it seemed a tough balancing act but for the rest of the world it was a supine foreign policy posture by a state that wants to be recognized as an emerging great power.

These episodes are symptomatic of the fundamental crisis facing Indian foreign policy at the beginning of this new millennium. As India's weight has grown in the international system in recent years, there's a perception that India is on the cusp of achieving "great power" status. It is repeated ad nauseam in the Indian and often in global media and India is already being asked to behave like one. There is just one problem: Indian policy-makers themselves are not clear as to what this status of a great power entails. At a time when the Indian foreign policy establishment should be vigorously debating the nature and scope of India's engagement with the world, it is disappointingly silent. This intellectual vacuum has allowed Indian foreign policy to drift without any sense of direction and the result is that as the world is looking to India to shape the emerging international order, India has little to offer except some platitudinous rhetoric that does great disservice to India's rising global stature.

As India makes its ascent in the global inter-state hierarchy, two issues have emerged as significant in defining its future trajectory. One, India will have to exploit the extant structure of international system to its advantage. Structural constraints are the most formidable ones a state encounters in its drive toward the status of a major power. Yet, Indian foreign policy continues to be reactive to the strategic environment and the constraints it imposes rather than trying to shape the strategic realities. While such an ad hoc response to the structural imperatives carried little cost when India was on the periphery of global politics, this can have grave consequences now when Indian capabilities have risen to a point where it seems poised to play a significant role in global politics. A second related constraint that India faces is its discomfort with the very notion of power and in particular its wariness of the use of "hard power." All major powers throughout history have demonstrated an ability to skillfully use military as an effective instrument of national policy. India's reluctance to evolve a more sophisticated understanding of power and of military power in particular will continue to underline the strategic diffidence that has come to be associated with Indian foreign and security policy.

India's rise

If the global balance of power is indeed shifting from the Atlantic to the Pacific, then the rise of India, along with China, is clearly the indisputable reality that few can dare to dismiss any longer. As a consequence, India is now being called upon to shoulder global responsibilities from the challenges of nuclear proliferation to the instability in the Persian Gulf and is increasingly being viewed as much more than a mere "South Asian" power. From a nation that was mortgaging its gold reserves in 1990 to one whose foreign exchange reserves are overfull, from a nation that was marginal in the global distribution of economic might to one that is increasingly emerging as one of the centers of modern global economy, India has indeed come a long way. Its economy is one of the fastest growing in the world; it is a nuclear weapon state (NWS), a status that is being grudgingly accepted by the world; its armed forces are highly professional, on the way toward rapid modernization; and its vibrant democratic institutions, with the world's second largest Muslim population, are attracting global attention at a time when the Islamic world is passing through some turbulent times.

According to the assessment of Goldman Sachs, by 2040, the four largest economies will be those of China, the United States, India, and Japan.[5] India will overtake the G-6 economies faster than earlier expected and India's GDP, in all likelihood, will surpass that of the United States before 2050, making it the second largest economy after China. After decades of marginalization due to the vagaries of the Cold War, its own obsolescent model of economic management and the seemingly never-ending tensions with Pakistan, India is starting to display flashes of self-confidence that come with growing capabilities. Its global and regional ambitions are rising and it is showing an aggressiveness in its foreign policy that had not been its forte before. Yet it remains far from obvious that in line with these trends the India of today is also crafting a foreign policy that is in tandem with its rising stature in the international system. The costs of ignoring the structural imperatives will only rise in the future as India continues its ascent in the global inter-state hierarchy.[6]

A nation's foreign policy flows from several sources: from the international system to its domestic political imperatives to the cultural factors that underlie its society to the personal characteristics and perceptions of individual decision-makers. Like most nations, India's foreign policy is also a result of these varied factors at different levels of analysis interacting and transforming each other. But as a nation's weight in the global balance of power rises, it becomes imperative to pay greater attention to the systemic constraints. As has been pointed out:

rising states have choices about whether to become great powers. However, a state's freedom to choose whether to become great power is in reality tightly constrained by structural factors. Eligible states that fail to attain great power status are predictably punished. If policy-makers of eligible states are socialised to the international system's constraints, they understand that attaining great power status is a pre-requisite if their states are be secure and autonomous.[7]

States do not emerge as great powers because they excel in one or another kind of capability. They have to rely on their combined capabilities in order to serve their interests. Therefore, the economic, military, territorial, demographic, and political capabilities of a state cannot be weighed in isolation of each other.[8] Great powers dominate and shape international politics and their behaviour is largely a product of their external environment. It is the structure of the international system that more than anything else shapes the foreign policies of great powers.

By any objective measure of material capability, India is a rising power in the international system and the consequences of an India that is rising are very visible in the international system. India is not a great power yet though it is most certainly a leading contender for great power status. India's rising wealth and large population are its latent power that India is and will be using to build up its military might.[9] As a result, it is not at all surprising that India is being asked to step up to the plate and shoulder global responsibilities in consonance with its rising global stature. What is less clear is whether Indian foreign policy is up to the task and whether Indian policy-makers are willing to make the right kind of choices.

Indian foreign policy: Cold War and after

Throughout the Cold War period, India was concerned about getting entangled in the superpower rivalry. It made sense to make a choice in favor of a non-aligned foreign policy posture that at least in theory preserved India's decision-making autonomy in the realm of international affairs. Behind all the rhetoric of the so-called Third World solidarity, there was a very cool-headed calculation that was aimed at protecting vital Indian interests, interests that were fairly limited in scope, given India's relatively limited economic and military capabilities. Pakistan's security strategy was India's most immediate threat and India's obsession with Pakistan was not all that surprising. But beyond Pakistan, there was little clarity, something that was vividly brought home in the stunning defeat at the hands of the Chinese in 1962. And even on Pakistan, there is little evidence to suggest that India had a coherent strategy.

Immediately at Independence, before any sort of foreign policy framework could be established, India's first Prime Minister, Jawaharlal Nehru, was required to address the inter-related problems of Kashmir and relations with Pakistan, which have remained an important strand in Indian foreign policy ever since. Yet there is little evidence to suggest that India has ever evolved a coherent policy for countering Pakistan's security strategy, still less for resolving the Kashmir problem. Instead, India has reacted to events. The wars with Pakistan kept coming and India kept fighting them without ever apparently making an assessment of whether a policy could be crafted to obviate the need for war. It is instructive to note how for the last six decades India has struggled to deal with the malevolence of a single hostile neighbor one-eighth its size.

More generally, Nehru wanted to construct a distinctive Indian approach to foreign policy issues, taking a certain distance from the views of the former colonial power. For almost two decades his concerns about getting entangled in the superpower rivalry found expression in support for the non-aligned movement (NAM) that, at least in theory, preserved India's decision-making autonomy in the realm of international affairs. The NAM was started when newly decolonized nations that did not want to join either of the two military blocs got together to assert their autonomy, their plea for disarmament, and greater development aid. The NAM did have a certain weight in the era of decolonization, yet mere reiteration of their non-aligned credentials did not prevent individual nations from having close relations with major powers such as the United States, the erstwhile Soviet Union, and the United Kingdom. For all their pious declarations on global peace, the non-aligned nations have rarely shared significant convergence of interests and have even fought among themselves. The NAM was an impotent observer to the eight-year Iran–Iraq conflict and several other direct and indirect conflicts among its member states. India's rhetoric about solidarity with the Third World was largely a function of India's limited capabilities and commensurate interests.

In 1962, the limitations of this policy were vividly brought home by the stunning defeat at the hands of the Chinese, which virtually spelled the end of the Nehru era in Indian politics. But there was no real change to the direction of Indian foreign policy and, in 1971, India was again forced to reckon with global forces, in the run-up to the war with Pakistan over Bangladesh. Since the very beginning Pakistan had been a close ally of the United States, thereby balancing Indian preponderance in the subcontinent rather effectively. When it became clear that the West, especially the United States, would not support India against Pakistan, Indira Gandhi was forced to court the Soviet Union to make sure that she would be able to carry forward her war without any involvement from the great powers. Thus, even though the United States dispatched the USS *Enterprise* to the Bay of Bengal as a show of support for Pakistan, India, with the Soviet Union on its side, successfully prosecuted its war against Pakistan and Bangladesh was born.

The one arena of foreign and security policy where India has had a long-term perspective is its approach to the nuclear question. Though at times the overall policy was contradictory and its various strands at cross-purposes, India was able to carve out a coherent policy that served its needs with great efficacy. The Chinese exploded their nuclear device in 1964. Coming on the heels of Indian defeat in 1962, this explosion shook the Indian foreign policy elite and gave a sense of urgency to the Indian nuclear program. The first option that Indian government went for was the support of the West, essentially seeking a nuclear umbrella. When the Indian efforts were rebuffed, there was no option but to consolidate its own indigenous nuclear weapons program. India's efforts in the nuclear realm culminated in what the then Indian government rather disingenuously termed the Peaceful Nuclear Explosion in 1974. Immediate sanctions were imposed by the international community on India and India was left out of the global high-technology regime, with long-term consequences for its economic and technological development.

These sanctions were also a result of India's opposition to the Nuclear Non-Proliferation Treaty (NPT) that India had argued was fundamentally discriminatory in nature by creating a two-tiered state system of nuclear haves and have-nots. The five states that were allowed to keep their nuclear programs had all become nuclear powers before 1968 while the remaining states were not to pursue nuclear weapons programs. India argued that only global and comprehensive nuclear disarmament was acceptable, and that in its absence it would not be willing to give up its right to pursue its nuclear weapons program if its security interests so demanded. India viewed the NPT as an instrument of the NWS to get their nuclear stockpiles legitimized by the comity of nations and therefore a tool to perpetuate their nuclear hegemony. It was a very *realpolitik* approach to the global nuclear politics and India successfully played this card until such time as it developed an indigenous nuclear weapons capability which it demonstrated to the world in 1998. Today, when India has emerged as a de facto nuclear weapons state, it wants to be a part of the same "hegemonistic" security architecture that it once decried so vociferously. The two mainstream political parties, the Congress and the Bharatiya Janata Party (BJP), have had a similar approach on nuclear issues ever since the former Indian Prime Minister, Rajiv Gandhi, initiated weaponization in the late 1980s. Traditionally, only the communist parties have not supported the Indian nuclear weapons program but they have generally been marginal in Indian national security decision-making.

The Bangladesh War was the beginning of twenty years of a close relationship between India and the Soviet Union, so close that India did not even dare to criticize the Soviet misadventure in Afghanistan in 1979. But India's balance of power approach, though skillful, was essentially reactive in nature, not based on any strategic assessment of its long-term foreign policy priorities. Though the era of decolonization had largely come to an end, the principles of the NAM were still upheld, and India's self-identification with the colonized found expression in Rajiv Gandhi's criticisms of Margaret Thatcher's policy on Rhodesia/Zimbabwe. In the mid-1980s Indian policy-makers seem to have been attracted by a more assertive policy toward India's neighbors, though this "Regional Gendarme" role had mixed results. The economic blockade of Nepal certainly helped bring down the absolute monarchy, but the intervention in Sri Lanka caused more problems than it solved, while incidentally leading to Rajiv's assassination. But, as it happened, the collapse of the Soviet Union and the consequent collapse of the Indian economy soon occupied center stage. In some ways, the end of the Cold War came as a blessing in disguise as Indian policy-makers were forced to adapt to the new global political and economic realities. The economic crisis that India faced in the early 1990s forced it to move away from the dominant Nehruvian socialist paradigm toward economic liberalization and a greater integration into the global economy. At the same time, the demise of the former Soviet Union changed the nature of the international system.

Many of the central assumptions of Indian foreign policy had to be reviewed in light of changed circumstances. The shape of the world changed, signaling the possibility of a new Indian foreign and national security strategy. A rapidly shifting geo-strategic landscape confronted India as it made its way up in the inter-state hierarchy. At the beginning of the new millennium, India is poised on the threshold of achieving the status of a major global power, emerging as an indispensable, albeit reluctant, element of the new global order exemplified not only by its growing economic and military might but also the attraction of its political and cultural values. But even as India's rise in the inter-state global hierarchy continues steadily, its policy-makers continue to act in the international arena as if India can continue to afford the luxury of responding to foreign policy challenges on a case-by-case basis without any requirement for a long-term strategic policy framework. The same ad-hocism that had characterized Indian foreign policy in the past continues. The problem, however, is India no longer has the luxury of time on its side and the issues that have gone unresolved since India's independence need a long-term resolution. Whatever the merits or otherwise of NAM, it is clear that the Indian foreign policy establishment continues to rigidly hold on to the concepts and intellectual frameworks which may have had some utility when they were developed but which have become outmoded in the present strategic context.

Power and interest

How states respond to their relative material rise or decline has long been central to understanding the forces that shape international politics. Structural constraints force states toward a particular set of foreign policies in line with their relative position in the international system. And as that position undergoes a change, so will change the foreign policy of that state. A state, therefore, will become more ambitious in defining the scale and scope of its foreign policy as its relative material power capabilities increase and vice versa. Indian policy-makers will have to make some crucial and necessary choices in the realm of foreign policy as India reaches a turning point in its relations with the rest of the world, the most important of which will deal with how best to exploit the extant structure of the international system to their nation's advantage.

But a fundamental quandary that has long dogged India in the realm of foreign affairs and that has become even more acute with India's ascent in the international order is what has been referred to as India's lack of an "instinct for power." Power lies at the heart of international politics. It affects the influence that states exert over one another, thereby shaping political outcomes. The success and failure of a nation's foreign policy is largely a function of its power and the manner in which that power is wielded. The exercise of power can be shocking and at times corrupting but power is absolutely necessary to fight the battles that must be fought. India's ambivalence about power and its use has resulted in a situation where even as India's economic and military capabilities have gradually expanded, it has failed to evolve a commensurate strategic agenda and requisite institutions so as to be able to mobilize and use its resources most optimally.

India faces a unique conundrum: its political elites desperately want global recognition for India as a major power and all the prestige and authority associated with it. Yet, they continue to be reticent about the acquisition and use of power in foreign affairs. This ambivalence about the use of power in international relations where "any prestige or authority eventually rely upon traditional measures of power, whether military or economic"[10] is curious as the Indian political elites have rarely shied away from the maximization of power in the realm of domestic politics, thereby corroding the institutional fabric of liberal democracy in the country.

In what has been diagnosed as a "mini state syndrome," those states which do not have the material capabilities to make a difference to the outcomes at the international level, often denounce the concept of power in foreign policy-making.[11] India had long been a part of such states, viewing itself as an object of the foreign policies of a small majority of powerful nations. As a consequence, the Indian political and strategic elite developed a suspicion of power politics with the word power itself acquiring a pejorative connotation in so far as foreign policy was concerned. The relationship between power and foreign policy was never fully understood, leading to a progressive loss in India's ability to wield power effectively in the international realm.

Inability to use force effectively

A nation's vital interests, in the ultimate analysis, can only be preserved and enhanced if the nation has sufficient power capabilities at its disposal. But not only must a nation possess such capabilities, there must also be a willingness to employ the required forms of power in pursuit of those interests.

India's lack of an instinct for power is most palpable in the realm of the military where unlike other major global powers of the past and the present India has failed to master the creation, deployment, and use of its military instruments in support of its national objectives.[12] Nehru envisioned making India a global leader without any help from the nation's armed forces, arguing, "the right approach to defense is to avoid having unfriendly relations with other countries – to put it differently, war today is, and ought to be, out of question."[13] War has been systematically factored out of Indian foreign policy and the national security matrix with the resulting ambiguity about India's ability to withstand major wars of the future.

Few nations face the kind of security challenges that confront India. Yet, since independence military was never seen as a central instrument in the achievement of Indian national priorities with the tendency of Indian political elites to downplay the importance of military power, India ignored the defense sector after independence and paid inadequate attention to its defense needs. Even though the policy-makers themselves had little knowledge of critical defense issues, the defense forces had little or no role in the formulation of defense policy until 1962.[14] Divorcing foreign policy from military power was a recipe for disaster as India realized in 1962 when even Nehru was forced to concede that "military weakness has been a temptation, and a little military strength may be a deterrent."[15] A state's legitimacy is tied to its ability to monopolize the use of force and operate effectively in an international strategic environment and India has lacked clarity on this relationship between the use of force and its foreign policy priorities.

Marginalization of the military

Indian politicians after independence in 1947 viewed the Indian Army with suspicion as the last supporters of the British Raj and did their best to isolate the military from policy and influence. This attitude was further reinforced by the views of two giants of the Indian nationalist movement, Mahatma Gandhi and Jawaharlal Nehru. Gandhi's ardent belief in non-violence left little room for accepting the role of the use of force in an independent India. It also shaped the views on military and defense of the first generation of post-independence political leaders in India. But more important has been the legacy of Nehru, India's first Prime Minister who laid the institutional foundations for civil–military relations in India. His obsession with economic development was only matched by his disdain and distrust of the military, resulting in the sidelining of defense planning in India.[16] He also ensured that the experiences in neighboring Pakistan, where military had become the dominant political force soon after independence, would not be repeated in India by institutionalizing civilian supremacy over the country's military apparatus. The civilian elite also did not want the emergence of a rival elite with direct access to political leadership.

Along with Nehru, another civilian who left a lasting impact on the evolution of civil–military relations was V.K. Krishna Menon, India's Minister of Defense from 1957 to 1962. During his tenure, which has been described as the most controversial stewardship of the Indian Defense Ministry, he heralded a number of organizational changes that were not very popular with the armed forces.[17] Despite any military experience, Nehru and Menon were actively involved in operational level planning before the outbreak of Sino-Indian war of 1962. They "directly supervised the placement of individual brigades, companies, and even platoons, as the Chinese and Indian forces engaged in mutual encirclement of isolated outposts."[18] As a consequence, when China won the war decisively, the blame was laid at the doors of Nehru and Menon. Menon resigned while Nehru's reputation suffered lasting damage. It also made it clear, both to the civilians and the military, that purely operational matters were best left to the military. Some have argued that since then a convention has been established whereby while the operational directive is laid down by the political leadership, the actual planning of the operation is left to the chiefs of staff.[19]

Stephen Rosen, in his study of the impact of societal structures on the military effectiveness of a state, argues that the separation of the Indian military from the Indian society, while preserving the coherence of the Indian army, has led to a reduction in the effective military power of the Indian state.[20] While India has been successful in evolving a sustained tradition of strict civilian control over the military since its independence, unlike its immediate neighbors, India has been unable to evolve institutions and procedures that would allow the military to substantially participate in the national security decision-making processes. This has significantly reduced the effectiveness with which India can wield its military as an instrument of national power.

Strategic culture deficit

A state can promulgate law and pursue strategy once it has not only achieved a legitimate monopoly on violence but also when it is free of the coercive violence of other states.[21] It is no surprise therefore that India's ability to think strategically on issues of national security remains at best questionable. George Tanham, in his landmark study on the Indian strategic thought, pointed out that Indian elites have shown little evidence of having thought coherently and systematically about national strategy. He argued that this lack of long-term planning and strategy owes largely to India's historical and cultural developmental patterns. These include the Hindu view of life as largely unknowable, thereby being outside man's control, and the Hindu concept of time as eternal, thereby discouraging planning. As a consequence, Tanham argued that India has been on the strategic defensive throughout its history, reluctant to assert itself except within the subcontinent.[22]

India's former Minister for External Affairs, Jaswant Singh, has also examined the evolution of strategic culture in the Indian society and in its political decision-making class, with a particular reference to post-independence India. He also finds Indian political elites lacking in the ability to think strategically about foreign policy and defense issues though he trains his guns on India's first Prime Minister, Jawaharlal Nehru, pointing to his "idealistic romanticism" and his unwillingness to institutionalize strategic thinking, policy formulation, and implementation.[23]

It is ironic, however, that even when Jaswant Singh was the External Affairs Minister, there was little evidence that anything of substance really changed in so far as the strategic dimension of India's foreign policy was concerned. For all the blame that Singh lays at Nehru's doorstep, even he and his government did not move toward the institutionalization of strategic thinking, policy formulation, and implementation. Perhaps, the Indian strategic culture became too powerful a constraint for even him to overcome.

Lack of institutionalization

A major consequence of the lack of any Indian strategic culture worth its name is a perceptible lack of institutionalization of the foreign policy-making in India. At its very foundation, Indian democracy is sustained by a range of institutions from the more formal ones of the executive, legislative, and the judiciary to the less formal ones of the broader civil-society. It is these institutions that in large measure have allowed Indian democracy to thrive and flourish for more than fifty years now despite a number of constraints that have led to the failure of democracy in many other societies. However, in the realm of foreign policy, it is the lack of institutionalization that has allowed a drift to set in without any long-term orientation. Some have laid the blame on Nehru for his unwillingness to construct strategic planning architecture because he single-handedly shaped Indian foreign policy during his tenure.[24] But even his successors have failed to pursue institutionalization in a consistent manner. The BJP-led National Democratic Alliance came to power in 1999 promising that it would establish a National Security Council (NSC) to analyze the military, economic, and political threats to the nation and to advise the government on meeting these challenges effectively.

While it did set up the NSC in the late 1990s and defined its role in policy formulation, it neglected the institutionalization of the NSC and the building up of its capabilities to play the role assigned to it, thereby failing to underpin national security with structural and systematic institutional arrangements. Important national security decisions were taken in an ad hoc manner without utilizing the Cabinet Committee on Security, the Strategic Policy Group (comprising of key secretaries, service chiefs, and heads of intelligence agencies), and officials of the National Security Advisory Board. Moreover, as has been rightly pointed out, the way the NSC is structured makes long-term planning impossible, thereby negating the very purpose of its formation and its effectiveness remains hostage to the weight of the National Security Advisor (NSA) in national politics.[25] The NSA has become the most powerful authority on national security, sidelining the institution of the NSC.

While the Congress-led United Progressive Alliance came to power in 2004 promising that it would make the NSC a professional and effective institution and blaming the National Democratic Alliance for making only cosmetic changes in the institutional arrangements, it too failed to make it work in an optimal manner whereby the NSC could anticipate national security threats, coordinate the management of national security, and engender long-term planning by generating new and bold ideas. An effective foreign policy institutional framework would not only identify the challenges but it would also develop a coherent strategy to deal with it, organize and motivate the bureaucracy, and persuade and inform the public. The NSC, by itself, is not a panacea particularly in light of the inability of the NSC in the United States to successfully mediate in the bureaucratic wars and effectively coordinate policy. But the lack of an effective NSC in India is reflective of India's ad hoc decision-making process in the realm of foreign policy. If there is any continuity in India's approach to foreign policy and national security, it is the inability and unwillingness of policy-makers, across political ideologies, to give a strategic vision to their nation's foreign policy priorities.

The myth of a debate

For long, there was a myth propagated by the political elites in the country that there has been a general consensus across political parties on major foreign policy issues. Aside from the fact that such a consensus has more been a result of intellectual laziness and apathy than any real attempt to forge a coherent grand strategy that cuts across ideological barriers, this is most certainly an exaggeration as until the early 1990s, the Congress Party's dominance over the Indian political landscape was almost complete and there was no political organization of an equal capacity that could bring to bear its influence on foreign and security policy issues in the same measure. It was the rise of the Hindu nationalist BJP that gave India a significantly different voice on foreign policy. But more importantly it is the changes in the international environment that have forced Indian policy-makers to challenge some of the assumptions underlying their approach to the outside world.

In debating the nature and scope of its engagement with the world India will have to bring its commitments and power into balance or, as Lippmann suggested in a different context of the United States, "its purposes within its means and its means equal to its purposes." India's foreign policy elite remains mired in the exigencies of day-to-day pressures emanating from the immediate challenges at hand rather than evolving a grand strategy that integrates the nation's multiple policy strands into a cohesive whole to be able to preserve and enhance Indian interests in a rapidly changing global environment. The assertions, therefore, that India does not have a China policy or an Iran policy or a Pakistan policy are plain irrelevant. India does not have a foreign policy, period. It is this lack of strategic orientation in Indian foreign policy that often results in a paradoxical situation where on the one hand India is accused by various domestic constituencies of angering this or that country by its actions while on the other hand India's relationship with almost all major powers is termed as a "strategic partnership" by the Indian government.

Moreover, the period of stable major power relations might also be coming to an end and soon difficult choices will have to be made and Indian policy-makers should have enough self-confidence to make those decisions even when they go against their long-held predilections. But a foreign policy that lacks intellectual and strategic coherence will ensure that India will forever remain poised on the threshold of great power status but won't be quite able to cross it.

The Modi factor

Since coming to office in May 2014, the Narendra Modi government has been successful in gradually dismantling India's default foreign policy legacy of non-alignment. Moving beyond ideological rhetoric, Modi is busy engaging confidently with all major global powers without inhibitions. The foreign policies of nations do not alter radically with changes in governments, but with the backing of the Indian electorate's decisive mandate, Modi has an opportunity to bring about a realignment of Indian foreign policy priorities and goals.

The Modi government has defied many expectations and confounded his detractors and supporters alike. But on the foreign policy front, remarkably for a politician who was considered provincial before elections, Modi hit the ground running from the very first day. On the security front, there is a new purposeful response against China with a focus on more efficient border management and defense acquisitions. Modi has reached out to the United States, despite his personal grievances over a visa denial by Washington when he was the chief minister of Gujarat, and there is a refreshing focus on immediate neighbors.

With India's immediate neighbors, there are certainly signs that there is a new dynamism in bilateral ties as New Delhi is putting renewed emphasis on revitalizing its regional profile. India's neighbors, barring Pakistan, are certainly looking at India with a new sense of expectation. New Delhi now has to operationalize the aspirations that have been articulated. Recognizing that the implementation phase has always been a problem for Indian credibility, the Modi government is focusing on completing projects in its neighborhood that are already in the pipeline rather than announcing new ones.

The biggest strategic challenge for India remains managing China's rise. The Modi government has concluded that the need of the hour is the right balance between enhancing economic and trade ties with Beijing while building a deterrent military might. Modi is confident of India's ability to emerge as a significant global player, allowing him to leverage ties with China and the United States to secure Indian interests. He has followed a dynamic foreign policy, developing closer ties with the United States and strengthening military cooperation with Australia, Japan, and Vietnam while working to regain strategic space in the Indian Ocean region. Modi's visits to Mongolia and South Korea after China in May 2015 signal that New Delhi remains keen on expanding its profile in China's periphery. To counter Chinese presence in the Gwadar port in Pakistan, which many in India view as a potential Chinese naval hub, India is building a port in Iran's Chabahar to gain access to Afghanistan. India has given a green light for collaborating with the United States on construction of its largest warship, the 65,000-ton aircraft carrier INS *Vishal*. For years, New Delhi was labeled as the obstacle to normalizing Sino-Indian ties. Modi has deftly turned the tables on Beijing by signaling that he is willing to go all out in enhancing cultural and economic ties, but the onus of reducing strategic distrust rests with Beijing.

Modi seems to be redefining the terms on which India is likely to engage with the world in the coming years. Pragmatism coupled with a more confident assertion of Indian interests has been his hallmark. He is not shy about reaching out directly to new constituencies such as the Non-Resident Indian and business communities in other states. For India's friends, a new outreach is in the offing. For India's adversaries, new red lines are being drawn.

Most significantly, Modi is gradually, but surely, marginalizing the idea of non-alignment as the bedrock of Indian foreign policy. He has indicated that he is willing to work with anyone and everyone to secure Indian interests, the most important of which for him is to take India on the path of rapid economic growth. For Modi and his government, however, the biggest challenge will remain to move away from an overly personalized foreign policy toward a more institutionalized foreign policy and national security decision-making, a weakness that previous governments have failed to tackle.

It would indeed be a tragedy if history would describe today's Indian policy-makers in the words Winston Churchill applied to those who ignored the changing strategic realities before World War II: "They go on in strange paradox, decided only to be undecided, resolved to be irresolute, adamant for drift, solid for fluidity, all-powerful to be impotent." India today, more than any other time in its history, needs a view of its role in the world quite removed from the shibboleths of the past. Despite the enormous challenges that it continues to face, India is widely recognized today as a rising power with enormous potential. The portents are hopeful if only the Indian policy-makers have the imagination and courage to seize some of the opportunities.

It is in this rapidly evolving context that this book provides an overview of Indian foreign policy landscape as it has evolved in recent times. The focus is on the twenty-first century with historical context provided as appropriate. It is an introductory book on Indian foreign policy and is not intended to be a detailed examination of any of its particular aspects. It examines India's relationships with major powers, with its neighbors and other regions, as well as India's stand on major global issues, underlining that with a gradual accretion in its powers, India has become more aggressive in the pursuit of its interests, thereby emerging as an important player in the shaping of the global order in the new millennium.

Notes

1 Raj Chengappa, "The Real Boss," *India Today*, December 11, 2008.
2 Shekhar Gupta, "No First Use Options," *Indian Express*, January 17, 2009.
3 "Pleasing Beijing, Govt tells its Ministers Don't Attend Dalai Lama Honour Function," *Indian Express*, November 4, 2007.
4 Somini Sengupta, "India Tiptoes in China's Footsteps to Compete but Not Offend," *New York Times*, April 4, 2008.
5 The report is available at www2.goldmansachs.com/insight/research/reports/99.pdf.
6 C. Raja Mohan, "India's Grand Strategy in the Gulf," India in the Gulf Project, The Nixon Center.
7 Christopher Layne, "The Unipolar Illusion: Why New Great Powers Will Rise?" *International Security*, Vol. 17, No. 4 (Spring 1993), pp. 9–10.
8 On the identification of great powers by the measurement of capabilities, see Kenneth Waltz, *Theory of International Politics* (Reading, MA: Addison-Wesley Publishing Company, 1979), pp. 129–31.
9 On why it makes sense to define power in terms of material capabilities rather than outcomes, see John J. Mearsheimer, *The Tragedy of Great Power Politics* (New York: W.W. Norton & Co, 2001), pp. 55–82.
10 Michael Sheehan, *The Balance of Power: History and Theory* (London: Routledge, 1996), p. 7.
11 K. Subrahmanyam, *Indian Security Perspectives* (New Delhi: ABC Publishing House, 1982), p. 127.
12 This point has been eloquently elaborated in Ashley J. Tellis, *Future Fire: Challenges Facing Indian Defense Policy in the New Century*, delivered at the India Today Conclave, New Delhi, March 13, 2004, available at www.ceip.org/files/pdf/futurefire.pdf.

13 Quoted in P.V.R. Rao, *India's Defence Policy and Organisation Since Independence* (New Delhi: The United Services Institution of India, 1977), pp. 5–6.

14 K. Subrahmanyam, *Perspectives in Defence Planning* (New Delhi: Abhinav, 1972), pp. 126–33.

15 Lorne J. Kavic, *India's Quest for Security: Defence Policies, 1947–1965* (Berkeley: University of Califirnia Press, 1967), p. 192.

16 Stephen P. Cohen, *India: Emerging Power* (New Delhi: Oxford University Press, 2001), pp. 127–30.

17 P.R. Chari, "Civil-Military Relations in India," *Armed Forces and Society*, Vol. 4, No. 1 (November 1977), pp. 13–15.

18 Stephen P. Cohen, *The Indian Army: Its Contribution to the Development of a Nation* (Berkeley: University of California Press, 1971), p. 176.

19 P.R. Chari, "Civil-Military Relations of India," *Link*, August 15, 1977, p. 75.

20 Stephen P. Rosen, *Societies and Military Power: India and Its Armies* (Ithaca, NY: Cornell University Press, 1996), pp. 250–3.

21 Philip Bobbitt, *The Shield of Achilles: War, Peace, and the Course of History* (New York: Anchor Books, 2003), p. 336.

22 George Tanham, *Indian Strategic Thought: An Interpretive Essay* (Santa Monica: RAND Corp., 1992).

23 Jaswant Singh, *Defending India* (New York: St. Martin's Press, 1999), pp. 1–58.

24 *Ibid.*, p. 34.

25 Ashley J. Tellis, *India's Emerging Nuclear Posture: Between Recessed Deterrent and Ready Arsenal* (New York: Oxford University Press, 2001), p. 658.

Snapshot 1: Indian foreign and security policy-making structures

Compared to many of its neighbors in South Asia, India enjoys stable foreign and security policy-making structures. India has not been witness to the military coups and weak civilian control that is often a feature of other states emerging from colonial control in the twentieth century, such as Egypt, Indonesia, Myanmar, and Pakistan. The policy-making authority of elected civilians at the apex of the Indian foreign and security policy systems is assured, as is the implementation authority of multiple layers of civilian officials flowing downward from this level.

The military and external analysts have marginal formal roles in these systems. This poses a stark contrast with the counterpart policy-making structures of the United States, which recognize the necessity of involving these actors in the process through the advisory roles of the US Joint Chiefs of Staff and of lateral entry of experts into senior policy-making positions. Indeed, by privileging the authority of the apex elected civilians to the extent that India does, the system has become largely only as effective and capable as its elected leaders of the day.

This ensures that the prime body for providing direction to both foreign and defense policy is the Prime Minister's Office. The Cabinet Committee on Security, consisting of the Prime Minister and Defense, External Affairs, Finance, and Home Ministers, further authorizes major defense policy and expenditure decisions. While all ultimate major foreign and defense policy actions must flow from these bodies, these issues must compete with the multiple other daily demands on the attention of these officials. When clear decisions on foreign and defense policy issues do not emerge from these levels, alongside sustained following attention paid to their implementation, the subordinate levels can become paralyzed by inertia.

The Ministry of External Affairs is the primary government interface for most international citizens and organizations concerned with Indian foreign policy. Its origins date back to before Indian independence, and the position of Minister for External Affairs is considered one of the most prestigious appointments for senior Indian politicians. However, it is structurally underpowered, both in policy-making influence and sheer headcount.

With authority in the foreign policy-making system gravitating toward the Prime Minister, the Ministry of External Affairs has become largely a policy implementation structure for the foreign policy decisions made by the Prime Minister's Office.

When the Prime Minister has intermittent or little interest in foreign policy, inertia and even uncoordinated improvisation can result within the Ministry of External Affairs, due to the remaining necessity of staking a coherent stance on an issue. The structural weakness of the Ministry of External Affairs in the foreign policy-making system is compounded by its recruitment policies. There is no specialized career track into the Ministry for experts; citizens can only join the general civil service through its application process, and are then assigned to the Ministry. This inhibits the recruitment of talented specialists that the Ministry needs. The overall headcount of India's foreign service is only around 50 percent of that for its counterpart departments in China and Brazil, and comparable to that of Singapore, which has a population of around 0.5 percent of that of India. These issues are not helped by the tendency of Ministers of External Affairs to have little previous experience of foreign policy, and be appointed instead on the basis of coalition or party political imperatives.

The defense policy-making system has a similar reliance on the Prime Minister's Office, and also the Cabinet Committee on Security, with paralysis emerging when decisions are not forthcoming. The Ministry of Defense is characterized by a highly limited military advisory role, with day-to-day management by several layers of non-specialist civil servants. The three military services largely plan and operate individually. Some half-hearted inter-service coordination measures have been introduced, such as an Integrated Defense Staff planning body and Chiefs of Staff Committee. However, true inter-service integration, such as the creation of a Chief of Defense Staff to speak for the armed services in a single voice to civilians, has yet to take place. Better coordination among the three military services would improve its advisory influence, but has been resisted by the civilian bureaucrats and apex political leaders for this reason.

The civilian bureaucracy within the Ministry of Defense has become famous for its inertia. This has become most visible in defense procurement. Military procurement requests cleared by the Defense Minister or Cabinet Committee on Security for the ongoing financial year, despite this authorization, are still subject to administrative queries and objections from lower levels of the civilian bureaucracy.

The resultant delays have led to significant elements of the defense budget being returned unspent to the Finance Ministry at the end of each financial year, with the services still missing the equipment. Indeed, only 5 percent of the armor in procurement requests was actually acquired over the period 1992–2007. In recognition of these problems, India's major procurement decision in April 2015, the purchase of 36 Rafale fighter jets from France, was instead directly handled by the Prime Minister's Office, with little involvement from India's formal defense procurement process or even reportedly from the Defense Minister.

The Rafale purchase underlines that the ultimate effectiveness of India's foreign and security policy-making structures is overdependent on the interest and political will that the individual Prime Minister is willing to devote to these issues. Whether the aforementioned shortcomings of the Indian foreign and defense policy-making system are addressed, remains largely reliant on the attention span of the Prime Minister.

PART I

India and major powers

2

India and the United States: an emerging partnership

During the visit of the Indian Prime Minister, Manmohan Singh, to the United States in July 2005, the George W. Bush administration declared its ambition to achieve full civil nuclear energy cooperation with India as part of its broader goals of promoting nuclear power and achieving nuclear security. In pursuit of this objective, the Bush administration agreed to "seek agreement from Congress to adjust U.S. laws and policies" and to "work with friends and allies to adjust international regimes to enable full civil nuclear energy cooperation and trade with India, including but not limited to expeditious consideration of fuel supplies for safeguarded nuclear reactors at Tarapur." India, for its part, promised "to assume the same responsibilities and practices and acquire the same benefits and advantages of other leading countries with advanced nuclear technology."[1] The Indo-US nuclear pact has virtually rewritten the rules of the global nuclear regime by underlining India's credentials as a responsible nuclear state that should be integrated into the global nuclear order. The nuclear agreement creates a major exception to the US prohibition of nuclear assistance to any country that does not accept international monitoring of all its nuclear facilities. It is a remarkable achievement not the least because it reveals the desire on both sides to challenge their long-held assumptions about each other so as to be able to strike a partnership that serves the interests of both India and the United States.

The Indian Prime Minister's visit to the United States was followed by the visit of US President Bush to New Delhi in March 2006. Together, these visits marked a new phase in the rather topsy-turvy bilateral relationship between the world's oldest and the world's largest democracies. It was during President Bush's visit to India that the two sides finally managed to reach a crucial understanding on the separation plan for India's nuclear facilities, the first crucial step toward putting the July 2005 agreement into effect.[2] This plan is part of India's obligation under the Indo-US nuclear agreement that requires separation of civil and military facilities in a phased manner and the filing of a declaration about the civilian facilities with the International Atomic Energy Agency (IAEA). The successful conclusion of the nuclear pact in 2008, though not without difficulty, underscores the great distance India's ties with the United States have traveled since the end of the Cold War. This chapter discusses the evolution in Indo-US ties over the last two decades and the key factors which are propelling this change.

US–India ties after the Cold War

The demise of the Soviet Union liberated Indian and US attitudes from the structural confines of Cold War realities. As India pursued economic reforms and moved toward global integration, it was clear that the United States and India would have to find a modus vivendi for a deeper engagement with each other. As Indian foreign policy priorities changed, US–India cooperation increased on a range of issue areas. India needed US support for its economic regeneration and the administration of former US President Bill Clinton viewed India as an emerging success story of globalization. Yet, relations could only go so far with the US refusal to reconcile itself to India's nuclear program and its inability to move beyond India's hyphenated relationship with Pakistan in its South Asia policy.

The Indian nuclear tests of 1998, while removing ambiguity about India's nuclear status, further complicated US–India bilateral relations. The Clinton administration wanted to improve US relations with India, but it did not want to compromise on its goal of non-proliferation. Protracted negotiations between the Deputy Chairman of the Planning Commission and later the Foreign Minister of India, Jaswant Singh, and the US Deputy Secretary of State, Strobe Talbott, emphasized this palpable difficulty.[3] While in concrete terms these negotiations achieved little, they set in motion a process that saw US–India bilateral engagement taking on a new meaning. Mutual trust developed in the US and Indian foreign policy bureaucracies that is so crucial to sustaining high-level political engagements. The visit of President Clinton to India in 2000 and the Next Steps in Strategic Partnership,[4] which was announced by the Indian Prime Minister and the US President in 2004, also laid the foundation for a dramatic upswing in Indo-US ties.

But it was the George W. Bush administration that redefined the parameters of US–India bilateral engagement. That India would figure prominently in the Bush administration's global strategic calculus was made clear by Condoleezza Rice in her *Foreign Affairs* article before the 2000 presidential elections in which she had argued that "there is a strong tendency conceptually [in the United States] to connect India with Pakistan and to think only of Kashmir or the nuclear competition between the two states."[5] She made it clear that India has the potential to become a great power and that US foreign policy would do well to take that into account. The Bush administration, from the very beginning, refused to look at India through the prism of non-proliferation and viewed India as a natural and strategic ally.[6]

But the events of September 11, 2001, and the subsequent dramatic changes in US foreign policy, prevented the Bush administration from following through with its new approach toward India. It was only when Rice became Secretary of State in 2005 that the United States started evolving a coherent approach in building its ties with India. Rice visited India in March 2005 as part of her Asia tour and put forth "an unprecedented framework for cooperation with India," something that took the Indian government by surprise.[7] Rice transformed the terms of the debate completely by revealing that the Bush administration was willing to consider civilian nuclear energy cooperation with India. A few days later, the State Department announced the administration's new India policy, which declared its goal "to help India become a major world power in the 21st century."[8] And the first step in that direction was removing the age-old distrust that has resulted between the two states over the nuclear issue. It was clear to both the United States and India that the road to a healthy strategic partnership between the two democracies was through nuclear energy cooperation.

US–India relations have been steadily strengthening in the last few years, with their interests converging on a range of issues. But the nuclear non-proliferation regime denying civilian nuclear technology to India, with its larger restrictive implications across the entire high technology spectrum, has been a fundamental irritant in this relationship. It was made clear to the US Congress that its failure to approve the deal would not only set back the clock on US–India relations but would also revive the anti-US sections of the Indian elite. In her testimonies before the House and Senate committees, Rice described India as "a rising global power that could be a pillar of stability in a rapidly changing Asia" and argued that the nuclear agreement was critical for forging a full-scale partnership between the world's two largest democracies.[9]

Aside from the fact that the United States is India's largest trading and investment partner,[10] US–India cooperation on strategic issues has also been growing. India is one of the top five donors to the Afghan government, and it contributed $2 million in response to the UN Secretary-General's appeal for help in Iraq, followed by another $10 million at the donor's conference in Madrid. India also contributed $10 million to the global democracy fund initiated by the UN Secretary-General.[11] The Indian and US navies are jointly patrolling the Malacca Straits, and India's rapid reaction to the Indian Ocean tsunami in 2004 won accolades from the Pentagon. It is by no means an exaggeration to suggest that the United States would like a strong US–India alliance to act as a "bulwark against the arc of Islamic instability running from the Middle East to Asia and to create much greater balance in Asia."[12]

The 2014 Quadrennial Defense Review (QDR) of the United States strongly emphasizes India's importance for the United States in the emerging global security architecture.[13] While a concern with China's rising military power is palpable throughout the defense review, it is instructive to note the importance that the QDR has attached to India's rising global profile. The report describes India as an emerging great power and a key strategic partner of the United States. Shared values such as the two states being long-standing multiethnic democracies are underlined as providing a foundation for increased strategic cooperation. This stands in marked contrast to the unease that has been expressed with the centralization of power in Russia and lack of transparency in security affairs in China. It is also significant that India is mentioned along with the United States' traditional allies such as the NATO countries, Japan, and Australia. The QDR goes on to say categorically that close cooperation with these partners (including India) in the war against terrorism as well as in efforts to counter weapons of mass destruction (WMD) proliferation and other non-traditional threats ensures not only the continuing need for these alliances but also the improvement of their capabilities.

It is in this context of burgeoning US–India ties that the nuclear pact between the two states assumed great significance, because it not only demonstrated the commitment of the two sides to take their bilateral ties out of the confines of Cold War nuclear realities, but it also revealed the complexities inherent in the process of doing so.

There was uneasiness in the Indian policy-making community on Obama's assumption of office, as much the result of administration change in the United States as of the economic crisis affecting Washington. While George W. Bush, deeply suspicious of communist China, was personally keen on building strong ties with India. He was willing to sacrifice long-held US non-proliferation concerns to embrace nuclear India and acknowledge it as the primary actor in South Asia, de-hyphenated from Pakistan. The Obama administration's concern about protecting the non-proliferation regime, the immediate challenge of dealing with the growing Taliban threat in Afghanistan and Pakistan, and unprecedented economic challenge led it to a very different set of priorities and agenda in which India had a marginal role. At least initially the only context in which Obama talked of India was the need to sort Kashmir out so as to find a way out of the West's troubles in Afghanistan. The talk of a strategic partnership between the two democracies disappeared. The new administration toyed with the idea of G-2, a global condominium of the United States and China whereby China can be expected to look after and "manage" Asia-Pacific.

Given the heavy US economic dependence on Beijing, a G-2 may have made perfect sense for the United States but it left India marginalized in the strategic scheme of things. From being viewed as a rising power and a balancer in Asia-Pacific, India in the early days of the Obama administration was back to being seen as a regional South Asian actor whose only relevance for the United States was in making sure that Pakistan fought the Taliban with full vigor without getting preoccupied in Kashmir. The smaller countries of

East and Southeast Asia, not to mention India's immediate neighbors being wooed by China, could not but note the shifting balance of power that Washington's maneuvering signaled and might adjust their own policies in response.

But soon the chimera of G-2 met its inevitable demise. Washington has been forced to fight back to retain its pre-eminence in the Asian balance of power. The choice of the four states that Obama visited in November 2010 – India, South Korea, Indonesia, and Japan – was aimed at reminding China that the United States still retains its role as principal balancing force in the region. All four worry about China's rise and recent attempts to assert its interests more forcefully in the region. There is a clamor for American leadership in the region as none of the regional states want China to emerge as the dominant actor. The expectation is that a stronger US presence in the region provides greater stability. The United States has tried to calm nerves in Asia with its recent moves and pronouncements vis-à-vis China. But there are still widespread doubts in the region about the United States' willingness and/or ability to provide counterbalancing capabilities vis-à-vis China.

One of the most remarkable aspects of Indian foreign policy in recent years has been New Delhi's gravitation toward Washington despite years of mistrust during the Cold War years. India's recent rise has been described by the US President, Barack Obama, as being in the best interests of both India and the United States as well as the world. Obama not only invited the Indian Prime Minister, Manmohan Singh, as the first state guest of his presidency in November 2009 but also visited India a year later.

The US President made all the right noises in India. The most significant was his declaration that that the United States will back India's bid for a permanent seat on an expanded United Nations Security Council. It was a major policy shift that India has long been clamoring for and Washington has been reluctant to offer. By suggesting that he looks "forward to a reformed UN Security Council that includes India as a permanent member," he warmed the hearts of Indian policy-makers who have long viewed American support as a litmus test.[14] There was no reservation and hesitation in Obama's gesture which was probably the strongest endorsement the United States has given to any state for permanent UN membership. On Pakistan too, Obama was deferential to Indian sensitivities. He maintained that "it is in the interest of India and Pakistan to reduce tensions between themselves and the US cannot impose solutions to these problems." He also put Pakistan on notice by making it clear that "there can be no safe haven for terror" and suggested that the United States "will continue to insist on Pak leadership to bring Mumbai attackers to justice."[15]

During Obama's visit, more than twenty deals worth $10 billion were signed by the corporate sectors of the two states. These deals included the sale of military transport aircraft, civilian airplanes, mining equipment, and jet engines. The issues of various barriers to trade and infrastructure bottlenecks were raised by Obama as problem areas in attracting greater American investment underlining the continuing problems in the US–India economic ties.

Other key agreements signed by New Delhi and Washington during Obama's visit include a pact on setting up a joint clean energy research and development center, memoranda of understanding (MoUs) on the Global Centre for Nuclear Energy Partnership, global disease protection center and energy cooperation, and a pact on technical cooperation for the study of monsoon. India and the United States also agreed to work closely on agricultural development and women's empowerment in Afghanistan as well as boosting joint efforts to promote a reliable information and communications infrastructure, with a goal of free, fair, and secure access to cyberspace.

The two states also decided to put in place a four-part export control reform program that includes American support for India's membership in multilateral export control regimes, removing India's defense and space-related entities from the American "Entities List," export licensing policy realignment and cooperation on export control. In line with Obama's declaration that India is no longer a rising power but has already "arrived," both countries have announced a dialogue on the Asia-Pacific, which will expand current consultations to include East Asia, West Asia, and Central Asia. It is also a signal to an increasingly assertive China that other states in the region will respond to Chinese projection of power.

However, while Obama has managed to make the right noises in New Delhi, many in India still wonder if he will be able to deliver on all that he has promised. The expansion of the UN Security Council is not happening anytime soon and there is no consensus among the five permanent members about the scale and scope of this expansion. China remains opposed to any new member from Asia sitting at the high table. The process is complicated and will take a long time to come to fruition. So in many ways it was a cost-free option for Obama to declare his support for India's membership and then wait and see what happens. Whatever the ultimate outcome, Obama did manage to ameliorate some of the concerns in New Delhi about his administration's earlier policies toward India. Obama's visit to New Delhi in January 2015 led to the finalization of the nuclear pact when the United States and India outlined a deal to limit the legal liability of US suppliers in the event of a nuclear power plant catastrophe.

A constellation of factors

A unique constellation of factors at the systemic, domestic political and individual level have enabled the United States and India to chart a new course in their bilateral relationship.

The most important determinant has been the changed structural realities as the international system evolved into a unipolar one after the demise of the Soviet Union that liberated Indian and US attitudes toward each other from the structural confines of Cold War realities. India's Cold War foreign policy posture of non-alignment lost its meaning in a world where there were no longer any blocs left to align against. There was one systemic reality and that was the US preponderance in the global hierarchy. As India pursued economic reforms and moved toward global integration, it was clear that the United States and India will have to find a modus vivendi for a deeper engagement with each other. As Indian foreign policy priorities changed, US–India cooperation increased on a range of issues areas. India needed US support for its economic regeneration and the Clinton administration viewed India as an emerging success story of globalization. Yet, the relations could only go so far in the absence of US reconciliation to India's nuclear status and the inability of the United States to move beyond the India–Pakistan hyphenated relationship in South Asia.[16]

Structural realists argue that because of the anarchic nature of the international system with no higher authority above the states, distribution of power defined in terms of material capabilities is the most important determinant of state behavior. The changing balance of power in Asia-Pacific made the Bush administration realize the importance of recalibrating its strategic posture vis-à-vis the region. The United States faces a prospect of an emerging power transition involving China and dealing with this is likely to be the most consequential challenge for US foreign policy in the coming decades. With this in mind, the United States has decided to pursue a policy of engaging China while simultaneously investing in increasing the power of other states located along China's periphery. This has involved not only reinvigorating its existing alliance with Japan but also reaching out to new partners such as India.[17] India, meanwhile, is also gearing up to face China. India and China are two major powers in Asia with global aspirations and some significant conflicting interests. As a result, some amount of friction in their bilateral relationship is inevitable. If India and China continue to rise in the next few years, there's a high likelihood of security competition between the two regional giants. And if India is serious about its desire to emerge as a major global power, then it will have to tackle the challenge of China's rise. Not only does the extant balance of power in Asia-Pacific adversely affect Indian interests but India also views a rising China with its aggregate strength (size, population, and economic capabilities), its geographical proximity, its offensive capabilities, and its offensive intentions as highly threatening.[18] It is to tackle this challenge that Indian foreign policy has been gearing up with its new approach toward the United States. And the Bush administration transformed the nature of the US–India partnership by advocating civilian nuclear energy cooperation with India, thereby incorporating India into the global nuclear order as well as declaring that the United States is committed to encouraging the growth of India as a great power.[19]

The second factor in the shaping of contemporary Indo-US ties emerges at the domestic political level with the coming into office of the Bush administration that had very different notions about global politics from its predecessor, thereby redefining the parameters of US–India bilateral engagement. That India would figure prominently in the Bush administration's global strategic calculus was made clear by Condoleezza Rice in her *Foreign Affairs* article before the 2000 presidential elections in which she had argued that "there is a strong tendency conceptually [in the United States] to connect India with Pakistan and to think of Kashmir or the nuclear competition between the two states."[20] She made it clear that India has the potential to become a great power and US foreign policy would do well to take that into account. The Bush administration, from the very beginning, refused to look at India through the prism of non-proliferation and viewed India as a natural and strategic ally.

But the events of 9/11 and the subsequent dramatic changes in the US foreign policy prevented the Bush administration from fully realizing its ambitions vis-à-vis India though bilateral engagement in the areas of counter-terrorism, joint military exercises, and trade continued to expand.[21] It was when Rice became the Secretary of State in 2005 that the United States started evolving a coherent approach in building its ties with India. Rice visited India in March 2005 as part of her Asia tour and put forth "an unprecedented framework for cooperation with India," something that took the Indian government by surprise.[22] While many in India were focused on the future of US–Pakistan ties, Rice transformed the terms of the debate completely by revealing that the Bush administration was willing to consider civilian nuclear energy cooperation with India. And a few days later, the State Department announced the administration's new India policy that declared its goal "to help India become a major world power in the 21st century."[23] And the first step in that direction was removing the age-old distrust that has engendered between the two states on the nuclear issue. It was clear to both the United States and India that the road to a healthy strategic partnership between the two democracies goes through nuclear energy cooperation.

The Bush administration's overture to India is also intricately linked to the way it redefined US non-proliferation policy in the aftermath of 9/11.[24] A basic tenet of this policy is that there are certain states that cannot be trusted with nuclear weapons technology given the nature of their domestic political regimes. On the other hand, states such as India, with its impeccable proliferation credentials, should be rewarded for their behavior. As domestic politics of other states became a central concern of the United States in recent years, especially after 9/11, a secular, pluralist, democratic India emerged as an attractive target to be wooed.[25]

On the Indian side, the reflexive anti-Americanism of the past has become much less pronounced. It's largely confined to the communist parties while the two main political parties, the Congress and the BJP, have taken a more pragmatic approach toward the United States, despite the constraints of coalition politics.

A third factor that is often neglected but has been no less crucial in shaping the trajectory of Indo-US nuclear pact is the role of key individuals. Top political leadership in both India and the United States have worked toward giving Indo-US ties greater substance in recent years. Despite the denial of the visa to Narendra Modi by the US government when he was the Chief Minister of Gujarat, Modi as Prime Minister has positioned himself well to boldly shape the contours of New Delhi's outreach to Washington. Modi's trip to the United States in September 2014 has ended up imparting a new dynamism to US–India ties. His approach was unconventional as he reached out to constituencies beyond the governmental level – the Indian Americans and the American corporate sector. Modi reached out to the 2.8 million-strong Indian American community in an unprecedented manner – by giving a rock star address to an expected audience of more than 18,000 people at Madison Square Garden in New York and making an appearance at the Global Citizen Festival in Central Park, where he was introduced by Hollywood actor Hugh Jackman. In another first, he penned a joint op-ed with Obama where the two leaders made a case that the time had come "to set a new agenda, one that realizes concrete benefits for our citizens."[26] During Modi's visit to Washington, the two nations not only renewed their 2005 defense cooperation agreement for another ten years but also expanded its scope by declaring that the two countries will "treat each other at the same level as their closest partners" on issues including "defense technology, trade, research, co-production and co-development." Both nations declared their support for freedom of navigation in the South China Sea in their joint statement, signaling that the Modi government is not hesitant to highlight New Delhi's convergence with Washington on regional issues. The United States also expressed its willingness to enhance technology partnership with the Indian Navy.[27] In a first, Modi then went on to invite the US President as the chief guest at India's Republic Day celebrations in January 2015.

On India's veto of the Trade Facilitation Agreement (TFA) at the World Trade Organization (WTO), both sides conceded that as they move forward they will need to take into consideration each other's points of view. Bilateral counter-terror and intelligence ties have taken a leap with the two sides deciding to undertake "joint and concerted efforts" for dismantling of safe havens of terrorists and criminal networks such as Lashkar-e-Toiba, Jaish-e-Mohamed, D-company, Haqqani Network, and Al Qaeda. Modi has articulated a vision of US–India ties as a relationship between equals: if America has a unique ability to absorb people from all parts of the world, argues the Indian Prime Minister, Indians too have a unique ability to become an integral part of the various societies to which they migrate and contribute to them in substantive ways. It is Modi's confidence in India's economic future and the American corporate sector's confidence in Modi's stewardship of the Indian economy that has already resulted in investments worth US$41 billion into India in 2015, only 20 percent of what is expected from the United States.[28]

Conclusion

As the United States repositions its leadership in an increasingly complex Asian strategic landscape, and as India starts to get its economic and military act together, the two states need each other more than ever. Modi has certainly signaled that he is not bogged down by the ideological predilections of his predecessors and is more than willing to rejuvenate bilateral ties. He is ready to confidently engage global powers, including the United States, in order to further India's developmental goals.

During his trip to India in 2006, President George W. Bush had claimed that the United States and India are "closer than ever before and this partnership has the power to transform the world."[29] It is this vision that had been the hallmark of the Bush administration's policy toward India from the very beginning and led it to proclaim openly that it would help India emerge as a major global player in the twenty-first century. India came to be viewed as a responsible rising power that needs to be accommodated in the global order.

With the global balance of power in flux, the United States and India are both trying to adjust to the emerging new realities. India, in many ways, is a natural partner of the United States as the world's pre-eminent power adjusts to a reconfiguration in the global distribution of power. However, neither the United States nor India are used to partnerships among equals and India remains too proud, too argumentative, and too big a nation to reconcile as a junior partner to any state, including the United States. How the two democracies adjust to this reality will shape the future of their relationship.

Notes

1 The details of the joint statement between US President George W Bush and the Indian Prime Minister Manmohan Singh, signed on July 18, 2005, can be found at www.whitehouse.gov/news/releases/2005/07/20050718-6.html.
2 The US–India joint statement, marking the completion of Indo-US discussions on India's separation plan, signed during US President Bush's visit to New Delhi in March 2006, is available at www.whitehouse.gov/news/releases/2006/03/20060302-5.html.
3 For a detailed account of these talks, see Strobe Talbott, *Engaging India: Diplomacy, Democracy and the Bomb* (Washington, DC: Brookings Institution Press, 2004).

4 Text of the joint US–India statement on "Next Steps in Strategic Partnership" is available at www.whitehouse.gov/news/releases/2004/01/20040112-1.html.

5 Condoleezza Rice, "Promoting the National Interest," Foreign Affairs, Vol. 79, No. 1 (January/February 2000), p. 56.

6 Robert D. Blackwill, "The Quality and Durability of U.S.-India Relationship," speech by the US ambassador to India, India Chamber of Commerce, Kolkata, India, November 27, 2002.

7 C. Raja Mohan, *Impossible Allies: Nuclear India, United States and the Global Order* (New Delhi: India Research Press, 2006), p. 57.

8 The transcript of the background briefing by administration officials on US–South Asia relations is available at www.state.gov/r/pa/prs/ps/2005/43853.htm.

9 The testimonies of Condoleezza Rice before the House International Relations and Senate Foreign Relations Committees can be found at www.state.gov/secretary/rm/2006/64146.htm and www.state.gov/secretary/rm/2006/64136.htm.

10 The details can be found at www.mea.gov.in/foreignrelation/usa.pdf.

11 K.P. Nayar, "What's in It for the U.S.?" Telegraph, March 8, 2006.

12 Alex Perry, "Why Bush Is Courting India?" Time, February 28, 2006.

13 The 2014 Quadrennial Defense Review Report is available at www.defense.gov/pubs/2014_Quadrennial_Defense_Review.pdf.

14 Emily Wax and Rama Lakshmi, "Obama Supports Adding India as a Permanent Member of U.N. Security Council," *Washington Post*, November 8, 2010.

15 *Ibid.*

16 On the glacial pace of improvement in US–India ties during this period, see Sunanda K. Datta Ray, *Waiting for America: India and the United States in the New Millennium* (New Delhi: HarperCollins, 2002).

17 Ashley Tellis, "India in Asian Geopolitics," in Prakash Nanda (ed.), *Rising India: Friends and Foes* (New Delhi: Lancer Publishers, 2007), pp. 123–7.

18 On the contention that states tend to ally with or against the foreign power that poses the greatest "threat," see Stephen M. Walt, *The Origins of Alliances* (Ithaca, NY: Cornell University Press, 1990).

19 Harsh V. Pant, *Contemporary Debates in Indian Foreign and Security Policy* (New York: Palgrave Macmillan, 2008), pp. 19–37.

20 Rice, "Promoting the National Interest," p. 56.

21 For a broad survey of the strategic convergence between India and the United States as well as important differences before 2006, see Sumit Ganguly, Brian Shoup, and Andrew Scobell, *US-Indian Strategic Cooperation into the 21st Century: More Than Words* (London: Routledge, 2006).

22 Mohan, *Impossible Allies*, p. 57.

23 The transcript of the Background Briefing by Administration Officials on US–South Asia relations is available at www.state.gov/r/pa/prs/ps/2005/43853.htm.

24 George Perkovich, "Bush's Nuclear Revolution: A Regime Change in Nonproliferation," *Foreign Affairs* (March/April 2003). Also, see The White House, *National Strategy to Combat Weapons of Mass Destruction* (Washington,

DC, December 2002). Unclassified version available online at www.fas.org/irp/
offdocs/nspd/nspd-17.html.

25 R. Nicholas Burns, "The US and India: The New Strategic Partnership,"
speech delivered at the Asia Society, New York, October 18, 2005, available at
www.asiasociety.org/speeches/burns05.html.

26 Narendra Modi and Barack Obama, "A Renewed US-India Partnership for the
21st Century," *Washington Post*, September 30, 2014, www.washingtonpost
.com/opinions/narendra-modi-and-barack-obama-a-us-india-partnership-for-the
-21st-century/2014/09/29/dac66812-4824-11e4-891d-713f052086a0_story.html.

27 The White House, Office of the Press Secretary, "U.S.-India Joint Statement,"
September 30, 2014, www.whitehouse.gov/the-press-office/2014/09/30/us-india
-joint-statement.

28 "US Investors Bet on PM Modi, to Invest $41 Billion in India in 3 Years,"
Times of India, October 5, 2014, http://timesofindia.indiatimes.com/india/
US-investors-bet-on-PM-Modi-to-invest-41-billion-in-India-in-3-years/article-
show/44360022.cms.

29 See the text of the US President's speech in India on March 3, 2006, at
www.whitehouse.gov/news/releases/2006/03/20060303-5.html.

3

India and China: an uneasy relationship

In recent years the world has grappled with the challenges posed by China's rapid rise, and India is no exception. The peculiar nature of Sino-Indian ties has been underscored by a sudden downturn in bilateral relations. The relationship has become so ruptured that some Indian strategists were contemplating a "year of the Chinese attack on India," suggesting that China would attack India by 2012 to divert attention from growing domestic troubles.[1] The Indian media, rather than interrogating these claims, further sensationalized this issue, which was then picked up by the official Chinese media.[2] Adding their own spin, voices in the Chinese media started suggesting that while a Chinese attack on India is highly unlikely, a conflict between the two neighbors could occur in one scenario: India's adoption of an aggressive policy toward China about their border dispute, thereby forcing China to take military action.[3] The Chinese media went on to speculate that the "China will attack India" line might actually be a pretext for India to deploy more troops to the border areas.[4]

As China and India have risen in the global inter-state hierarchy, their bilateral relationship has become uneasy as they attempt to come to terms with each other's rise. The distrust between the two is actually growing at an alarming rate, notwithstanding the rhetoric of official pronouncements. Growing economic cooperation as well as bilateral political and socio-cultural exchanges have done little to assuage each country's concerns about the other's intentions.

This chapter discusses the contemporary state of Sino-Indian relations with a focus on the changing trajectory of Indian policy toward the rise of China and explores how India is responding to this rise across a range of issue areas central to its strategic calculus.

Historical and diplomatic interactions

As two ancient civilizations, India and China have had cultural and trade ties since at least the first century. The famous Silk Road allowed for economic ties to develop between the two neighbors, with the transmission of Buddhism from India to China giving a further cultural dimension to the relationship. Political ties between China and India, however, remained underdeveloped. During the colonial period, British trade and diplomacy linked India to China in both positive and nefarious ways as India emerged as the jumping off place for the British exploitation of China, mostly by the East India Company. This history has continued to influence Chinese thinking about India and the perception that India still serves as the "cat's paw" for the West.

In the early Cold War period, independent India's first Prime Minister, Jawaharlal Nehru, saw an anti-imperialist friendship between the two largest states of Asia as imperative in order to avoid interference by the two external superpowers.[5] Solidarity with China was integral to Nehru's vision of Asian leadership. After the People's Republic of China (PRC) was founded in 1949 and India established diplomatic ties with it in 1950, India not only advocated for PRC membership at the United Nations but also opposed attempts to condemn the PRC for its actions in Korea. Yet the issue of Tibet soon emerged as a major bone of contention between China and India. New Delhi sought to allay Beijing's suspicions about Indian designs on Tibet by supporting the Seventeen-Point Agreement between Tibetan delegates and China in 1951, which recognized PRC sovereignty over Tibet and guaranteed the existing socio-political arrangements. India and China signed the famed Panchsheel Agreement in 1954 that underlined the five principles of peaceful coexistence as the basis of their bilateral relationship.[6] These principles included mutual respect for each other's territorial integrity and sovereignty, mutual nonaggression, mutual noninterference in each other's internal affairs, equality and mutual benefit, and peaceful coexistence. This was the heyday of Sino-Indian ties, with the phrase *Hindi-China bhai-bhai* (Indians and Chinese are brothers) being a favorite slogan for the seeming camaraderie between the two states.

But that camaraderie did not last long. Soon the border dispute between China and India escalated, leading to the 1962 Sino-Indian War.[7] Though short, the war would have a long-lasting impact on Sino-Indian ties. It demolished Nehru's claims of Asian solidarity, and the defeat by China psychologically scarred Indian military and political elites. The war also led China to develop close ties with India's neighboring adversary, Pakistan, resulting in what is now widely considered an "all-weather" friendship. China supported Pakistan in its 1965 and 1971 wars with India and helped Islamabad in the development of its nuclear weapons arsenal. Meanwhile, India accelerated its own nuclear weapons program following China's testing of nuclear weapons in 1964.

The border issue continues to be a major obstacle in Sino-Indian ties, with minor skirmishes at the border occurring since 1962. As China and the United States grew closer after their rapprochement in 1972, India gravitated toward the former Soviet Union to balance the Sino-US-Pakistan axis.

In 1988, then Indian Prime Minister Rajiv Gandhi turned a new leaf in Sino-Indian ties when he went to Beijing and signed an agreement aimed at achieving a "fair and reasonable settlement while seeking a mutually acceptable solution to the border dispute."[8] The visit saw a joint working group (JWG) set up to explore the boundary issue and examine possible solutions to the problem.

However, bilateral relations between India and the PRC reached their nadir in the immediate aftermath of India's nuclear tests in May 1998. Just before the tests, the Indian Defense Minister had identified China as his country's top security threat.[9] Afterward, Indian Prime Minister Atal Bihari Vajpayee wrote to US President Bill Clinton justifying Indian nuclear tests as a response to the threat posed by China.[10] Not surprisingly, China reacted strongly, and diplomatic relations between the two countries plummeted to an all-time low.

Today relations between the two countries, at least on the surface, seem to be on a much firmer footing as they have tried to reduce the prospect for rivalry and expand areas of cooperation. The visit of the Indian External Affairs Minister to China in 1999 marked the resumption of high-level dialogue and the two sides declared that they were not threats to each other. A bilateral security dialogue was also initiated that has helped the two countries in openly expressing and sharing their security concerns with each other. Both China and India continue to emphasize that neither side should let differences act as an impediment to the growth of functional cooperation between the two states. India and China also decided to expedite the process of demarcation of the Line of Actual Control (LAC) and the JWG on the boundary question, set up in 1988, has been meeting regularly. As a first step in this direction, the two countries exchanged border maps on the least controversial middle sector of the LAC. Both nations have finalized a set of political "guiding principles" that will govern the parameters of the dispute settlement. China has expressed its desire to seek a "fair" resolution to the vexed boundary issue on the basis of "mutual accommodation, respect for history, and accommodation of reality."[11]

The visit by former Indian Prime Minister Atal Bihari Vajpayee in June 2003 was the first by an Indian premier in a decade. The joint declaration signed during this visit expressed the view that China was not a threat to India.[12] The two states appointed special representatives in order to impart momentum to border negotiations that have lasted now for more than twenty years, with the Prime Minister's principal secretary becoming India's political-level negotiator, replacing the India–China JWG. India and China also decided to hold their first joint naval and air exercises. More significantly, India acknowledged China's sovereignty over Tibet and pledged not to allow "anti-China" political activities in India. On its part, China has acknowledged India's 1975 annexation of the former monarchy of Sikkim by agreeing to open a trading post along the border with the former kingdom and later by rectifying its official maps to include Sikkim as part of India.[13] After being closed for sixty years, the Nathu La pass, a centuries-old trading post between Tibet and Sikkim, was reopened in 2006. High-level political interactions have continued unabated since then. The two states have set up institutionalized defense consultation mechanisms to reduce suspicions and identify areas of cooperation on security issues.

Soon after assuming office in 2004 the Manmohan Singh government too made it clear that it desired closer ties with China and would continue to work toward improving relations. When Singh visited China in 2008, the two states signed the "shared visions on the 21st century" declaration "to promote the building of a harmonious world of durable peace and common prosperity through developing the Strategic and Cooperative Partnership for Peace and Prosperity between the two countries,"[14] while also reiterating support for the 2005 boundary settlement agreement.

This positive trajectory has been helped by growing economic ties between the two have been burgeoning with China emerging as India's largest trading partner. The Sino-Indian trade stands at $70 billion in 2015, providing a basis for long-term engagement.

Global engagement

It is at the international level, however, that India and China have found some real convergence of interests. Both share similar concerns about the international dominance of the United States, the threat of fundamentalist religious and ethnic movements in the form of terrorism and the need to accord primacy to economic development. India and China have both expressed concern about the US use of military power around the world and both were publicly opposed to the war in Iraq. Both China and India, much like other major powers in the international system, favor a multipolar world order where US unipolarity remains constrained by the other "poles" in the system. China and India share an interest in resisting interventionist foreign policy doctrines emanating from the West, particularly the United States, and display "conservative attitudes on the prerogatives of sovereignty."[15]

China and India have coordinated their efforts on issues as wide-ranging as climate change, trade negotiations, energy security, and the global financial crisis. Both nations favor more democratic international economic regimes. Sino-Indian coordination on climate change, global trade negotiations as well as in demanding a restructuring of financial institutions in view of the world economy's shifting center of gravity has had a significant impact on the course of international politics over the last few years. It is being argued that the forces of globalization have led to a certain convergence of Sino-Indian interests in the economic realm, as the two nations become even more deeply engaged in the international trading economy and more integrated in global financial networks.[16] The two have strongly resisted efforts by the United States and other developed nations to link global trade to labor and environmental standards, realizing clearly that this would put them at a huge disadvantage in relation to the developed world, thereby hampering their drive toward economic development, the number one priority for both countries. Both have committed themselves to crafting joint Sino-Indian positions in the WTO and global trade negotiations in the hope that this might provide them greater negotiating leverage over other developed states. They would like to see further liberalization of agricultural trade in the developed countries, tightening of the rules on anti-dumping measures and ensuring that non-trade-related issues such as labor and environment are not allowed to come to the WTO. Both have fought carbon emission caps proposed by the industrialized world and have resisted Western pressure to open their agricultural markets.

The Doha talks had collapsed in 2008 after coming very close to an agreement primarily because of differences between Washington and emerging economies, led by India, over proposals to help farmers in poor nations. China teamed up with India to scuttle the Doha round. Because of their much greater economic power compared to the past, states like China and India now have much greater bargaining power. The United States has suggested that developing nations such as India need to provide greater market access for the talks to advance. India and China argue that they cannot compromise on food security and livelihood concerns even as the United States and the EU remain resistant to scale down their own agricultural subsidies for fear of offending their domestic farm lobbies. China and India have made it clear that they would be able to make unpopular concessions at home only if the developed world provides reciprocal concessions by phasing out its own agricultural subsidies, something that is highly unlikely in the present climate of economic turmoil in the developed world.

This convergence is also reflected in the postures China and India have adopted on issues related to climate change. As the date neared for the UN climate treaty to be negotiated in Copenhagen in December 2009, the West led by the United States and emerging powers such as China and India tried to bridge their differences on how to curb greenhouse gas emissions. The United States wanted developing countries such as India and China to agree to control the emissions being produced by their rapidly growing economies, setting time-bound targets to this effect. China and India argued that this would hurt their economic growth and wanted the industrialized world to curb its pollution as well as fund new technologies in the developing world by underlining that they had low emissions per capita. There was no appetite in Beijing and New Delhi to concede on this issue with both finding it politically difficult to agree on binding targets. Though around 80 percent of world growth in carbon emissions is coming from fast-growing economies like India and China, their governments argue that even if these economies continue to grow at current levels for the next decade or two, their per cap-ita emissions would still be below those of the developed countries.

China and India together blocked such a protocol that called for a more ambitious climate target and mandatory greenhouse gas cuts from both industrialized and major emerging economies. China and India joined Brazil and South Africa in drawing up a basic draft for negotiating cuts in green-house gas emissions on the principle of differentiated responsibility.[17] As a result, the West found it difficult to get its way at Copenhagen. India has followed China in devising its own domestic climate change policies and toward this end, the two have been conducting regular dialogues to exchange views on their respective action plans. China has declared that it is pursuing its National Climate Change Program, which includes manda-tory targets for reducing energy intensity and discharge of major pollutants as well as increasing forest coverage and share of renewable energy during the time period 2005–10. India followed suit by committing itself to a man-datory fuel efficiency cap to begin in 2011, a change in its energy matrix whereby renewable sources will account for 20 percent of India's power usage by 2020, as well as announcing an ambitious solar energy plan.

It is against an increasingly complex strategic background that states such as China and India are trying to shape their own energy policies. Their approach toward their energy predicament remains rather traditional in so far as it is largely state-centric, supply-side biased, mainly reliant on oil, and tends to privilege self-sufficiency.[18] It is toward an aggressive pursuit of energy resources, particularly oil, across the globe that China and India seem to have focused their diplomatic energies in recent years, with some far-reaching implications.

Both China and India are feeling the pressure of diminishing oil discover-ies and flat-lined oil production at a time when expansion of their domestic economies is rapidly increasing demand for energy. They have made energy the focal point of their diplomatic overtures to states far and wide. More sig-nificantly, faced with a market in which politics has an equal, if not greater, influence on price as economics, the two have also decided to coordinate their efforts to secure energy resources overseas. In essence, China and India plan to work together to secure energy resources without unnecessarily bid-ding up the price of those resources, thereby agreeing to a consumer's car-tel representing 2.3 billion potential consumers. Together, their combined markets and purchasing power offers an extremely attractive partner to energy-producing states, especially the ones that face Western pressure over their human rights records or the nature of their political institutions.

From global to bilateral: without much success

The attempt on the part of China in recent years has been to build its bilateral relationship with India on the basis of their larger worldview of international politics. As New Delhi and Beijing discovered a distinct convergence of their interests on the world stage, they have used it to strengthen their bilateral relations. They have established and maintained regular reciprocal high-level visits between political leaders. There has been a serious attempt to improve trade relations and China has sought to compartmentalize intractable issues with India that make it difficult for their bilateral relationship to move forward.

Growing frictions

And yet, despite this changing atmosphere, uneasiness exists between the two Asian giants as they continue their ascent in the global inter-state hierarchy. Even as they sign loftily worded documents year after year, the distrust between the two is actually growing at an alarming rate. True, economic cooperation and bilateral political, as well as socio-cultural exchanges, are at an all-time high; China is India's largest trading partner. Yet this cooperation has done little to assuage each country's concerns about the other's intentions. The two sides are locked in a classic security dilemma, where any action taken by one is immediately interpreted by the other as a threat to its interests.

At the global level, the rhetoric is all about cooperation, and indeed as discussed earlier the two sides have worked together on climate change, global trade negotiations, and demanding a restructuring of global financial institutions in view of the global economy's shifting center of gravity. At the bilateral level, however, mounting tensions reached an impasse in 2009, when China took its territorial dispute with India all the way to the Asian Development Bank. There China blocked India's application for a loan that included money for development projects in the Indian state of Arunachal Pradesh, which China continues to claim as part of its own territory.[19] China's efforts to block the US–India civilian nuclear energy cooperation pact in the Nuclear Suppliers Group (NSG) and its obstructionist stance on bringing to justice the masterminds of the November 2008 terrorist attacks in Mumbai seem to have further confirmed Indian suspicions about China's lack of sensitivity to India's security interests and its failure to recognize India as a global power. This perception was only reinforced by China's suggestion to the US Pacific Fleet commander in 2009 that the Indian Ocean be recognized as part of a Chinese sphere of influence.[20]

Sino-Indian frictions are growing, and the potential for conflict remains high. Alarm is rising in India because of frequent and strident Chinese claims about the LAC in Arunachal Pradesh and Sikkim, where Indians have complained of a dramatic rise in Chinese intrusions into Indian territory over the last few years, most along the border in Arunachal Pradesh, which China refers to as "Southern Tibet." China has also upped the ante on the border issue. It has been regularly protesting against the Indian Prime Minister's visits to Arunachal Pradesh, asserting its claims over the territory.[21] What has caught most observers of Sino-Indian ties by surprise, however, is the vehemence with which Beijing has contested recent Indian administrative and political actions in the state, even denying visas to Indian citizens of Arunachal Pradesh. The recent rounds of boundary negotiations have been a disappointing failure, with a growing perception in India that China is less willing to adhere to earlier political understandings about how to address the boundary dispute.

Pakistan, of course, has always been a crucial foreign policy asset for China, but with India's rise and US–India rapprochement, its role in China's grand strategy is bound to grow even further. Not surprisingly, China's shift away from its old, more cautious approach on Jammu and Kashmir, its increasing military presence in Pakistan, planned infrastructure linking Xinjiang and Gwadar, issuing stapled visas to residents of Jammu and Kashmir and supplying nuclear reactors to Pakistan, all confirm a new intensity behind China's old strategy of using Pakistan to secure its interests in the region.[22]

Strained economic ties

Even the much vaunted economic ties have come under strain as the economic disparities between China and India have increased. Though India has achieved some remarkable growth rates in the last few years, indeed enjoying average annual rates of real income growth of 6 percent in the last two decades of the twentieth century, it still lags far behind China and will need many more years to match China's impressive economic performance. China has outperformed India in terms of levels of growth, of the education, health, and living standards of its population, and integrating its economy with the global economy. In sectors where India and China compete with each other for export markets, such as textiles, China is far ahead even as Sino-Indian competition for third markets is bound to further intensify. China's GDP is four times that of India's. India accounts for less than 1 percent of world trade in goods and services and has been unable to market itself as attractive a destination for foreign direct investment (FDI) as China. Meanwhile, investments by China account for merely 0.01 percent of total foreign investment in India. China's annual trade with India is only a fraction of its trade with Europe, Japan, and the United States. Indian exports to China are primarily dominated by raw materials and iron ore. India's challenge is to match Chinese exports to India and diversify India's export basket.[23] A rising trade deficit that is in favor of China is problematic for India, as is the Indian failure to use its core competencies to enter the Chinese market.

Sino-Indian trade tensions have also risen, especially as the economic downturn that started in 2008 began to make its effect palpable in China and India. Economic nationalism is on the rise in China and the business environment is deteriorating, with China attempting to force foreign companies to hand over their intellectual property and other trademarks if they want to keep selling their goods in China. As the two states compete across the globe for export markets, energy assets, and investment projects, some amount of competition is inevitable. This economic rivalry has intensified as both intrude into each other's strengths, with China shifting its economy toward services and high-tech industries and India trying to rapidly expand its manufacturing base. India remains concerned about the Chinese imports flooding Indian markets and has accused Chinese companies of swamping its markets with low-quality products, even banning, albeit briefly, Chinese-made toys in early 2009 for safety reasons, and is the largest initiator of anti-dumping investigations against China under the WTO.[24] In the words of the Indian commerce secretary, "Cooperation [between China and India] hasn't really worked."[25]

India remains reluctant to open its domestic industries that haven't faced foreign competition and remains ambivalent about allowing Chinese firms a level playing field. The Indian security establishment continues to view Chinese firms with suspicion as potential security hazards given that the People's Liberation Army (PLA) holds a stake in a number of Chinese companies. China has complained that its investments are subjected to rigorous security reviews and work visas for its executives are not swiftly processed. China has been vocal about its concerns about the investment climate in India as it relates to the Chinese firms though most of the FDI proposals from Chinese companies have managed to receive clearance from the Indian government in recent years.[26] There has been talk of a Sino-Indian Free Trade Agreement (FTA) for some time now, but it is not readily evident that it would be a good idea. Given China's manipulation of its currency exchange rate, some see in the FTA a "yuan trap."[27] Though some argue that the long-term economic prospects of India are much better than China's and Chinese policy-makers, under pressure from the United States to revalue their currency, are increasingly worried about India's competitive advantage, China remains the undisputed economic powerhouse of the moment driving the Asian and global economy with India lagging somewhere behind.

Energy competition

China is aggressively working to satisfy its energy requirements in the future. Recent Indian attempts notwithstanding, China has clearly left India far behind in so far as its international diplomacy in the energy realm is concerned. Despite all the talk of Sino-Indian cooperation on energy security, the two sides are actually competing aggressively as their energy demands surge. While there have indeed been some attempts at cooperation, engendering a lot of enthusiasm in some quarters, these developments form a small part of a much broader China–India energy relationship, which remains largely competitive, if not conflictual.

Indian concerns about rising Chinese influence across the globe are derived from the Indian perception that it is losing out to China in the energy race. The Chinese have an upper hand over India in bidding, because they can clinch a deal at any cost, while Indian public sector companies need to ensure that the investment provides at least a 12 percent rate of return. The Chinese companies not only enjoy a head start over their Indian rivals but also have deeper pockets. India is only a recent entrant into the global bidding process, because it was only in 2002 that the Indian government deregulated the domestic oil sector. For China, buying foreign oil and gas fields for energy security has become a central mission, and the Chinese government has allowed its oil majors unprecedented freedom to achieve that goal. China has realized that its energy interests lie in geopolitical relations and has thus decided to focus on these much more intently to address its security needs. And in that pursuit, Chinese oil companies have used all sorts of government aid, including non-oil commitments, transfer of missile technologies, the veto of UN sanctions against countries where China has oil interests, and even education and development aid, to lure energy-rich states. The results are fairly evident.

As a consequence, Sino-Indian relations have reached a stage where tensions are visible in almost all aspects of their bilateral relationship. The Chinese engagement policy of relying on economics and a selective convergence on global issues has reached a dead end. While India has not yet achieved the economic and political profile that China enjoys regionally and globally, it is increasingly bracketed with China as a rising or emerging power – or even a global superpower. Indian elites who have been obsessed with Pakistan for more than sixty years suddenly have found a new object of fascination. India's main security concern now is not the increasingly decrepit state of Pakistan but an ever more assertive China, a shift that is widely viewed inside India as one that can facilitate better strategic planning. China is viewed by a large section of the Indian policy elite as a growing, aggressive nationalistic power whose ambitions are likely to reshape the contours of the regional and global balance of power with deleterious consequences for Indian interests.

India balances a rising China

China's recent hardening toward India might well be a function of its own internal vulnerabilities, but that is hardly a consolation to Indian policy-makers who have to respond to an Indian public that increasingly wants the country to assert itself in the region and beyond. New Delhi has responded to the challenge posed by a rising China by adopting a more hard-nosed policy vis-à-vis Beijing.

While there has always been and continues to be a range of opinions in India on how best to deal with China, a consensus seems to be evolving among the highest echelons of military planners and policy-makers.[28] For a long time now, Indian defense officials have been warning their government in rather blunt terms about the growing disparity between the two Asian powers. The naval chief had warned that India neither has "the capability nor the intention to match China force for force" in military terms, while the former air chief had suggested that China poses more of a threat to India than does Pakistan. But the political leadership in India continued to act on the assumption that Beijing is not a short-term threat to India but rather needs to be watched over the long term. However, that assessment seems to be undergoing a change. After trying to ignore significant differences with China, Indian decision-makers are finally acknowledging that the relationship between the countries is becoming increasingly contentious. Former Indian Prime Minister Manmohan Singh had suggested that "China would like to have a foothold in South Asia and we have to reflect on this reality ... It's important to be prepared."[29] Former Indian Defence Minister, A.K. Antony, had argued that China's increasing assertiveness is a "serious threat."[30] And a former national security advisor and special envoy to China, M.K. Narayanan, has openly accused Chinese hackers of attacking his website as well as those of other government departments.[31]

An elite consensus is evolving in India that China's rise is posing problems for the country. "We are friends, not rivals," said the Chinese premier in India.[32] But a growing number of Indians now see China as a competitor, if not a rival. A 2010 Pew poll suggested that only 34 percent of Indians held a favorable view of China, with four in ten viewing their neighbor as a "very serious threat."[33] More damaging is the perception gaining ground in India that China is the only major power that does not accept India as a rising global player that must be accommodated. The discord between the two countries thus remains entrenched, and their increasing economic strength and geopolitical standing has only underlined their rapidly growing ambitions. Though it is not entirely clear if China has well-defined policy objectives vis-à-vis India, Beijing's means, both economic and military, to pursue its goals are greater than at any time in the recent past. In response, a process of military consolidation and build-up of key external partnerships is underway in India.

With a new robustness in its dealings with Beijing, New Delhi is signaling that there are limits to what is negotiable in Sino-Indian ties. In particular, it has adopted a harder line on Tibet by making it clear to Beijing that it expects China to reciprocate on Jammu and Kashmir just as India has respected Chinese sensitivities on Tibet and Taiwan. Overriding Chinese objections, for example, the Indian government went ahead and allowed one of its central universities, the Indira Gandhi

National Open University, to confer an honorary doctorate on the Dalai Lama.[34] This is the same government that just a few years back sent a note to all its ministers advising them against attending a function organized by the Gandhi Peace Foundation to honor the Dalai Lama so as to not to offend China.[35]

Likewise, after Beijing began issuing stapled visas to the residents of Jammu and Kashmir and then denied a visa to the head of the Indian Army's Northern Command, New Delhi reacted forcefully and hinted that it was ready to review its long-standing Tibet and Taiwan policies. India also declined to endorse the "one China" policy during Wen's visit to India, a departure from past statements.[36]

During Prime Minister Narendra Modi's visit to China in May 2015, he openly "stressed the need for China to reconsider its approach on some of the issues that hold us back from realizing full potential of our partnership" and "suggested that China should take a strategic and long-term view of our relations."[37] In his speech at Tsinghua University too, Modi went beyond the rhetorical flourishes of Sino-Indian cooperation, pointing out the need to resolve the border dispute and to "ensure that our relationships with other countries do not become a source of concern for each other." This is a shift in Indian traditional defensiveness vis-à-vis China, underscoring a recalibration in policy by squarely putting the blame for stalemate in bilateral ties on China's doorstep.

India is reassessing its policy toward China as the latter's faster-than-expected rise has challenged the fundamentals of New Delhi's traditional approach to Beijing. India's robust partnership with the United States, its burgeoning ties with East and Southeast Asian nations as part of its "Look East" policy, and its military modernization are all aimed at managing China's dramatic rise.

Conclusion

India is gearing up to respond to China's rise with its own diplomatic and military overtures, setting the stage for a Sino-Indian strategic rivalry. Indian policy trajectory toward China is evolving as India starts to pursue a policy of internal and external balancing more forcefully in an attempt to protect its core interests. The government is trying to fashion an effective response to the rise of China at a time of great regional and global turbulence. Though it is not entirely clear if there is a larger strategic framework shaping India's China policy, India's approach toward China is indeed undergoing a transformation, the full consequences of which will only be visible a few years down the line.

Both India and China have a vested interest in stabilizing their relationship by seeking out issues on which their interests converge, but pursuing mutually desirable interests does not inevitably produce satisfactory solutions to strategic problems. A troubled history coupled with the structural uncertainties engendered by their simultaneous rise is propelling the two Asian giants into a trajectory that they might find rather difficult to navigate in the coming years. For India, symbolism matters, especially in the context of acknowledging India's rise as a major global power. And that has not come from China. Sino-Indian ties have entered turbulent times, and they are likely to remain there for the foreseeable future.

Notes

1 "Nervous China May Attack India by 2012: Defence Expert," *Indian Express*, July 12, 2009.
2 See for example, "China Could Attack India by 2012, Claims Analyst," Press Trust of India, July 12, 2009.
3 Li Hongmei, "Veiled Threat or Good Neighbor?" *People's Daily Online*, June 19, 2009, http://english.peopledaily.com.cn/90002/96417/6682302.html.
4 *Ibid.*
5 For a detailed discussion of early Sino-Indian ties, see John Rowland, *A History of Sino-Indian Relations: Hostile Co-Existence* (Princeton: D. Van Nostrand Company, 1967).
6 "India and the People's Republic of China: Agreement (with Exchange of Notes) on Trade and Intercourse between Tibet Region of China and India" (Beijing, April 29, 1954), recorded in United Nations, *Treaty Series* 299 (1958), 57.
7 For a detailed account, see Steven A. Hoffmann, *India and the China Crisis* (Berkeley: University of California Press, 1990). For an earlier account that is quite critical of Nehru and his "forward policy," see Neville Maxwell, *India's China War* (London: Jonathan Cape, 1970).
8 "Sino-Indian Joint Press Communiqué," Ministry of Foreign Affairs of the People's Republic of China (PRC), December 23, 1988, www.fmprc.gov.cn/eng/wjdt/2649/t15800.htm.
9 "China is Threat No.1, Says Fernandes," *Hindustan Times*, May 3, 1998.
10 "Nuclear Anxiety; Indian's Letter to Clinton on the Nuclear Testing," *New York Times*, May 13, 1998, www.nytimes.com/1998/05/13/world/nuclear-anxiety-indian-s-letter-to-clinton-on-the-nuclear-testing.html.
11 Anil K. Joseph, "Wen to Seek Resolution of Border Dispute," *Indian Express*, March 15, 2005.
12 "Declaration on Principles for Relations and Comprehensive Cooperation Between the People's Republic of China and the Republic of India," Ministry of Foreign Affairs of the PRC, June 23, 2003, www.fmprc.gov.cn/eng/wjdt/2649/t22852.htm.
13 Amit Baruah, "China Keeps Its Word on Sikkim," *Hindu*, May 7, 2004.
14 "A Shared Vision for the 21st Century of the People's Republic of China and the Republic of India," Ministry of Foreign Affairs of the PRC, January 14, 2008, www.fmprc.gov.cn/eng/wjdt/2649/t399545.htm.

15 James Clad, "Convergent Chinese and Indian Perspectives on the Global Order," in Francine R. Frankel and Harry Harding (eds), *The India-China Relationship: What the United States Needs to Know* (New York: Columbia University Press, 2004), pp. 267–93.

16 *Ibid.*

17 K.G. Narendranath, "Jairam has a Copenhagen Axis: India, China, Brazil, South Africa," *The Indian Express*, December 8, 2009.

18 Edward R. Fried and Philip H. Trezise, *Oil Security: Retrospect and Prospect* (Washington, DC: Brookings Institution Press, 1993), p. 1.

19 "China Blocked India's ADB Plan over Arunachal, Confirms Krishna," *Indian Express*, July 10, 2009.

20 Yuriko Koike, "The Struggle for Mastery of the Pacific," Project Syndicate, May 12, 2010, www.project-syndicate.org/commentary/koike5/English.

21 "China 'Strongly' Protests over PM's Visit to Arunachal Pradesh," *Daily News and Analysis*, October 13, 2009.

22 On the China–Pakistan–India triangle, see Harsh V. Pant, "The Pakistan Thorn in China-India-US Relations," *The Washington Quarterly*, Vol. 35, No. 1 (Winter 2012), pp. 83–95.

23 Amit Mitra, "An Unequal Relationship," *Times of India*, January 12, 2008.

24 Peter Wonacott, "Downturn Heightens China-India Tension on Trade," *Wall Street Journal*, March 20, 2009.

25 *Ibid.*

26 Shishir Gupta, "Contrary to What Left Says, 87% of FDI Proposals from Chinese Firms Cleared," *Indian Express*, November 13, 2006.

27 Swaminathan S. Anklesaria Aiyar, "Free Trade Area or Yuan Trap?" *Times of India*, November 26, 2006.

28 For a good typology of India's China debate, see Mohan Malik, "Eyeing the Dragon: India's China Debate," Asia-Pacific Center for Security Studies, Special Assessment, December 2003, www.apcss.org/Publications/SAS/ChinaDebate/ChinaDebate_Malik.pdf.

29 "PM Warns on China's South Asia Foothold," *Indian Express*, September 7, 2010.

30 Rajat Pandit, "Assertive China a Worry, says Antony," *Times of India*, September 14, 2010.

31 "Chinese Hacked PMO Computers, says Narayanan," *Indian Express*, January 19, 2010.

32 Jim Yardley, "In India, Chinese Leader Pushes Trade," *New York Times*, December 16, 2010.

33 The details of this poll are available at "Key Indicators Database: Opinion of China, Percent Responding Favorable, All Years Measured," Pew Global Attitudes Project, http://pewglobal.org/database/?indicator=24&survey=12&response=Favorable&mode=table.

34 Anubhuti Vishnoi, "MEA Gives Nod to IGNOU for Doctorate to Dalai Lama," *Indian Express*, April 24, 2011.

35 "Pleasing Beijing, Govt Tells its Ministers Don't Attend Dalai Lama Honour Function," *Indian Express*, November 4, 2007.
36 Pramit Pal Chaudhuri, "China's Flip-Flop on Kashmir," *Hindustan Times*, April 15, 2011.
37 James T. Areddy and Niharika Mandhana, "India's Modi Prods China to Change Tack on Strategic Issues," *Wall Street Journal*, May 15, 2015.

4

India and Russia: convergence across time

There are few examples of a relationship between countries that has been as stable as the one between India and Russia. Despite the momentous changes in the international environment after the end of the Cold War, there remains a continued convergence of interests that makes it advantageous for both India and Russia to maintain close ties. Barring a fleeting hiccup during Boris Yeltsin's term as Russia's president, New Delhi and Moscow have been extraordinarily successful in nurturing a friction-free relationship that harks back to the Soviet era. This chapter examines the factors that have been the main historical drivers of India–Russia ties and that are likely to shape the trajectory of this relationship in the coming years.

The Soviet era: alignment in the non-alignment phase

India enjoyed a multifaceted relationship with the Soviet Union which ranged from the political and, economic to technological and strategic ties. In many ways, it was a special and unique relationship. For India, the Soviet Union contributed an irreplaceable counterbalancing force in facing up to its regional and international concerns and an added source of strength in pushing economic and scientific development with India receiving valuable assistance in establishing basic industrial infrastructure. The relationship with the Soviet Union offered protection against perceived external adversaries, Pakistan and China, even as Soviet military support allowed India to emerge as a military power of some consequence. It is not surprising, therefore, that despite trying to emerge as a leader of the NAM, India sought to cultivate a "special relationship" with the Soviet Union. For the Soviet Union, ties with India were aimed at counterbalancing Chinese and American influence in the region, as well as securing support among the Third World states via Indian leadership of NAM. As the ties between the ruling communist parties in Moscow and Beijing deteriorated in the 1950s and 1960s, the Indo-Russian partnership gathered momentum.

It was the death of Stalin in 1953 that allowed the Soviet–Indian relationship to grow. Prior to that Soviet elites viewed India's Congress Party

leaders as "reactionaries" under the influence of "Anglo-American imperial-
ism." India was too preoccupied with domestic issues to devote attention to
foreign policy.[1] The Indian position on the Korean conflict when it strongly
protested at the United Nation's decision to extend the war north of the
38th parallel and Jawaharlal Nehru's forceful support for the PRC's admis-
sion into the UN saw Soviet and Indian policy converging on two crucial
global issues.

As the US tilt toward Pakistan became more pronounced with the
American decision to extend military assistance to Pakistan in 1954 followed by Pakistan's subsequent accession both to the Southeast Asia Treaty
Organization (SEATO) in 1954 and the Baghdad Pact (later CENTO), Indian
concerns grew about the interventionist approach of the United States and
the concomitant downgrading of New Delhi's own pre-eminent role in the
sub-continent.[2] India's opposition to the US arming of Pakistan was based
on India's desire to try to keep both superpowers out of the subcontinent
to the extent possible. The United States not only brought the Cold War
to India's doorstep, as Nehru noted, but was also striving to negate India's
natural pre-eminence in the subcontinent. At one stage, Nehru said that the
Baghdad Pact and the Manila treaty were tantamount to encircling India.[3]
India's drift away from the United States and toward the communist powers
became more pronounced.

Given the US policy toward the subcontinent in the 1950s, Nehru was
forced to involve the Soviet Union in India's affairs to a greater extent than
he had wanted to. Later, Moscow had to be used as a counter-weight to
China's hostility. Nehru also wanted to diversify India's economic links with
other nations, specifically reducing the dependence on the West. Instead of
minimizing the superpowers' role in the subcontinent, India had to opt for
maximizing it to give the policy of bi-alignment.[4]

India's pro-Soviet position at the Bandung conference in 1955 further
consolidated these ties. The Soviet leadership started voicing support for
India's general foreign policy orientation, as well as its position on specific
issues such as Kashmir and Goa.[5] As a result, while the Soviet policy toward
India was a response to American and Chinese diplomatic moves in the
region, Indian foreign policy was also responding to the rapidly shifting
great power alignments.

The Soviet support outside the UN and threat or use of veto inside the
Security Council acted as an umbrella against a determined Western pressure in favor of Pakistan and to the detriment of India. And this Soviet policy
of close and friendly relations with India remained singularly stable despite
occasional problems. In 1955, the Soviet Union unequivocally accepted the
position that Kashmir was an integral part of India. Moscow became an
indispensable source of supply of military hardware not available elsewhere.

Recognizing the importance of the Soviet Union in its foreign policy calculus, India acted accordingly. While it strongly condemned the Anglo-French

intervention in Egypt, its response to Soviet intervention in Hungary was weak, to say the least. It even joined the communist bloc to vote against a UN General Assembly resolution calling for the withdrawal of Soviet troops from Hungary though Nehru was later forced to criticize the Soviet policy toward Hungary. The Soviet Union also adopted a neutral position in Indian disputes with China, much to Chinese annoyance. As border clashes erupted between China and India in 1959, the Soviet Union called for direct negotiations between the two to settle the problem, angering the Chinese and pleasing India. During the 1962 war, the fact that the Soviet Union had not proffered open support to its ostensible communist ally was used by the Nehru government to buttress its claims that non-alignment was a good policy for India.

Despite bureaucratic and military resistance, Indo-Soviet defense ties gathered momentum in the early 1960s. This was as much due to India's failure to obtain similar military technology under comparable terms from the West as it was due to the need for diversification of arms sources. Meanwhile, the Soviet Union was concerned that American and British military aid to India during the 1962 war with China might tilt New Delhi toward the West and so a renewed push was given to India–Soviet ties after 1962. The Congress Party and Nehru however had no such intention for they were convinced that a strong relationship with the Soviet Union was essential to further Indian foreign policy aims across a broad spectrum of issues.[6]

The Soviet role as a mediator in Tashkent after the Indo-Pak conflict of 1965 was appreciated in India as the Soviet Union provided clear assurances that Indian interests would not be compromised. By the late 1960s, the Soviet Union had emerged as India's primary supplier of defense equipment and India's second largest trading partner. On global issues New Delhi and Moscow adopted identical positions. For example, joint Soviet–Indian communiqués from 1965 onwards registered their opposition to the US bombing campaign in Vietnam. On the other hand, India did not condemn the Soviet invasion of Czechoslovakia in 1968. Though there was widespread popular sympathy for the Czechs in India, the Indian government only expressed mild "regret" and even abstained in the Security Council vote.

The Soviet agreement to set up a plant in India for the production of MiG-21 was also a product of geopolitical realities. The Russian agreement to let India produce MiGs was a valuable symbol of Soviet support against China. It was not entirely clear to New Delhi that the West would be willing to permit India to emerge as a strong military power. Moreover, Moscow was the only arms supplier sympathetic to India's philosophy of a self-sufficient military establishment.[7]

The 1971 treaty: India's balance of power strategy

As the regional security environment deteriorated in the early 1970s, India sought even closer ties with Moscow. India had realized that without unfettered access to Soviet arms it would not be able to pursue the military option. On the other hand, the Sino-American rapprochement facilitated by Pakistan was constraining India's room to maneuver. It was under these circumstances that India mooted the possibility of a bilateral treaty of Peace and Friendship with Soviet Union. Finally, the twenty-year Soviet–Indian treaty of Peace, Friendship and Cooperation was signed by the two states in August 1971.[8]

The Nixon administration viewed the crisis in the subcontinent in 1969–70 through the prism of a strategic relationship it hoped to build with China and so its tilt toward Pakistan was understandable given the help Pakistan was providing as a conduit to China.[9] Moscow's backing of New Delhi's position on Bangladesh was of critical importance for India, confronted as it was with the combined opposition of the United States and China who along with Pakistan were striving to evolve a new equation in Asia for themselves. The new strategic relationship Beijing sought with the United States exacerbated Sino-Soviet rivalry and caused anxiety in New Delhi.

India desperately needed Soviet diplomatic and strategic support in the event of war with Pakistan. Kissinger had warned India, "If war broke out between India and Pakistan, and China became involved on Pakistan's side, we would be unable to help you against China."[10] This pushed India into making some hasty overtures toward the Soviet Union and the latter was surprised if not taken aback by the speed with which India wished to formalize the Indo-Soviet treaty that had been in discussion since 1969. The dramatic announcement of Kissinger's secret visit to Beijing in July 1971 and President Nixon's slated visit in 1972 made the Sino-US alignment a very real possibility.

The treaty precluded either country from entering into military alliances directed against the other party. Both sides were to "abstain from providing any assistance to any third party that engages in armed conflict with the other party. In the event of either party being subjected to attack or threat thereof, the high contracting parties shall immediately enter into mutual consultations in order to remove such a threat and to take effective measures to ensure peace and security of their countries." For India, the treaty served the strategic purpose of deterring Chinese or American intervention in a possible Indo-Pakistani war. It also provided an insurance of Soviet diplomatic support in the UN if the issue reached the world body. It has also been argued that Moscow's intention to expand its military aid program to Pakistan in the late 1960s was a more potent factor in India deciding to sign this treaty. Sisson and Rose suggest that the much publicized Pakistan–China–US "axis" was in fact concocted by New Delhi and was not of great concern to decision-makers in India as not only was such an alliance unlikely to emerge in the early stages of a US–China rapprochement, the continuing disagreements between Washington and Beijing over the American involvement in the Vietnam War was a much more critical issue for them both.[11]

Whatever the motives, the treaty led the Soviet Union toward providing India with the requisite military support should the military option became necessary and by late 1971 the Soviet Union started supporting India's contention that the refugees from East Pakistan were no longer an internal affair of Pakistan.[12] Once the war started, the Soviet Union attributed sole responsibility for the war to Pakistan and warned other governments to avoid becoming involved in the conflict. Giving India crucial time to consolidate its military position in East Pakistan, the Soviet Union vetoed the UN resolutions calling for a ceasefire and the withdrawal of Indian and Pakistani forces from each other's territories. Soviet naval vessels were sent to the Bay of Bengal to counter the movement of an American naval task force into the same area. Indian military victory would not have been possible without the deterrent posture adopted by the Soviet Union vis-à-vis extra-regional powers. In essence, the 1971 Treaty of Peace, Friendship and Cooperation helped India win its third war against Pakistan, safeguard its territorial integrity and neutralize external threats stemming from the Sino-American rapprochement, the China–Pakistan nexus as well as the US alliance with Pakistan. Soviet support in the diplomatic and military realm stemmed from a convergence of Indo-Russian national interests.

India continued to adopt positions on international issues in accord with those of the Soviet Union and even when the Indian and Soviet interests diverged, India tried to publicly minimize those differences by refraining from open criticism of Soviet policy. Indira Gandhi realized the true extent of Indian dependence on the Soviet Union and modified India's position on Vietnam from linking a halt to the bombing of Vietnam with a ceasefire in South Vietnam to an immediate and unconditional halt to American bombing.

The Soviet Union did not seek to create a balance in its ties with India and Pakistan. Its limited attempts at reaching out to Pakistan were intended to make it not solely dependent on the United States or China. The Soviet Union did not condemn the Indian nuclear test of 1974 and in fact seemed to be justifying it, lending support to the theory of Chinese nuclear blackmail. After American and Canadian shipments of heavy water to India were halted in the wake of Indian nuclear tests in 1974, the Soviet Union stepped in to fill the void by readily agreeing to provide heavy water for its nuclear reactors.

A relationship unaffected by domestic politics

Despite its ups and downs, the Indo-Soviet relationship remained largely insulated from the vicissitudes of the Indian domestic political situation.

Across the party-political dividing lines, the relationship with the Soviet Union was viewed as special, as one that served important national interests. It has been rightly observed that Indian internal developments did not per se constitute a major determinant of the Indo-Soviet relationship.[13] Though the President of the Janata Party, Morarji Desai, had openly criticized the 1971 Indo-Soviet treaty and had declared that if his party came to power the treaty would be scrapped, once in power the Janata government led by Desai himself realized that a change from Indira Gandhi's policy toward Moscow was not possible in light of the arms, trade, and security linkages with the USSR.[14] Despite some internal opposition, the Janata government continued to view India's relationship with the Soviet Union as serving Indian national interests and sought to assure Moscow that no major shift in the country's foreign policy orientation would be contemplated.

Indira Gandhi government's attitude toward the Soviet occupation of Afghanistan was largely sympathetic. India abstained on the UN General Assembly resolution calling for the immediate termination of armed intervention in Afghanistan despite an overwhelming 104–18 vote in favor of the motion. India's stance was widely viewed as tacit support for the Soviet position. India linked Soviet occupation of Afghanistan to the expansion of American facilities in Diego Garcia and the evolving Sino-American security relationship.[15]

While New Delhi had reacted vociferously to the American decision to expand existing British facilities on Diego Garcia it was muted in its response to the Soviet invasion of Afghanistan. Many Third World states wondered aloud if there was an erosion in India's non-aligned status.

Indian foreign policy elites viewed the Soviet intervention in Afghanistan in December 1979 as a defensive move, accelerated by the turmoil in Iran and possible military action against it, to ensure that Afghanistan does not harbor an anti-Soviet regime. India abstained on the General Assembly resolution condemning the Soviet action not only to repay Soviet support to India at the UN but also to safeguard India's security interests in a region that had become highly unstable by not weakening the Soviet link. India ended up almost endorsing the Soviet action in Afghanistan.[16]

Despite ritual condemnations of the "balance of power," India used it to retain leverage with the Soviet Union. It was the Soviet Union that helped India build a heavy industry and arms technology base and ultimately enabled India to win the Bangladesh war. India, for its part, made the Soviet Union acceptable to the Third World and muted its criticism of Moscow on major world issues. The relationship therefore served the interests of both states during the entire Cold War period.

The post-Cold War era

After the end of the Cold War, Russia had little strategic interest in South Asia except as a potential market for arms and missile technology sales in exchange for hard currency. The rapid rise of India's trade with the United States and the even more spectacular rise of US investments in India constrained Indo-Soviet strategic cooperation. It took India and Russia a few years to come to terms with the post-Cold War international environment and it was only when Vladimir Putin assumed office did seriousness return to bilateral ties.

In sharp contrast to the erratic ties India had with Russia when Boris Yeltsin was at the helm, Putin refocused attention on India. While maintaining continuity in ensuring a substantive and incremental pattern of relations with the United States and Western Europe, Putin revived equations with other major Asian nations like China, Japan, and India. It was under Putin's leadership that Russia established a strategic partnership with India in 2000. Putin's re-election to the Russian presidency in March 2012 has only helped in sustaining continuity in Indo-Russian relations, especially as Putin has described India as a "key strategic partner in the Asia-Pacific region."[17] But there are new parameters that have defined and will continue to shape the trajectory of India's ties with Russia in the post-Cold War era.

Changing balance of power
After the Cold War, both India and Russia struggled for several years to define their relations with other major players on the global stage, where the rules of international politics were in a state of flux and where the terms of the economic interaction between nations were being reset. As India rose in the global inter-state hierarchy, many in India continued to rely on Russia for opposing the "unipolar world order." The most visible manifestation of this tendency was an attempt to carve a Russia–China–India "strategic triangle."[18] The proposal for a Moscow–Beijing–Delhi strategic triangle had originally come from the former Russian Prime Minister, Yevgeny Primakov, during his visit to India in 1998, arguing that such an arrangement would be a force for greater regional and international stability. But as every state in the triangle needed the United States to further its own interests, this project could not move beyond platitudinous rhetoric.

And now with the United States in relative decline and China emerging as its most likely challenger, Russia and India are struggling to come to grips with the implications of a possible Chinese hegemony over the Asian strategic landscape. Russia shares a common strategic objective with India for a stable power balance in Asia where China is increasingly looming large. It is this geopolitical imperative that is forcing New Delhi and Moscow to ramp up their partnership. While this has not been discussed openly, this is the hidden subtext behind the rapidity with which the two states are trying to revise their relationship. The rise of China is the new reality that India and Russia are trying to come to grips with and this will shape the contours of Indo-Russian ties in the future. This is reflected in both bilateral and multilateral initiatives being proposed by the two sides. At the bilateral level, after completing a decade of strategic partnership, inaugurated in 2000, New Delhi and Moscow decided to elevate their relationship to a "Special and Privileged Strategic Partnership" in 2010. At the multilateral level, Russia's promotion of the Russia–China–India trilateral initiative and now the Brazil, Russia, India, China, and South Africa (BRICS) grouping is aimed at enhancing its international status vis-à-vis the West and the need for a realignment of the post-World War II global order that was based on the untrammelled supremacy of the United States. Given China's growing dominance of the global economy and polity, it is not readily evident if such initiatives, in and of themselves, will be enough to shape the evolving regional and global balance of power in Russia and India's favor.

New expectations from defense
Defense, of course, remains central to Indo-Russian relations. Not only is Russia the biggest supplier of defense products to India, but the India–Russia defense relationship also encompasses a wide range of activity that includes joint research, design, development, and co-production.[19] India, for its part, was one of the few nations ready to finance the production of weapons in Russia at a time when the Russian arms industry was facing virtual disarray due to the collapse of the Soviet Union. The old buyer–seller defense relationship is now being transformed into a defense industrial collaboration that emphasizes joint development of weapons. Russia is the only country with which India has an institutionalized mechanism at the defense minister level fostering transfer of high technology and joint production. India is now locally producing several Russian defense products including the Brahmos supersonic missile, the T-90 tank, and Sukhoi fighter aircrafts. Russia has agreed to further expand defense supplies ties with India, both in content and range, and has also agreed to give its nod to cooperation in sophisticated spheres of technology about which the United States and other Western nations have seemed reticent.

Significant defense deals signed in recent years include a $2.34 billion contract for the refit of the Gorshkov aircraft carrier; a $1.2 billion deal to procure twenty-nine additional MiG 29 K naval fighter aircraft; and an agreement for an additional forty Su MKI fighters for the Indian Air Force. The contract for the preliminary design of the fifth generation fighter aircraft has been signed between India's Hindustan Aeronautics Limited and Russia's Rosoboronexport and Sukhoi and will lead to the development of a next generation fighter with features like advanced stealth, ultra-maneuverability and high-tech avionics.[20] Other deals include the delivery of seventy-one Mi-17V-5 transport helicopters from Russia to India, another shipment of Mi-17V-5 helicopters, supply of Kamov Ka-31 (Helix) helicopters to be used on the Vikrant-class aircraft carriers, and a deal on the second batch of twenty-nine MiG-29K/KUB carrier based fighters. Indo-Russian cooperation on space is gathering momentum with India participating in the commercial as well as military segments of Glonass, the Russian version of the US-controlled Global Positioning System (GPS), in its quest for strategic autonomy in advanced technology.[21]

The bilateral defense relationship has indeed come under pressure as India has adjusted to the changing nature of modern warfare and shifted its defense priorities to the purchase of smart weaponry, which Russia is ill equipped to provide. Already, India's increasing defense ties with Israel and the gradual opening of the US arms market for India has made Russia relatively less exciting for India. The US offer to India of F-16s, the Patriot antimissile system, C-130 stretched medium-lift transport aircraft, and P-3C Orion maritime surveillance planes may only be a reflection of what is still to come. In contrast to more than sixty naval exercises with the United States, India has conducted only five such exercises with Russia.[22] India rejected a Russian bid for a US$10.4 billion sale to India of 126 medium multi-role combat aircraft in favor of Rafale from Dassault of France. Though Moscow did not discuss its disappointment in public, it did cancel a few important military exercises with India, signaling its disappointment.[23]

The Indian military has been critical of an over-reliance on Russia for defense acquisition which was reflected in the Indian Naval Chief's view that there should be a rethink on India's ties with Russia in light of the Russian demand of US$1.2 billion more for the aircraft carrier, *Admiral Gorshkov*, purchased by India in 2004.[24] India has had to pay US$2.34 billion for *Gorshkov*'s retrofitting instead of the US$974 million agreed upon in 2004 and it was handed over to India only in 2013.[25] Russia had promised to handover to India an Akula-II class nuclear-powered submarine in 2009 on a ten-year lease but it came to India only in 2012. There have also been complaints from the Indian Air Force and the Indian Army about the delays in delivery and repair of Russian equipment and a shortage of spare parts. Though there is certainly disquiet among the Indian armed forces about Russian behavior on these issues, it is also clear that Russia is the only state that is willing to share defense technology of a strategic nature with India including aircraft carriers and nuclear submarines. It is equally significant that Russia is probably the only major global power that has not sold defense technology to Pakistan. Despite repeated delays in Russia's implementation of major weapon orders, India continues to rely on Russia for strategic weaponry. Russia will remain India's major defense partner in the foreseeable future as the two states move toward joint development and production of new weapon systems to sustain their historically strong defense ties. This will be key to sustaining Indo-Russian cooperation given the changing technological needs of the Indian defense sector.

India is sensitive to the fact that Russia also enjoys an excellent defense relationship with China and that Russia has even been reaching out to Pakistan. It is the largest supplier of defense equipment to China, with the result that the modernization of Chinese military owes a lot to Russian supplies.[26] Not only is this of direct strategic consequence for Indian security but it also creates a cascading effect whereby Russian military technology and know-how gets transferred to Pakistan via China. Therefore, the prospects of Indo-Russian defense and political cooperation will be assessed by India in the light of Russia's defense supplies and cooperation arrangements with China. On the other hand, there are concerns in Russia about the growing Indian strategic alignment with the United States even as Russia has been adopting an increasingly confrontational posture vis-à-vis the United States and the West. But the rapid rise of China has upended the regional balance of power in Asia and Moscow and New Delhi have already started to work together to counter the possibility of Chinese regional hegemony. China has been importing a significant quantity of advanced weapons from Russia over the last two decades but is now producing Russian-designed weapons and is poised to export much of this weaponry to the developing world, thereby undercutting Russia. This has strained ties between the two states, with Russia suggesting that one of China's latest fighters, the J-11B, is a copy of the Su-27 that it had supplied to Beijing in the 1990s.[27] Given the steady deterioration in Sino-Indian ties in recent years, the threat of China will be one of the most important factors in determining India's outreach to Russia in the defense sector.

Sub-optimal economic ties

The most challenging aspect of Indo-Russian relations today is, perhaps, the upgrading of bilateral economic and trade relations, which fails to reflect the potential that exists and is a major challenge that the two countries are trying to address on a priority basis. Bilateral trade stood at US$10 billion in 2013 and after years of persistent decline has only recently picked up with the two states aiming to achieve a trade target of US$30 billion by 2025. On the other hand, China is now Russia's largest trading partner and the two sides have signed a thirty-year agreement under which Russia will supply China with 68 billion cubic meters of gas annually from 2015.[28] To address this problem, Russia has not only been trying to woo Indian investors but has also agreed to use the amount that India owes it as debt from the past to fund joint ventures in the fields of telecommunications, aluminium, and information technology.[29] The two states are also studying the possibility of a Comprehensive Economic Cooperation Agreement between India and the Belarus–Kazakhstan–Russia customs union. Moscow is promising greater access to Indian investment in high-technology sectors where Russia needs all the help it can get. Information technology and the financial sector are where Indian companies are trying to get a foothold in Russia. But the dynamic Indian private sector is not attracted to Russia as the Russian economy is not yet as innovative and technologically advanced compared to the West.

India is looking to Russia as a major supplier of the much-needed energy resources in the future, with India investing in Russia's Sakhalin-1 hydrocarbon project in one of its highest public sector investments abroad. Russia is also stressing its role as a key energy supplier. The two states are collaborating to align India's oil and gas companies with powerful Russian state-owned energy companies such as Gazprom. A consortium of Indian oil companies including ONGC Videsh, GAIL, and Petronet LNG, is investing in Russia's independent gas producer Novatek's US$30 billion liquefied natural gas (LNG) project in Yamal peninsula in order to secure a share in Russia's gas sector.[30] Russia's state-owned nuclear corporation is planning to set up joint ventures with Indian companies to manufacture power generation equipment. Civilian nuclear energy cooperation has also gathered momentum with a comprehensive nuclear deal between India and Russia and a pact to build two power plants in the Indian state of Tamil Nadu.[31] Russia is already constructing four nuclear reactors in India and this nuclear pact will lead to more than a dozen Russian nuclear power plants in India. Russian Atomic Energy Corporation, Rosatom, is working toward the construction of two nuclear power reactors of the Kudankulam Nuclear Power Plant. Russia will remain India's main partner in the civilian nuclear energy sector given the problems American and French companies will face in investing in India in the absence of an India–Japan civilian nuclear pact. Given the involvement of Japanese firms in the American and French nuclear industry, an Indo-Japanese pact is essential if US and French civilian nuclear cooperation with India is to be realized. Japanese approval, for instance, is needed if GE-Hitachi and Toshiba-Westinghouse are to sell nuclear reactors to India.[32]

The "Af-Pak" challenge

The rapidly deteriorating security situation in Afghanistan is another key factor shaping India's priorities vis-à-vis Russia in recent years. Moscow's assertion that the security situation in Afghanistan "does impact the security" of India and Russia underscores the convergence of views between the two states on the evolving situation in Afghanistan.[33] Both have consistently maintained that "the fight against terrorism cannot be selective, and drawing false distinctions between 'good' and 'bad' Taliban would be counter-productive."[34] As a consequence, India and Russia have stepped up cooperation on Afghanistan. This comes at a time when Indian disenchantment with the West on "Af-Pak" is growing and it is looking at alternative policy options to secure its interests.[35] To preserve its interests in such a strategic milieu, India is re-assessing its options. Reaching out to Moscow is one step in that direction.

Much like New Delhi, Moscow has, time and again, laid down certain "red lines" on the integration of the Taliban that include renunciation of violence by the Taliban, cessation of armed struggle, acceptance of the

Afghan constitution, and a complete break with Al Qaeda.[36] Where India recognizes that a victory by pro-Pakistan Pashtun groups, Taliban or otherwise, in Afghanistan is a defeat for its outreach to the Afghans, Russia hopes to leverage the Afghan crisis into an acceptance of Moscow's security leadership by the Central Asian nations vulnerable to Taliban-inspired Islamist militancy.

Moscow is refocusing on Afghanistan as Islamist extremism and drug trafficking emanating from Central Asia have emerged as major threats to its national security. Moscow hosted the presidents of Afghanistan, Pakistan, and Tajikistan in August 2010, promising to invest significant resources in Afghanistan to develop infrastructure and natural resources. After keeping itself aloof from Af-Pak for years after Taliban's ouster, Russia is back in the game and even the United States seems to be supporting greater Russian involvement. This has prompted greater cooperation between India and Russia on Afghanistan.[37] India and Russia have their own proxies in Afghanistan. There is worry that integrating the Taliban will come at the expense of their Afghan proxy, the Northern Alliance of ethnic Uzbeks and Tajiks. Russia remains concerned about the growing instability in the region and its spillover effects into its southern periphery.

Conclusion

The India–Russia relationship enjoys consensual support in both countries and has managed to withstand the test of time. If India and Russia managed to have a strong bilateral partnership during the Cold War years and are coming closer again, it is based on a commonality of interests. India remains determined to preserve and strengthen its special relationship with Russia. Much like the Cold War period, the contemporary state of Indo-Russian ties is also being shaped by a new convergence across a whole range of factors that are fundamental to the security interests of both states. But challenges are mounting as a new balance of power shapes the global political landscape.

Notes

1 Arthur Stein, *India and the Soviet Union: The Nehru Era* (Chicago: University of Chicago Press, 1969).
2 For a seminal account of Indian policy toward the United States and its implications for larger Indian foreign policy during the Cold War, see Dennis Kux, *India and the United States: Estranged Democracies, 1941–1991* (Washington, DC: National Defense University Press, 1992).
3 S. Nihal Singh, *The Yogi and the Bear* (London: Mansell Publishing Ltd, 1986), p. 9.

4 *Ibid.*, p. 40.
5 V.P. Dutt, *India's Foreign Policy* (New Delhi: Vikas Publishing House, 1984), pp. 131–2.
6 Bimal Prasad, *Indo-Soviet Relations, 1947–1972: A Documentary Study* (Bombay: Allied Publishers, 1973), pp. 73–6.
7 Singh, *The Yogi and the Bear*, p. 29.
8 For the full text of this agreement, see *Survival*, Vol. 13, No. 10 (October 1971), pp. 351–3.
9 On Pakistan's key role in Sino-US rapprochement, see William Burr, "Sino-American Relations, 1969: The Sino-Soviet Border War and Steps Towards Rapprochement," *Cold War History*, Vol. 1, No. 3 (April 2001), pp. 73–112.
10 Singh, *The Yogi and the Bear*, p. 87.
11 For a detailed explication of this argument, see Richard Sisson and Leo E. Rose, *War and Secession: Pakistan, India, and the Creation of Bangladesh* (Berkeley: University Press, 1990, pp. 196–202.
12 Robert H. Donaldson, *Soviet Policy Toward India: Ideology and Strategy* (Cambridge, MA: Harvard University Press, 1974), p. 230.
13 Timothy George, Robert Litwak, and Shahram Chubin, *Security in Southern Asia: India and the Great Powers* (Aldershot: Gower Publishing Company Ltd, 1984), p. 135.
14 Sumit Chakravarty, "Indo-Soviet Summits," in Vinod Bhatia (ed.), *Indo-Soviet Relations: Problems and Prospects* (New Delhi: Humanities Press, 1984), pp. 96–8.
15 *Ibid.*, p. 112.
16 *Ibid.*, pp. 111–16.
17 "Putin Puts Forward a Realistic Foreign Policy," *Russia Beyond the Headlines*, March 12, 2012, available at http://rbth.ru/articles/2012/03/12/putin_puts_forward_a_realistic_foreign_policy_15042.html.
18 An explication of the Russia–China–India strategic triangle can be found in Harsh V. Pant, "The Moscow-Beijing-Delhi 'Strategic Triangle': An Idea Whose Time May Never Come," *Security Dialogue*, Vol. 35, No. 3 (September 2004), pp. 311–28.
19 For a detailed account of the Indo-Russian defense ties, see Vinay Shukla, "Russia in South Asia: A View from India," in Gennady Chufrin (ed.), *Russia and Asia: The Emerging Security Agenda* (Sweden: SIPRI, 1999), pp. 34–30.
20 Manu Pubby, "Biggest Ever: Russia, India Seal Record Fighter Deal," *Indian Express*, December 22, 2010.
21 Sandeep Dikshit, "India Strikes Deal with Russia on Glonass," *The Hindu*, December 19, 2011.
22 Sandeep Unnithan, "Russia Snubs India," *India Today*, May 27, 2011.
23 "Russia Snubs India," *Times of India*, May 30, 2011.
24 Sandeep Unnithan, "Battle over Gorshkov," *India Today*, December 7, 2007.
25 Manu Pubby, "Gorhskov Arrival Further Delayed," *Indian Express*, September 18, 2012.

26 Paradorn Rangsimaporn, "Russia's Debate on Military-Technical Cooperation with China," *Asian Survey*, Vol. 46, No. 3 (May/June 2006), pp. 477–95.

27 C. Raja Mohan, "Defence Diplomacy," *Indian Express*, December 8, 2010.

28 Dmitri Trenin, "China, Russia Ties on Sound Base," *China Daily*, June 14, 2011.

29 J.N. Dixit, "Moscow Reaches Out," Indian Express, December 12, 2002.

30 Anupama Airy, "Oil Giants May Put Rs 15, 500 cr in Russia Gas Project," *Hindustan Times*, May 26, 2011.

31 This could, of course, be possible after the landmark civilian nuclear energy cooperation pact India signed with the United States. For details, see Harsh V. Pant, *The US-India Nuclear Pact: Policy Process, and Great Power Politics* (Oxford: Oxford University Press, 2011).

32 Harsh V. Pant, "The Japan Roadblock to Nuclear Cooperation," *Wall Street Journal*, October 28, 2010.

33 "Deals Signed, Putin Reminds India: Never Sold Arms to Pak," *Indian Express*, March 13, 2010.

34 Joint communiqué issued by Singh and Medvedev.

35 For a detailed explication of Indian interests in Afghanistan, see Harsh V. Pant, "India in Afghanistan: A Test Case for a Rising Power," *Contemporary South Asia*, Vol. 18, No. 2 (June 2010), pp. 133–53.

36 Vladimir Radyuhin, "India, Russia to Step Up Cooperation in Afghanistan," *The Hindu*, August 3, 2010.

37 Jason Motlagh, "With US Approval, Moscow Heads Back to Afghanistan," *Time*, August 24, 2010.

5

India and the European Union: a relationship in search of meaning

As the global balance of power shifts to East, India is fast emerging as one of main pillars of the new international order. Because of its size, population, economic and military capabilities, India is today being viewed as an emerging global power of the new century. As one of the recent reports suggests, the international community will soon have to confront the military, political, and economic dimensions of the rise of China and India, likening the emergence of these two states in the twenty-first century to the rise of Germany in the nineteenth and the United States in the twentieth, with impacts potentially as dramatic.[1] As a consequence, major global powers, including the European Union (EU) are re-evaluating their policies toward these two regional giants. The United States has taken the lead and has been the first to adapt its strategies to the emerging global realities. While on the one hand, it has tried to craft a stable relationship with China, it has also, as discussed in Chapter 2, vigorously courted India in recent years to an extent where it has made a major exception for India in the global nuclear non-proliferation order.

The EU due to some inherent limitations has been slower in responding to the new strategic realities. It has been focusing on China for some time now and has only recently started taking India seriously. This chapter examines the India–EU relationship, focusing on the implications of the EU initiatives toward New Delhi over the last two decades and constraints that continue to circumscribe the relationship.

An important experiment

The EU is the successor to what was initially the European Coal and Steel Community, which was established in 1952 with the aim of integrating the market in coal and steel amongst the member states.[2] It became the European Economic Community (EEC) in 1957, and widened its focus to greater economic integration. The Maastricht Treaty, which came into force in 1993, established the organization as the EU. Contrary to public perception, the EU has always been a "security organization." It was established in the wake of World War II with the aim of allowing Germany to recover economically in a supra-national structure. The logic was that by integrating the industries of war, it would be too costly for the member states to go to war with one another again.

The EU has traditionally focused on security through economic integration, and has become one of the world's most important economic organizations. It is the world's most integrated single market (i.e. there are no barriers to trade amongst the member states), and is also the world's largest donor of development aid. The issue of defense policy and military security was kept off the EEC agenda during the Cold War. As a result, the EU has come to be known as a "civilian power."

The end of the Cold War brought new threats, but also new opportunities. As well as bringing the EU into existence, the Maastricht Treaty also established the Common Security and Foreign Policy (CFSP).[3] The CFSP outlines the foreign and security objectives adopted by the EU's member states. It commits the EU to not only safeguard its own security but promote state and human security around the world. At the Maastricht Intergovernmental Conference, proposals were put forward for the development of a defense policy within the EU. Divisions of opinion and fears about what this would imply for the North Atlantic Treaty Organization (NATO) and, for the character of the EU, prevented further developments in the area of defense.

In 1998 the British and French governments issued the St. Malo Declaration in which they called for the creation of a "capacity for autonomous action, backed up by credible military forces, the means to decide to use them, and a readiness to do so, in order to respond to international crises."[4] The St. Malo Declaration led to the development of the European Security and Defence Policy (now the Common Security and Defence Policy; CSDP).[5] The CSDP offers a framework for cooperation within which the EU can conduct operational missions in third countries. Specifically, the aims of these missions are peace-keeping and strengthening international security. They rely on civil and military assets provided by member states.

Though arrangements to manage the EU–NATO partnership are in place, there remain tensions and issues at the political level. In particular, some non-EU NATO member states make it difficult for the EU to use NATO infrastructure for EU-led operations (as provided for in the Berlin Plus agreement).[6] Some member states fear that an enhanced EU capability to deal with its own defense will reduce the commitment of the United States to Europe. Other member states are reluctant for the EU to become associated with the use of military force. EU military operations are therefore often small-scale, and are more traditional peace-keeping than stabilization. There are concerns that EU capabilities would lead to duplication of NATO capabilities, which would have cost implications. Although many member states commit resources in principle, in practice the EU often struggles to generate the military resources it needs for operations. Operations also tend to be undertaken on an ad-hoc basis, rather than being based on a systematic calculation of the EU's security needs.

The EU is the only European security organization with the resources to potentially provide a comprehensive approach to security, including economic and trade agreements, as well as development aid. It has also undertaken a number of security sector reform operations, which are recognized as vital in the contemporary security environment. It cannot, however, carry out the type of operations that NATO, underwritten by US capabilities, can undertake.

The EU and the new global order

As the EU comes to terms with a changing geopolitical landscape being shaped by emerging powers such as China and India, it has tried to restructure its foreign policy priorities. Ties between the EU and India have significantly strengthened in recent years. Though India was amongst the first countries to establish diplomatic relations with the EEC, it was only recently that the EU has formalized its ties with India into a "strategic partnership."[7] The EU and India decided to launch a strategic partnership initiative in 2004. This is very significant as the EU has strategic partnerships with only five other countries – the United States, Canada, Russia, Japan, and China. Under politically congenial conditions, India–EU bilateral relations have progressed from trade in merchandise and development cooperation during the Cold War to a political dialogue in the 1990s culminating in a comprehensive strategic partnership. Bilateral ties have grown exponentially since 2004 when it was decided to hold annual EU–India summits. The aim is to have a much stronger and intensive relationship over the entire gamut of exchanges from political to multilateral, economic to science and technology, academic, cultural and civil society.

As the largest open societies in the world, the EU and India share a commitment to participatory democracy, human rights, good governance, and rule of law. The EU's gradual gravitation toward India is also the result of a growing unease with China's economic dominance. Not only is India seen as a better enforcer of Intellectual Property Rights laws but diversification also seems to be a better strategy for Europe. While China is not seen as being fully integrated into the international system, India being a liberal democracy is considered as almost a fellow traveler.

India has been a major beneficiary of the EU's Generalized System of Preferences scheme that provides duty reduction, and duty-free and quota-free access to products from developing and least developing countries. The EU is India's largest trading partner with the value of EU–India trade growing from €28.6 billion in 2003 to €72.5 billion in 2014 and one of the largest sources of FDI for India, accounting for over one-fourth of the total.[8] It is hoped that in the coming years India and the EU will explore the possibility of implementing a coordinated call for climate change research so that experts on both sides can work on collaborative research projects.

Apart from the 1994 cooperation agreement that the EU has signed with India and that provides the institutional basis for the EU–India ties, India has signed several other bilateral agreements including Bilateral Investment Protection Agreements with sixteen of the twenty-seven EU member states, Double Taxation Avoidance Agreements with eighteen EU member states, a Science and Technology Cooperation Agreement, a Joint Vision Statement for promoting cooperation in the information and communications technology, and a Customs Cooperation Agreement. At their sixth summit meeting in 2005, the EU and India adopted an ambitious and wide-ranging joint action plan, setting the course for the future EU–India strategic partnership. The action plan covered a range of issues including:

- strengthening dialogue and consultation mechanisms;
- political dialogue and cooperation;
- bringing people and cultures together;
- economic policy dialogue and cooperation; and
- developing trade and investment ties.[9]

The two sides have set up several working groups in sectors such as textiles and clothing, steel, agricultural and marine products, sanitary and phyto-sanitary issues, technical barriers to trade and customs cooperation with the aim of resolving contentious issues on both sides and to help in improving market access. An agreement was reached to launch formal talks on a broad-based bilateral trade and investment agreement that would be wider in scope than a mere free-trade agreement, encompassing investment, trade facilitation, transparency in regulatory frameworks, and the investment-related movement of natural persons.[10] During the 2012 EU–India summit, the two sides reinforced cooperation in security, in particular counter-terrorism, cybersecurity and counter-piracy, as well as trade, energy, research, and innovation. Against the backdrop of Western forces preparing to complete the ongoing transition and Afghan authorities assuming full security responsibility for the country beginning in 2014, India and the EU underscored the long-term commitment of the international community to Afghanistan in the Transformation Decade from 2015 to 2024.[11]

India is also trying to leverage India's "Asian identity" in the economic sphere and the strong geopolitical underpinnings between India's rising economic profile and global vision on the one hand and the EU's integrated foreign and defense policies on the other. India is a partner in the European satellite navigation project, Galileo, and in the international thermo-nuclear experimental reactor, ITER, set up by a consortium, led by the EU. Both the EU and India have a vision of a global order that is multipolar in structure and where multilateral institutions such as the UN and the WTO deliver effective global governance. In this context, the EU considers itself a natural ally of India in the ongoing WTO negotiations despite sharp differences over farm subsidy policies of the EU as well as on issues relating to market access.

While for a long time the EU–India relationship was largely viewed through the prism of economic and trade ties, the EU is now keen on enlarging and deepening the dialogue on political issues. Being the world's two biggest democracies, the EU and India share a host of common values on which the relationship is now being built. For example, one of the key areas for dialogue is democracy and human rights, which is not only considered to be the "core" of the EU foreign policy but also an area where there is much to share with India. Both the EU and India are examples of the strength that multiculturalism can bring in today's world. India with its twenty-two official languages and many religious and ethnic identities is matched by an equally diverse union of European citizens speaking a diverse range of languages and practicing many different faiths. Both are founded on stable democratic institutions and rule of law. As a consequence, there is much potential in the EU–India ties that remains to be tapped into.

Despite the well-intentioned attempts by the EU to engage India more productively in recent years, there are significant constraints that have prevented these ties from reaching their full potential.

Limits to EU–India Partnership

It took the EU a long time to recognize that India also matters in the long term and should be taken seriously. For too long, the EU single-mindedly focused on China, ignoring the rise of India in Asia-Pacific. India's rising economic profile, the US overtures to India, its growing role on the global stage from the UN to the WTO, all finally forced the EU to make it one of its strategic partners. The EU–India relationship is getting a long-term focus with the recognition that there are enough mutual benefits to ensure that small areas of friction are smoothed over.

The EU as an organization has been reluctant to support India's bid for permanent membership in the UN Security Council. This is partly because different member states have different views on this issue and partly because the EU is still testing the waters to see which way the wind will blow. This is despite the fact that the EU has been supportive of the UN attempts to reform its functioning and organizational structure to meet the changing global realities.

The EU and India also find themselves on the opposite sides in trade negotiations in the WTO and there are strong differences over the EU's farm subsidy policy and on issues related to market access.[12] The EU's reluctance to reduce the massive agricultural subsidies to its farmers that distort fair competition in trade in agriculture continues to be a major bone of contention between the EU and India. India is a member of G-20 and G-33, groupings of developing countries resisting the agenda of the developed world in the WTO.

The EU is India's largest trading partner, accounting for 19 percent of trade. The FDI from the EU into India has also grown considerably in recent years but total FDI into India still amounts to only 1 percent of EU outflows and is less than a tenth of that into China.[13] The EU's economic ties with India are yet to reach their full potential.

India and the EU continue to struggle to conclude a bilateral FTA several years after the negotiations were first launched in 2007. There is a new momentum in the talks after the visit of the Prime Minister, Narendra Modi, to Germany in April 2015 where he, along with the German Chancellor, Angela Merkel, emphasized the importance of concluding the ongoing India–EU Broad-based Investment and Trade Agreement (BITA) talks expeditiously. BITA will be India's first bilateral agreement (including services) with a large trading partner and the EU's first comprehensive agreement with a large emerging economy. Negotiations on the FTA came to a halt after fifteen rounds in April 2013 when the talks ran into a deadlock. India feels it is in a stronger negotiating position after the Indian parliament approved raising the foreign investment cap in the insurance sector to 49 percent from 26 percent, a key demand of the EU. India gave the option of an incremental approach to the FTA, which means signing whatever has been achieved and taking up the pending issues later. But the EU was keen on getting the entire agreement as a package.

India has an interest in getting a favorable package on services, including declared interests in IT and movement of Indian professionals. Market access for agricultural products, pharmaceuticals, and textiles is also a priority for India. For the EU, concessions in the financial services are key. The EU is also keen on the automobile sector where it is seeking a reduction in tariffs, much to the consternation of the Indian automobile industry, as well as a strong intellectual property regime. India is likely to take a "flexible approach" on tariffs on wines and spirits, as well as on auto components in the FTA negotiations with the EU, marking a shift from the hard stance it adopted until the talks broke down.[14] The BITA will be very significant for India–EU ties as this will be the first FTA for India not merely focused on the liberalization of trade but also on investment. The conclusion of BITA will be important not only for India's further integration into the global economy but also to a give a boost to India–EU ties which have failed to achieve their full potential.

Finally, there is the issue of the EU mindset, which still views India as a regional South Asian power and continues to equate India with Pakistan. The tendency to equate India and Pakistan, which until recently affected Washington and marred all policy initiatives in the past, has hurt the EU's attempts to reach out to India in any significant manner. Despite some belated efforts, the EU continues to see security issues through the old lens, trying to find a fine balance between New Delhi and Islamabad. India remains uncomfortable with the EU's position on the issue of Kashmir despite some changes in the EU's posture after the events of 9/11. In recent years, a shift can be discerned. A report titled "Kashmir: Present Situation and Future Prospects" was released and adopted by the European Parliament in 2007. It radically changed the EU's position on Kashmir by calling Pakistan's bluff on Kashmir as it focuses on human rights abuse in Pakistan Occupied Kashmir and rejects the doctrine of the right to self-determination propagated by Pakistan for long. In many ways, it was a vindication of the Indian position on this very contentious issue and should go a long way in remolding EU–India ties.[15]

On another crucial issue, with the exception of France and Britain, the other member states of the EU have not been enthusiastic about the US–India nuclear deal that is aimed at ending India's isolation from the global nuclear technology regime in return for India putting its civilian nuclear plants under international inspections.[16] This granting of an extraordinary exception to India by the United States has not gone down very well with the EU that has been a strong votary of the non-proliferation regime.

India's ties with the EU have also suffered because of the acrimony over delays to the trial of two Italian marines for murder in the 2012 killing of two Indian fishermen. Marines Massimiliano Latorre and Salvatore Girone, part of a military team protecting a privately owned cargo ship, have maintained that they mistook Indian fishermen for pirates and fired warning shots into the water. India's Supreme Court has allowed Latorre to temporarily return to Italy for heart surgery, but Girone remains in India awaiting trial. New Delhi has taken exception to the role of EU Foreign Affairs High Representative Federica Mogherini in the case, which has made headlines in her home country, Italy.[17] A European Parliament resolution has called for the return of the marines and a change of jurisdiction in the case. Italy argues that the incident took place in international waters off India's southwestern coast, a claim New Delhi rejects.

While India recognizes the growing importance of the EU as an economic entity, it does not take the EU very seriously as a political unit. India considers getting close to the United States a much more important foreign policy priority and it is toward this end that it has diverted its diplomatic energies in recent times. There is a belief in India that, as a rising power, it is much more important for India to cultivate its ties with the United States, especially as both of them have to deal with the consequences of a rising China. As a result, the EU has at best been a second-order priority for India. Instead, India has preferred to deal with European states on an individual basis and New Delhi's three main interlocutors in Europe have been France, Germany, and the United Kingdom.

India's bilateral outreach

Indian Prime Minister Narendra Modi visited France and Germany in April 2015, where used his "Make in India" initiative to encourage investment from Europe's two largest economies. Defense, energy, and infrastructure took center stage in Paris as Modi went on a boat ride with the French President on the Seine and interacted with French business leaders before visiting a World War I memorial, where he paid tribute to 10,000 Indians who lost their lives fighting with the French. In Germany, the real European powerhouse, Modi met Chancellor Angela Merkel and inaugurated the Hannover Messe, considered one of the world's largest congregations of industry gurus, in which India was a partner country in 2015.

Modi's unabashed promotion of India as an investment destination is the most striking aspect of his outreach to Europe. Pledging a stable and transparent tax regime, Modi has been busy wooing global investors, arguing that development is "not a mere political agenda" but an "article of faith" for his government and has sought international support to achieve the objectives crucial for growth. He has also been underlining that his government means business. "India is a now changed country ... our regulatory regime is much more transparent, responsive and stable," Modi said in Germany as he promised investors that his government is working on a "war footing" to improve the business environment further.[18] This is something that global investors, including Europeans, have long wanted to hear from Indian leaders. In Modi they see a leader who has the mandate to deliver on his commitments.

In France, Modi's pragmatic instincts were unleashed as he tried to move forward on projects that have been stuck for a long time. The Rafale fighter jet deal has been in limbo since 2012 over terms of procedures and pricing negotiations even as the Indian Air Force has been worried about meeting its "critical operational necessity." Modi managed to break the deadlock with his out of the box approach when he signed a government-to-government deal with France for the supply of thirty-six Rafale fighter jets in "fly-away" condition "as quickly as possible."[19] Though this goes against his "Make in India" pitch, he understood the urgency of the Indian Air Force's demands. In some ways, this was compensated by the support Modi's "Make in India" campaign received from Airbus which declared that the company was "ready to manufacture in India, for India and the world."[20] Airbus Group is likely to increase its sourcing of aerospace parts from Indian companies to US$2 billion in the next five years. India and France also signed deals aimed at the early operationalization of a civil nuclear cooperation agreement. The Jaitapur project, a proposed 9,900 MW power nuclear project to be designed and designed by Areva of France, has been stuck because of differences over the cost of electricity generation. With the new pacts, there is likely to be swift movement on this front as well.

India and Britain had forged a "strategic partnership" during the former British Prime Minister Tony Blair's visit to India in 2005 but it remained a partnership only in name. The Conservative Party and Prime Minister David Cameron have been keen on giving Britain's ties with India new momentum. The UK is the largest European investor in India and India is the second largest investor in the UK. Indian students are the second largest student group in Britain. There are significant historical, linguistic, and cultural ties that remain untapped. But the Labour government's legacy on India was very complex and Cameron's government needed great diplomatic finesse to manage the challenges. This was particularly true of the issue of Kashmir where the Labour government could not help but irritate New Delhi. As late as 2009, the former Foreign Secretary, David Miliband, was advising the Indian government that the resolution of the Kashmir dispute was essential to solving the problem of extremism in South Asia.[21] Miliband's complete lack of sensitivity to Indian concerns raised some fundamental questions in New Delhi about the trajectory of British foreign policy. Miliband was merely trying to assuage the concerns of Labour Party's domestic constituents, in particular the Pakistani Muslims who form the largest share of British Muslims. But such an approach merely reinforced Indian perceptions of Britain being on the side of Pakistan on this critical issue.

David Cameron's government made a serious effort to jettison the traditional British approach toward the subcontinent in so far as it has decided to deal with India as a rising power, not merely as a South Asian entity that needs to be seen through the prism of Pakistan. David Cameron made all the right noises in India during his two trips to India in his first term. He warned Pakistan against promoting any "export of terror," whether to India or elsewhere, and said it must not be allowed to "look both ways."[22] He has proposed a close security partnership with India and underlined that Britain, like India, was determined that groups like the Taliban, the Haqqani network or Lakshar-e-Toiba should not be allowed to launch attacks on Indian and British citizens in India or in Britain. More significantly, the British Prime Minister has also rejected any role for his country in the India–Pakistan dispute.[23] Indian Prime Minister Narendra Modi reciprocated Cameron's outreach by visiting Britain in November 2015, becoming the first Indian Prime Minister to visit the UK in nearly a decade.

Conclusion

As the center of gravity shifts to Asia-Pacific and the international system undergoes a profound re-ordering, the EU is trying hard to accommodate these new global realities. The rise of China and India has presented the EU with several opportunities that it's trying its best to harness. But while trade and economics seems to have given the EU a reference point vis-à-vis the two Asian giants, politically it seems adrift as it is finding it difficult to speak with one voice on the political issues that confront the world today.

Europe is finding it difficult to formulate a coherent foreign policy across the EU nations and this has made it difficult for the EU to respond as effectively to the rise of China and India as it would like to.

The EU's worldview is, not surprisingly, shaped by its historical experiences and seems intent on exploiting the opportunities provided by the liberal global economic order. Nonetheless, to think of foreign policy as nothing more than an outcome of economic policy and to consider international politics as nothing but a sum total of global trade and economic cooperation is a liberal fallacy that assumes that only if nations trade with each other more, the world would become more prosperous and peaceful. The problem with these assumptions is that not only is there little empirical evidence to prove that more trade leads to peace and tranquillity, but also that while politics and economics are certainly inter-related, the international economic system rests upon international political order and not vice versa. The EU's lack of a strategic direction in foreign policy makes it difficult for it to respond effectively to new challenges such as the rise of China and India.

At a time when Europe and the wider West is struggling economically and the Western world is jittery about China's growing global heft, strong ties with India are now a cornerstone of the foreign policies of most European nations and support for strong bilateral ties with India cuts across party political divides. India and Europe will not always agree but it's a sign of mature partnerships when partners can gracefully agree to disagree. New Delhi stands to benefit from leveraging partnerships rather than shunning them. Today India is well positioned to define its bilateral partnerships on its own terms and would do well to continue engaging more closely with those countries that can facilitate its rise in regional and global prominence. And European countries retain their importance in that context.

Notes

1 The report is available at www.cia.gov/nic/NIC_globaltrend2020.html.
2 On the origins of the EU and its evolution, see Andrew Moravcsik, *The Choice for Europe: Social Purpose and State Power from Messina to Maastricht* (Ithaca, NY: Cornell University Press, 1998).
3 Details of the treaty are available at www.eurotreaties.com/maastrichtec.pdf.
4 The St. Malo Declaration is available at www.cvce.eu/obj/franco_british_st_malo_declaration_4_december_1998-en-f3cd16fb-fc37-4d52-936f-c8e9b-c80f24f.html.
5 Details of the CSDP are available at http://europa.eu/legislation_summaries/institutional_affairs/treaties/lisbon_treaty/ai0025_en.htm.
6 Details of the Berlin Plus agreement are available at http://eeas.europa.eu/csdp/about-csdp/berlin/index_en.htm.
7 Sushma Ramachandran, "The Expanding EU-India Relationship," *The Hindu*, July 5, 2005.

8 For details on India–EU trade relationship, see http://ec.europa.eu/trade/policy/
   countries-and-regions/countries/india/.

9 The full text of the Joint Action Plan signed by the EU and India in 2005 is available at http://commerce.nic.in/India-EU-jap.pdf.

10 See the Joint Statement issued at the end of the Sixth EU–India Summit held in
   Helsinki on October 13, 2006, available at http://commerce.nic.in/India-EU-jap.pdf.

11 The India–EU joint statement at the February 2012 summit is available at http://
   eeas.europa.eu/india/sum02_12/docs/20120210_joint_statement_en.pdf.

12 "India, EU Cross Swords Over Trade Barriers," *Financial Express*, September
   8, 2005.

13 Batuk Gathani, "India, EU Determined to Boost Trade Ties," *The Hindu Business
   Line*, February 2, 2006.

14 Dilasha Seth, "Free-Trade Agreement with European Union: India May Relax
   Tariffs on Spirits, Auto Parts," *Economic Times*, March 19, 2015.

15 See the draft report titled "Kashmir: Present Situation and Future Prospects,"
   available at www.europarl.europa.eu/meetdocs/2004_2009/documents/pr/640/
   640763/640763en.pdf.

16 For details on the US–India nuclear deal and strategic imperatives behind it, see
   Harsh V. Pant, *The US-India Nuclear Pact: Policy, Process, and Great Power
   Politics* (Oxford: Oxford University Press, 2011).

17 Douglas Busvine, "EU-India Summit Off as Italian Marines Case Rankles,"
   Reuters, March 16, 2015.

18 Press Trust of India, "Will Make Corrections in Rules, Regulations: Modi in
   Germany," *Business Standard*, March 13, 2015.

19 John Irish and Elizabeth Pineau, "India Orders 36 French-Made Rafale Fighter
   Jets – PM Modi," Reuters, April 11, 2015.

20 Santanu Choudhury, "Modi's 'Make in India' Gets $2 Billion Vote of Confidence
   From Airbus," *Wall Street Journal*, April 12, 2015.

21 Jane Merrick, "Miliband's Trip to India 'a Disaster', after Kashmir Gaffe,"
   Independent, January 18, 2009.

22 Rosa Prince, "David Cameron: Pakistan is Promoting the 'Export of Terror',"
   Telegraph, July 28, 2010.

23 *Ibid.*

Snapshot 2: The BRICS fallacy

Representing around 40 percent of the world's population and nearly a quarter of its economic output, BRICS does offer promise of clout. The economic profile of the five nations, especially that of China, has continued to grow with suggestions that BRICS collectively could become bigger than the United States by 2018 and by 2050 even surpass the combined economies of G-7 states.

Yet a major challenge for ongoing influence from BRICS is China's dominance over the other four members. For all its promise, BRICS has remained a talking shop aspiring to greatness.

The first formal summit meeting was held in Russia in June 2009 with South Africa joining the group in December 2010, changing the nomenclature from BRIC to BRICS. The Yekaterinburg summit called for "a more democratic and just multipolar world order based on the rule of international law, equality, mutual respect, cooperation, coordinated action and collective decision-making of all states." Since then the joint statements of the various BRICS summits have repeatedly underscored need for a realignment of the post-World War II global order based on the untrammelled supremacy of the United States. As the United States is preoccupied with internal troubles and the eurozone is mired in a debilitating debt crisis, a vacuum is increasingly being felt in the international system. This presents an opportunity for the BRICS to emerge as major global players. Plans are underway for some joint projects. A joint BRICS development bank that would finance investments in developing nations is on the anvil.

But overall momentum for BRICS, a much-hyped initiative, seems to be flagging. Growth-rate estimates for all the BRICS are steadily declining. In fact, as Brazil, Russia, and China hit hurdles, it's the poorest member of the emerging-market group that's proving a darling of global investors. The International Monetary Fund has predicted that India in 2016 will grow faster than each of its BRICS counterparts for the first time since 1999. Fluctuating economic trends, however, are not the leading reason behind the unworkability of the BRICS idea, but rather the structural disparity at the heart of the grouping.

China's rise has been so fast and so spectacular that others are still trying to catch up. The Chinese economy is not only the second largest in the world but also larger than the economies of the other four members combined. China's power makes the other members nervous, leading them to hedge bets by investing in alternative alliances and partnerships even as China's rapid accretion of economic and political power adds to its own challenges to make friends. Given the leverage that China enjoys in BRICS, it should come as no surprise that Beijing has suggested that IBSA – the grouping of democracies India, Brazil, and South Africa – be shut down in favor of BRICS.

China's manipulation of its currency has resulted in significant problems for manufacturing sectors of other emerging powers. India, Brazil, and South Africa all have expressed disenchantment with Beijing's economic policies at various times. New Delhi has even imposed anti-dumping duties on a range of Chinese goods. China's dominance of the intra-South trade remains overwhelming, with other emerging powers struggling to get a share of the pie. Central bankers from Brazil and India spoke against the undervalued yuan in 2009 and 2010 to little effect.

Economic ties between China and Brazil have grown, but so have frictions. China is not viewed as a fair competitor with Brazilian manufacturers accusing China of dumping diverted exports from Europe even as Brazilian manufacturers face steep non-tariff barriers in trying to export to China. Worried about the influx of investment and cheap imports from China, Brazilian manufacturers are losing market share to Chinese counterparts, and Brazil is also wary of China's growing economic profile in South America, which Brazil considers its own sphere of influence.

Russia and China are united in their aversion to a US-led global political order, but elite distrust of each other remains. Though they coordinate in trying to scuttle Western policies, as has been the case in Iran and Syria, the partnership is one of convenience. Russia's failure to develop its Far East has allowed China to gain a toehold in this strategic region and allowed Beijing to define the Asian security landscape. And though China is the largest buyer of Russian conventional weaponry, many in Russia see this as counterproductive: China could emerge as the greatest potential security threat to Russia.

Likewise, Sino-India ties have witnessed a steady deterioration over the last few years on a variety of issues – from land border to maritime disputes. Despite the public pronouncements by the two sides, New Delhi remains skeptical of China's intentions. Beijing's refusal to acknowledge India's rise and a lack of sensitivity on core security interests are leading to pushback.

South Africa's relations with China are also not as wrinkle-free as so often made out in the popular media. Concerns have been rising that China's economic power is strangling South African manufacturing while locking up vital resources for years, as the flood of Chinese finished goods to Africa has created a large trade imbalance. Textile mills in South Africa have closed down under the onslaught of inexpensive Chinese imports, leading to public protests. In a somewhat surprising outburst, former South African President Thabo Mbeki warned that Africa risked becoming an economic colony of China if the growing trade imbalance between the two was not rectified. Though China has its share of supporters in South Africa, its extractive economic policy is leading to growing calls for a more equitable economic relationship.

The fascination with BRICS is partly an offshoot of the discussion on the emerging so-called post-American world. Many commentators argue multipolarity is likely to be the norm. Yet while BRICS may have growing economies, it's not clear this can translate into power at the global level. Even if the BRICS get their economic act together, the grouping will find it difficult to turn that strength into a unified political force. China's dominance makes most of the goals articulated by the BRICS states wobbly. The point of this coalition was always to show that the balance of power is shifting toward emerging countries, away from the West's historical dominance. But a multipolar world isn't the same as China just trying to tilt the balance of power toward itself.

The narrative surrounding the rise of BRICS is as exaggerated as that of decline of the United States. The tectonic plates of global politics are certainly shifting, but their movements are unpredictable. BRICS will remain an artificial construct, merely an acronym coined by an investment banking analyst, for some time to come.

PART II

India and its neighborhood

6

India and Pakistan: a road to nowhere

The surprise invitation to Pakistani Prime Minister Nawaz Sharif, along with other South Asian leaders, by the newly elected Indian Prime Minister, Narendra Modi, to his government's inauguration in May 2014 had led some to hope that this might be a new beginning in India–Pakistan relations. But that was not to be. The Indian Foreign Secretary was scheduled to travel to Islamabad for talks with her Pakistani counterpart in August 2014, the first meeting at this level since September 2012. India decided to call off these talks with Pakistan soon after Pakistan High Commissioner in India, Abdul Basit, met Kashmiri separatist leaders under the umbrella of the Hurriyat Conference.

Indian response was sharp:

Foreign Secretary conveyed to the Pakistan High Commissioner today, in clear and unambiguous terms, that Pakistan's continued efforts to interfere in India's internal affairs were unacceptable. It was underlined that the Pakistani High Commissioner's meetings with these so-called leaders of the Hurriyat undermines the constructive diplomatic engagement initiated by Prime Minister Modi in May on his very first day in office. Therefore, under the present circumstances, it is felt that no useful purpose will be served by the Indian Foreign Secretary going to Islamabad next week. Foreign Secretary's visit to Islamabad for talks on 25 August stands cancelled.[1]

Arguing that the Pakistani High Commissioner did not interfere in India's internal affairs, Pakistan's Foreign Office retorted that Kashmir was not part of India. It went on to underline that "Pakistan is not subservient to India" and is "a legitimate stakeholder in the Jammu and Kashmir dispute."[2]

There was nothing new in what had happened. It happens after every few years when India and Pakistan decide that they need to talk. Either the talks happen and nothing comes out of them or even before the talks start, something happens to derail them. It can be considered the biggest strategic failure of Indian diplomacy that even after more than six decades, India has not found a way to neutralize the challenge posed by a neighbour one-eighth its size. India's Pakistan policy in recent years has struggled to move beyond cultural exchanges and cross-border trade. Pakistan has continued to drain India's diplomatic capital and military strength and India has continued to debate whether Pakistani musicians should be allowed to enter India. This disconnect between Pakistan's clear strategic priority and India's magnificently short-sighted approach has continued to exact its toll on India and its global ambitions. This chapter surveys the trajectory of India–Pakistan relations and underlines the factors that have made it difficult for the two neighbors to resolve their differences.

A history of wars and conflicts

Conflict, in many ways, was inherent in the very nature of the birth of independent India and Pakistan. Since 1947, India and Pakistan have gone to war four times, with three of these wars directly related to the dispute over Kashmir.[3] When India was partitioned, states were given the option to join either India or Pakistan, or remain free. Maharaja Hari Singh, the Hindu ruler of Jammu and Kashmir, wished to remain independent, thus stalling decision. However, the internal revolt amongst his majority Muslim subjects, along with the threat of external invasion of the Lashkars (armed tribesmen from what is today called Khyber Pakhtunkhwa) compelled him to act. He requested military assistance from India, in exchange for acceding to India. The war came to an end on January 1, 1949, by a UN-mandated ceasefire line, along with the deployment of a UN peace-keeping group at the ceasefire line. This was the first Indo-Pakistani war of 1947. This proved to be the longest-running war over Kashmir, but was also the least costly as a result of the limited nature of the firepower employed by both sides; there were no naval engagements and the use of air power was minimal. As a result of the ceasefire agreement, a Line of Control (LoC) was established between the opposing armies, which left Pakistan occupying about a third of the country.[4] The UN-brokered ceasefire called for a withdrawal from Kashmir, although, much to India's irritation, Pakistan was not explicitly named as the aggressor.

After the war concluded, both Pakistan and India abided by the ceasefire agreement and dropped back to the LoC. Pakistan therefore achieved the buffer zone between her boundary and the Indian forces stationed in Kashmir. India, despite remaining adamant that her sovereign territory had been invaded, did not attempt to drive the invaders from Kashmir. It can be deduced that both sides wished to ensure that the conflict remained limited to the Kashmir region itself and would not spill over into general war. They also both appeared to accept the now established situation of both sides opposing each other along the LoC in Kashmir.

India and Pakistan were to proceed to war again in 1965 after a period of sporadic border skirmishes in Kashmir. An Indian thrust into Pakistani controlled "Azad" Kashmir led to Pakistani forces attacking the south of

Kashmir in order to strangle the Indian logistical chain. As a result of the success of this mission, the Indian forces realized that they could well suffer defeat and attempted to draw Pakistani attention away by attacking targets within the Punjab. Attack and counter-attack followed and the Pakistani forces were beginning to run out of ammunition. Before Pakistan was led to the negotiating table, Islamabad appealed to the Chinese government which had fought a war with India only three years previously.

Subsequent Chinese threats against India forced the UK and US governments to pledge assistance to India against possible Chinese involvement. A UN-brokered ceasefire came into effect in September.[5] This time, casualties were relatively high with over 6,000 troops killed, mainly as a result of the effective employment of air power by both sides. Despite the heavy losses, in the Tashkent agreement of 1966 both countries were persuaded to return to the pre-war positions along the LoC.[6]

The engagement between the two countries was again, initially, limited geographically to the Kashmir region. It was only when India realized that, as a result of Pakistan's attacks on the supply chain, she might lose the military advantage and suffer a further loss of territory, that she took offensive action outside Kashmir and in Pakistani territory. Even then, there was no attempt to stage a strategic strike against Pakistan and action was solely intended to split the main effort of the Pakistani forces. More significant was the fact that China was ready to become militarily engaged in the dispute against India. This may have opened up a further front on the east of Jammu and Kashmir and this would have seriously weakened India's ability to defeat the Pakistani action; this forced the UK and US pledges of military assistance. In any future conflict, India would therefore have to take account of the potential for the involvement of China and India's own requirement for external assistance, particularly if Pakistan felt that her own territory was under threat. To address this, New Delhi later signed a pact with Russia that would provide her with a counter to the Chinese.[7]

The war of 1971 was different to the previous Indo-Pakistan wars in that it was not directly related to the Kashmir issue. The origins of this war lie with the loosening of ties between East and West Pakistan. The Bengali East Pakistanis began to feel increasingly isolated, particularly after the 1966 Tashkent agreement. East Pakistanis felt that they were vulnerable to India as a result of Pakistan's venture in Kashmir.[8] Unrest and discontent grew to such an extent that open calls were made for independence. In response, West Pakistan imposed a State of Emergency and the ensuing crackdown resulted in thousands of Bengalis fleeing into Indian West Bengal. Faced with this exodus, India considered direct military intervention into East Pakistan and deployed forces along the border. The first engagement occurred at Boyar on November 21, 1971 along the West Bengal–East Pakistan border. On December 3, fearing Indian involvement, Pakistan launched a pre-emptive strike against air bases in India. Simultaneously, ground operations were conducted in the Punjab and Kashmir. In response, Indian forces struck back hard with a naval blockade of East Pakistan and a direct naval bombardment of Karachi in West Pakistan. The United States, concerned this time not with the threat of Chinese involvement, but more with the Russian pact with India, deployed a carrier battle group to the Bay of Bengal in order to deter India from a total annihilation of the Pakistani state. If deterrence was the aim of this action then it was not required as subsequent records have unearthed no desire of India to seek territorial gains in the West.[9] Unable to contain the superior military might of India, Pakistani resistance in East Pakistan crumbled and the Indian Army effectively overran the country. The total cost in lives was over 10,000. As a result of the war, the State of Bangladesh was born.[10]

Despite a full-scale engagement between the two countries, military action did not attempt to solve the Kashmir issue under the smokescreen of the war. Indian forces did not try to oust the occupying Pakistani forces from the LoC. India appeared not to have the total defeat of Pakistan as a strategic objective. The threat of external involvement from China never materialized as a result of the pact that India had signed with Russia. The Chinese may in the past have been content to involve themselves militarily against India alone, but were more hesitant when confronted with Russia. Similarly, the Russian influence did not develop militarily following the United States' overtly deterrent posture.

The Simla agreement signed by the Pakistani Prime Minister Zulfiqar Ali Bhutto and Indian Prime Minister Indira Gandhi in 1972 committed the two nations to abjure conflict and confrontation which had marred relations in the past, and to work toward the establishment of durable peace, friendship, and cooperation.[11] It was much more than a peace treaty seeking to reverse the consequences of the 1971 war (i.e. to bring about withdrawals of troops and an exchange of prisoners of war) and was a comprehensive blueprint for good neighborly relations. Both countries also committed themselves to "settle all their differences by peaceful means and through bilateral negotiations or by any other peaceful means mutually agreed upon." Bhutto reneged on his promise to Gandhi a lot earlier than some had anticipated, and from then onwards, all Pakistani governments – including that of General Zia-ul-Haq, who first overthrew Bhutto in July 1977 and then executed him in April 1979 – have maintained that the promise attributed by India to Bhutto was never made.[12]

As the covert nuclearization of the subcontinent continued in the 1980s and the 1990s, the conflict in South Asia attained nuclear dimensions. For the international community, South Asia emerged as one of the most dangerous global flashpoints. And in May 1998 the two nations decided to formally cross the nuclear Rubicon. Recognizing the challenges, the two states decided to assuage global anxiety by reaching out to each other. Early in

1999 the governments of India and Pakistan met at Lahore and agreed to "intensify efforts to resolve all issues including Jammu and Kashmir" and to "refrain from intervention in each other's internal affairs."[13] During the winter months of 1998–99, the Indian Army vacated its posts at very high peaks in Kargil sector in Kashmir as it used to do every year. The Pakistani Army intruded across the LOC, which served as a de facto border between the two states as specified in the Simla agreement, and occupied the posts. The Indian Army discovered this in May 1999 when the snow thawed. This resulted in intense fighting between Indian and Pakistani forces, known as the Kargil conflict. Backed by the Indian Air Force, the Indian Army regained some of the posts that Pakistan has occupied. Pakistan later withdrew from the remaining portion under international pressure.[14]

Though this conflict was fought after both India and Pakistan became nuclear capable, as with previous Kashmir wars, the action was isolated to the region itself and did not spill over into each other's territory or have a measure of strategic attack. Given the previous reluctance of either Pakistan or India to act strategically, it is interesting that Pakistan did not dismiss the use of nuclear weapons.[15] After the end of the Cold War, as the world seemed to be losing interest in the Kashmir dispute, Pakistan saw the chance to thrust the issue to the fore and the mere mention of nuclear weapons was sufficient to achieve the attention. The policy backfired as the rest of the world resented the nuclear blackmail and this distracted from the Kashmir dispute. Additionally, the mention of nuclear weapons led to India mobilizing her forces and this may have escalated the conflict unintentionally.

On December 13, 2001, the Indian parliament was attacked by militants affiliated to Pakistan-based Lashkar-e-Toiba and Jaish-e-Mohammed, resulting in the amassing of military forces on both sides of the LOC and a ten-month standoff. And then, on November 26, 2008, ten terrorists affiliated to Pakistan-based Lashkar-e-Toiba carried out a series of coordinated attacks in Mumbai, targeting civilians in hotels and the railway station.[16] During the attack, the Indian intelligence intercepted the satellite conversations between the terrorists and their handlers in Pakistan. In the wake of this horrendous attack, India suspended talks with Pakistan.

A crude nuclear stability has emerged in South Asia as India's calibrated responses to the three crises since the two sides openly crossed the nuclear Rubicon in 1998 demonstrate. Indeed, a state of recessed/non-weaponized deterrence had existed since the time of the border crisis in early 1987 that led to the 1988 India–Pakistan agreement not to strike each other's nuclear installations. Nuclear weapons have contributed to regional strategic stability by reducing the risk of full-scale war in the region. Despite repeated provocations by Pakistan in 1999, 2001–02, and 2008, and a resentful Indian public that wanted its government to retaliate, Indian policy-makers have demonstrated an extraordinary measure of restraint in the aftermath of all three crises, refusing to launch even small-scale limited attacks against

Pakistan. The Indian government forbade the military to cross the LOC despite Indian military officials clearly wanting to pursue such a posture.

For a long time, the West has viewed nuclear weapons in South Asia with dread because of the possibility that conventional warfare between India and Pakistan might escalate into a nuclear war. Indian and Pakistani officials, on the other hand, have continued to argue that, just as the threat of Mutual Assured Destruction resulted in "hot peace" between the United States and the former Soviet Union during the Cold War, nuclear weapons in South Asia will also have a stabilizing impact. Since 9/11, however, the nature of the problem for the region and the world at large has changed, in so far as the threat now appears to be Pakistan's nuclear arsenal being used by radical Islamists if they can manage to wrest control of it. There is little hope that the rational actor model on which classical nuclear deterrence theory is based would apply as much to Islamist terrorist groups as it would to the Pakistani government. In the immediate aftermath of 9/11, there were suggestions that the United States had explicitly sought guarantees from the Musharraf government that its nuclear arsenal was safe.

The present turmoil in Pakistan continues to raise concerns about the safety, security, and command of its nuclear stockpile. Though Pakistan's government is always quick to dismiss reports that its nuclear weapons are in danger of falling into the wrong hands as "inspired" and stresses that Pakistan provides the highest level of institutionalized protection to its strategic assets, the credibility of such claims remains open to question in the context of Pakistan's rapidly evolving domestic political context.

Pakistan's domestic vulnerabilities

Pakistan has been in political turmoil for years now as the civilian government struggles to achieve legitimacy and credibility even as radical Islamist forces continue to strengthen their control in large parts of the country. The Nawaz Sharif government, elected in 2013, is struggling to establish its authority over the militarized state institutions. For the first time in its history Pakistan witnessed a transfer of power from one elected government to another when Sharif assumed the premiership. His critics, however, have attacked the elections as being rigged.[17]

The Pakistani military remains keen to retain its pre-eminence in the nation. Since 2012, it has been carrying out an offensive in the tribal areas of North Waziristan. The aim is to retake territory from the Taliban and punish those groups which have carried out attacks against the army and the general civilian populace from their bases in North Waziristan and the tribal belt bordering Afghanistan. Despite allegations that the Afghan Taliban, the dreaded Afghan Haqqani network and even some Pakistani groups fighting in Afghanistan have been left alone, the Pakistani Army claims to have targeted all groups and killed more than 1,000 militants – although it does not identify those killed and bans all media coverage of the operations.[18]

For the West, and the United States in particular, democracy in Pakistan can be a complicated issue. To have political currency in Pakistan, it is essential for political leaders to demonstrate their independence from Washington. There is a danger that anti-Americanism will be further inflamed once democratic forces come into full play in the country, more so because mainstream political parties have been discredited and marginalized in the last few years as the Islamist forces have gathered momentum.

Pakistan is struggling to lift a dismally low rate of economic growth, expected to be 4.3 percent in 2016, placing the country at the bottom of a region that is poised to witness the fastest rate of economic growth in the world. Thanks to a stagnant economy, millions of young Pakistanis are without jobs or regular incomes, especially in the burgeoning cities. Poverty and bleak prospects are also contributing to the extremist violence that daily rocks the country.

Reflecting some improvement in electricity supply that facilitated increased industrial production, growth in the gross domestic product (GDP) of Pakistan reached an estimated 4.1 percent in Fiscal Year 2014 (ended June 30, 2014), unexpectedly accelerating from 3.7 percent the previous year.[19] Reform initiated by the government helped improve economic conditions during the year. Renewed support from development partners has helped stabilize the currency and rebuild foreign exchange reserves from very low levels. The continuation of economic reforms and efforts to improve the security can certainly improve business confidence and help revive private investment.[20] However, even concerted reform will need several years to eliminate electricity and gas shortfalls and to effect the change needed to lift structural constraints on growth.

Pakistan is riven with social conflicts, the most prominent of them being the Shia–Sunni divide. Home to 188 million people, 95 percent of Pakistan's population is Muslim and they are predominantly Sunni. Only 13 percent of its citizens are Shiite. Conflict between Sunnis and Shiites has escalated over the last few years, with Taliban forces repeatedly targeting Shiite processions and places of worship and Iran-backed Shiite groups retaliating. In the 1980s, several radical groups sponsored by Pakistani intelligence began a systematic assault on Shia symbols and mosques in Pakistan. Pakistani Shia, with Iranian assistance, have responded by forming their own militias. The continued Sunni terrorist targeting of Pakistani Shia also remains an Iranian concern. This Shia–Sunni strife in Pakistan has provoked Iran to provide clandestine support to its co-religionists there.[21]

Balochistan is also becoming a battleground for Sunni–Shia violence. Since 2012, sectarian violence has become a more serious issue than the ongoing nationalist insurgency in Balochistan, with Sunni militant groups increasingly active in the province and targeting Shias, particularly the local Hazara community.[22] The increase in sectarian violence in Balochistan indicates an escalating rivalry between Saudi Arabia and Iran, which is being fought by proxies in Pakistan. Although much of the bloodshed can be traced to Sunni militant groups, there is growing concern that the Shiite minority is also starting to organize militant groups.[23] Sectarian tension in Pakistan could easily spill over into Afghanistan, where security remains perilous and where religious and ethnic rivalries simmer, too.

For decades Balochistan had been fighting for provincial autonomy while remaining within the federation of Pakistan. Since 2006, when prominent Baloch political and tribal leader Nawab Akbar Bugti was killed, the demand for provincial autonomy has transformed into an organized call for a separate Baloch state.[24] Those who are calling for separation are mostly young, educated people who no longer see a future for themselves in Pakistan. Baloch women have also begun to actively participate in the pro-independence movement. Balochistan is the richest Pakistani province in terms of natural resources, but it is still one of the poorest regions in South Asia. It is Pakistan's least-educated province, with extremely depressing social indicators on health and education. People do not have access to clean drinking water. Employment opportunities are tight and limited. The conflict has left hundreds of thousands of people internally displaced.

Political institutions in Pakistan remain underdeveloped. Pakistan's real power center is its military-industrial complex and it has had no real incentives to enter into a serious dialogue with India. In this anti-India posture, Pakistan has been helped by its external partners, in particular China.

The China–Pakistan axis

Ever since an understanding was reached between Chinese and Pakistani leaders at the Bandung conference of Asian and African states, which took place in Indonesia in 1955, Pakistan has occupied a unique position in China's foreign policy calculus. China's relations with Pakistan have been described as "arguably the most stable and durable element of China's foreign relations."[25] India has been the main factor that has influenced China and Pakistan's bilateral relations. Whereas Pakistan has gained access to civilian and military resources to balance the Indian might in the subcontinent, China, viewing India as potential challenger in the strategic landscape of Asia, has tended to use Pakistan to counter Indian power in the region.

Sino-Pakistan ties gained particular momentum in the aftermath of the 1962 Sino-Indian War, when the two nations signed a boundary agreement recognizing Chinese control over portions of the disputed Kashmir territory, and since then the ties have been so strong that former Chinese President Hu Jintao has described the relationship as "higher than mountains and deeper than oceans." Much like his predecessors in recent times, Nawaz Sharif chose China as the destination for his first official overseas visit as Pakistan's Prime Minister, in July 2013, where at the Great Hall of the People in Beijing, Sharif declared that his welcome "reminds me of the saying, our friendship is higher than the Himalayas and deeper than the deepest sea in the world, and sweeter than honey."[26]

In one of the largest defense deals for China, it is selling eight diesel-electric submarines to Pakistan as well as 110 latest JF-17 Thunder fighter jets. The much talked about US$46 billion investment package in the China–Pakistan Economic Corridor, between Pakistan's Gwadar port on the Arabian Sea and China's western Xinjiang province, is part of Beijing's ambitious Maritime Silk Road initiative. Over the years China has emerged as Pakistan's largest defense supplier. Military cooperation between the two countries has deepened with joint projects to produce armaments ranging from fighter jets to guided missile frigates. China is a steady source of military hardware to the resource-deficient Pakistani Army. China has played a major role in the development of Pakistan's nuclear infrastructure and has emerged as Pakistan's benefactor at a time when increasingly stringent export controls in Western countries have made it difficult for Pakistan to acquire materials and technology. As such, the Pakistani nuclear weapons program is essentially an extension of the Chinese one.[27] This is perhaps the only case where a NWS has given weapons-grade fissile material – as well as a bomb design – to a non-NWS.

There are calls in Pakistan to adopt a foreign policy that considers China – not the United States – to be Pakistan's strongest ally and most significant stakeholder. China's emergence as the leading global economic power, coupled with increased cooperation between India and the United States, has helped this suggestion gain traction. Washington has historically been accused of using Pakistan in times of need and then deserting it in exchange for stronger relations with India to serve its larger strategic agenda. China is considered a reliable ally that has always come to Pakistan's aid when India has seemed in the ascendant – so much so that China has even tacitly supported Pakistan's strategy of using terror as a policy instrument against India. Not surprisingly, Pakistan has given China a "blank check" to intervene in India–Pakistan peace talks.[28]

With India ascending in the global hierarchy and strengthening its ties with the United States, China's need for Pakistan is likely to grow. This has been evident in China's polices toward Pakistan on critical issues in South Asia. A rising India makes Pakistan all the more important in China's strategy for the subcontinent. It is highly unlikely that China will give up playing the Pakistan card vis-à-vis India anytime soon. The China–Pakistan partnership serves the interests of both partners by presenting India with a potential two-front theater in the event of war with either country.

No sign of resolution

Bilateral relations between India and Pakistan have been a source of concern for the international community for a long time and attract international scrutiny unlike any other bilateral relationship, with the possible exception of the Israeli–Palestinian one. It is no surprise, therefore, that every time India and Pakistan decide to talk with each other, it is hailed as a new beginning in their relationship.

Various structural and institutional factors have indeed been pushing India and Pakistan toward some sort of a dialogue for some time now. The international and regional environment has changed dramatically after 9/11 and 26/11 with little or no tolerance in the international community for the use of terrorism as an instrument of foreign policy. The United States, in particular, has been pushing Pakistan toward ending its support for terrorists in Kashmir, though not as strongly as many in India would like. Pakistan is finding it increasingly hard to justify its moral and logistical support to extremists in Kashmir under the watchful eyes of the United States. The United States, meanwhile, is also busy cultivating a close relationship with India. Despite Pakistan's utility for the United States in the war in Afghanistan, it is India that is seen as a long-term partner with an eye toward the containment of rising Chinese power and influence. The strategic situation in South Asia has also changed with the overt nuclearization of the subcontinent. Notwithstanding these factors propelling the Indo-Pak peace process, there are equally, if not more, significant constraints that continue to prevent normalization.

The idea of Pakistan was premised on the belief that Muslims of South Asia needed a separate homeland from what was seen as a Hindu-dominated India. And so a Muslim-majority state, Pakistan, came into being that derived its identity in opposition to India. This need to view India as an adversary has been a constant in Pakistan's politics and foreign policy since its inception. The armed forces of Pakistan have historically viewed themselves as guardians of Pakistani identity.

Like any other state in the international system, Pakistan also aimed to preserve and enhance its security vis-à-vis its much stronger regional rival, India. The two states have been in a perpetual state of security dilemma ever since their independence in 1947. Given India's enormous economic, military, and geographical advantages, Pakistan has relied on non-conventional means to limit India's influence and power. It pursued nuclear weapons in order to prevent India from using its overwhelming conventional military superiority, thereby leveling the playing field. Under the nuclear umbrella, Pakistan has used terrorism as an instrument of its foreign policy, especially in Jammu and Kashmir which Pakistan has coveted since 1947.

Despite recent attempts by India and Pakistan to patch up their differences, nothing much has changed in so far as the above narrative is concerned.

Significant sections of Pakistani military and intelligence services continue to see themselves in a permanent state of conflict with India and have little incentive to moderate their behavior as a continuing conflict with India is the *raison d'être* of their pre-eminent position in Pakistani society.[29] At a time when Pakistan's Islamic identity is under siege because of its cooperation with the United States in the war on terror, the need to define itself in opposition to India remains even stronger. Militarily, Pakistan's strategy of low-intensity conflict based on supporting terrorism can be seen as successful in so far as it has prevented India from achieving its full potential as a major military power.

The Indo-Pak peace process also hinges on the ability of Pakistan's political establishment to control terrorist groups from wreaking havoc in India. It is doubtful how much control the civilian government in Islamabad can exert given that various terrorist outfits have vowed to continue their jihad in Kashmir. The Frankenstein monster that the Pakistani state had created to further its strategic objectives vis-à-vis its adversaries has now turned against it and threatens to devour any future attempts at Indo-Pak reconciliation. Moreover, there is little evidence of any significant Pakistani effort to dismantle the infrastructure of terrorism such as communications, launching pads, and training camps on its eastern border with India.

Finally, and perhaps most important from the point of view of the resolution of the Kashmir dispute, is the very different strategic goals India and Pakistan have in pursuing a peace process. Pakistan has a revisionist agenda and would like to change the status quo in Kashmir while India would like the very opposite. India hopes that the negotiations with Pakistan would ratify the existing territorial status quo in Kashmir. At its foundation, these are irreconcilable differences and no confidence-building measures are likely to alter this situation. India's premise largely has been that the peace process will persuade Pakistan to cease supporting and sending extremists into India and start building good neighborly ties. Pakistan, in contrast, has viewed the process as a means to nudge India to make progress on Kashmir, a euphemism for Indian concessions. While Pakistan has a clear position on Kashmir and it shows little sign of budging from that, nobody really knows what India wants as it lacks clarity in its objectives and consistency in its plans. It is obvious that India would not give up its control over the Kashmir valley. However, it remains unclear as to what it is that India is bringing to the negotiating table for Pakistan to take it seriously. And just as India has had difficulty thinking of what it would offer, Pakistan also has had a hard time articulating what it would be satisfied with, short of wresting control of Kashmir.

And this is primarily a function of the lack of national political consensus on this issue in both states. In Pakistan, not only radical Islamic groups but also many mainstream political parties are against what they view as Islamabad's soft line toward the Kashmir issue. In India, the Congress-led governments have found it difficult to make any concessions as it would have to protect its flank from the right of the Indian political establishment. While there is a general political consensus in India on opening up trade routes and bus services, the threat of terrorism keeps all political parties on guard as no one would want to be held responsible for a terrorist attack that might come. The Narendra Modi government with a decisive mandate is viewed by many as India's best hope of resolving long-term problems with Pakistan. But if Pakistan fails to resolve its internal contradictions, even the Modi government will find it difficult to tackle the Pakistan challenge.

Notes

1 Shubhajit Roy, "Upset India Calls Off Foreign Secy Talks, Says 'Unacceptable'; Islamabad Terms it a Setback to Peace Efforts," *Indian Express*, August 18, 2014.
2 *Ibid.*
3 For a detailed examination of the centrality of Kashmir to the India–Pakistan conflict, see Victoria Schofield, *Kashmir in Conflict* (London: I.B. Tauris, 2000).
4 Sumit Ganguly, *The Origins of War in South Asia* (Boulder: Westview Press, 1994), p. 14.
5 Schofield, *Kashmir in Conflict*, pp. 110–11.
6 *Ibid.*, p. 112.
7 Ganguly, *The Origins of War in South Asia*, pp. 104–5. US Secretary of State, Kissinger, predicted that the Chinese would intervene if India attacked Pakistan and it could not expect US assistance as in 1962.
8 *Ibid.*, p. 78.
9 *Ibid.*, p. 112.
10 *Ibid.*, pp. 81–4.
11 The text of the Simla agreement of July 2, 1972 is available at www.mea.gov.in/in-focus-article.htm?19005/Simla+Agreement+July+2+1972.
12 Inder Malhotra, "The Collapse of the Shimla Accord," *Indian Express*, June 9, 2014.
13 The statement of the Lahore Declaration is available at www.indianembassy.org/SouthAsia/Pakistan/lahoredeclaration.html.
14 V.K. Sood and Pravin Sawhney, *Operation Parakram: The War Unfinished* (New Delhi: Sage, 2003), pp. 65–77.
15 Schofield, *Kashmir in Conflict*, p. 215.
16 For a vivid account of these attacks, see Cathy Scott-Clark and Adrian Levy, *The Siege: 68 Hours Inside the Taj Hotel* (New York: Penguin Books, 2013).
17 Salman Masood, "Khan's Call for Long March," *The Nation*, June 28, 2014.
18 Ahmed Rashid, "Pakistan's India Rivalry Harms its Anti-Terrorism Strategy," *Financial Times*, November 4, 2014.
19 "Pakistan Economy," The Asian Development Bank, March 31, 2014, www.adb.org/countries/pakistan/economy.
20 *Ibid.*

21 Zahid Hussain, *Frontline Pakistan: The Struggle with Militant Islam* (London: I.B. Tauris, 2007), pp. 89–101.

22 "Increased Sectarian Violence in Pakistan's Balochistan Province Likely to Raise Risk of Wider Sunni-Shia Conflict," *IHS Jane's Intelligence Weekly*, April 8, 2014.

23 Tim Craig, "Sectarian Killings Soar in Pakistan, Raising Fears of Regional Spillover," *Washington Post*, January 15, 2015.

24 Ahmed Rashid, "Balochistan: The Untold Story of Pakistan's Other War," BBC, February 22, 2014, www.bbc.co.uk/news/world-asia-26272897.

25 S.M. Burke, *Pakistan's Foreign Policy* (London: Oxford University Press, 1973), p. 213.

26 "China-Pakistan Friendship 'Sweeter than Honey', Says Nawaz Sharif," *Telegraph*, July 5, 2015.

27 R. Jeffry Smith and Joby Warrick, "A Nuclear Power's Act of Proliferation," *Washington Post*, November 13, 2009.

28 "Pak Now Hands China a 'Blank Cheque', India Says No Way," *Indian Express*, February 23, 2010.

29 Christine Fair, *Fighting to the End: The Pakistan Army's Way of War* (New York: Oxford University Press, 2014).

7

India and Bangladesh: a difficult partnership

India's relations with Bangladesh have suffered as New Delhi has failed to capitalize on the propitious political circumstances in Bangladesh in recent years with the coming to power of Sheikh Hasina of the Bangladesh Awami League (AL), who has taken great political risks to restore momentum in bilateral ties since 2008. Bureaucratic inertia and lack of political will on India's part has prevented serious progress on outstanding bilateral issues. Bangladesh is seeking an expeditious Indian response to its demand for the removal of tariff and non-tariff barriers on Bangladeshi products. There has also been slow movement on transit rights and on a water-sharing agreement for the Teesta river, which is crucial to agricultural production in north-western Bangladesh. India has failed to reciprocate fully Hasina's overtures. Meanwhile, the opposition Bangladesh Nationalist Party (BNP) has used the India–Bangladesh cordiality under Hasina to criticize the government for perceived subservience to India. India–Bangladesh ties had reached their lowest ebb during the 2001–06 tenure of the BNP government.

Since she first came to power as the nation's Prime Minister in December 2008, Sheikh Hasina has faced challenges to her authority from right-wing parties as well as the fundamentalist organizations such as Jamaat-e-Islami and Jamaat-ul-Mujahideen which enjoy Pakistan's support. The greatest challenge that Sheikh Hasina overcame in her first year was the mutiny by the paramilitary Bangladesh Rifles, which erupted in February 2009. It soon became clear that the mutineers were being instigated by supporters of the opposition led by the BNP and others connected to the Jamaat-e-Islami. The parliamentary elections of January 2014 were boycotted by the opposition parties. All elections since 1991 have been held under a neutral caretaker administration to ensure that voting is not fixed. But the AL abolished the caretaker system in 2010, arguing that it was no longer necessary. This led the opposition parties to boycott the elections, resulting in the eroding of the electoral process in the country.[1] The mainstream political parties, because of their dysfunctionalities, have failed to resolve the problems of weak political institutions and rising Islamic radicalism and hindering not only Bangladesh's evolution into a stable secular democracy but also impinging on the future of India–Bangladesh ties. This chapter examines the factors which have shaped the trajectory of India–Bangladesh ties in the last two decades.

Balancing India's predominance

Bangladesh is surrounded on three sides by India along a 4,094-kilometer land border. This results in near total geographical domination by India except for the 193-kilometer land border that Bangladesh shares with Myanmar. India's overarching presence in South Asia, in fact, has been a cause for concern for all of its smaller neighbors. Bangladesh is no exception. For India, the struggle against Pakistan in 1971 was a strategic imperative, in which India further marginalized Pakistan by cutting it in half with the emergence of Bangladesh. India may have expected Bangladesh to remain indebted to it for its role in assisting Bangladesh to achieve independence, but this did not happen. Structural constraints are the most important determinant of state behavior in international politics and Bangladesh soon began "balancing" against Indian preponderance in the region. Like other states in South Asia, Bangladesh has tried to counter India's regional hegemony through a variety of means.

Bangladesh's relations with Pakistan in the years immediately after independence were severely strained for obvious reasons, but their ties eventually began to improve quite dramatically. A major impetus for this was the desire of both countries to balance India's power and influence in the region. In 1974 Pakistan and Bangladesh signed an accord to recognize each other and two years later established formal diplomatic relations. The two states have maintained high-level contacts ever since. It has been correctly observed that popular fears of Indian domination in both countries outweigh any lingering animosity between them, resulting in closer Pakistan–Bangladesh ties.[2] Thus Bangladesh started cultivating Pakistan in an effort to counterbalance India because it sees India as its main potential threat. In contrast, India's foreign policy obsession with Pakistan has led it to ignore Bangladesh. There is some suspicion that then Pakistani President General Pervez Musharraf used his 2003 visit to Bangladesh to forge covert military ties with Dhaka and obtain authorization for Pakistan's premier intelligence agency, the ISI, to operate from Bangladeshi territory.

More significant are Bangladesh's attempts to woo an extra-regional power – namely, China – to prevent New Delhi from asserting regional supremacy in its relations with Dhaka; something that other states in the region – including both Pakistan and Nepal – have also frequently used China for. For its part, China has been quite willing to play this role because it not only enhances Beijing's influence in South Asia but also keeps India bogged down in regional affairs and hobbled in its efforts to become a major global player.

Since China and Bangladesh established ties in 1976, their bilateral relationship has grown steadily, culminating in the signing of a *Defense Cooperation Agreement* in 2002 that covers military training and defense production.[3] China has also provided Bangladesh with substantial resources to bolster its civil service and law enforcement agencies. The two states have signed an agreement on peaceful uses of nuclear energy in the fields of medicine, agriculture, and biotechnology. Energy-hungry China views Bangladesh's large natural gas reserves as a potential asset to be tapped. Much to India's discomfort, Bangladesh supports China's full entry into the South Asian Association of Regional Cooperation (SAARC). China is also helping Bangladesh in the construction of a deep water port at Chittagong, further heightening Indian fears of "encirclement."

In this context, it is interesting to note the proposal to revive the Stilwell Road (also known as the "Old Burma Road") which stretches from the Indian state of Assam through Bangladesh and Myanmar, extending all the way to Yunnan Province in southern China. In 1999 China, India, Myanmar, and Bangladesh all came together in what is known as the "Kunming Initiative" to push this proposal forward, mainly because of the potential trade advantages that would derive from linking those countries to Southeast Asia via a long land route.[4] But India has been reconsidering this proposal, fearing that it might give a fillip to insurgents in northeastern India who receive support from Bangladesh and might also allow Chinese goods to potentially flood Indian markets.

Bangladesh's ties with China have continued to flourish even under the AL administration, which has been careful to avoid appearing to be too close to India. Sheikh Hasina has described China as the "most dependable and consistent friend of Bangladesh" ever since the two states established their diplomatic ties more than three decades ago. A close relationship with China is one of the most potent ways by which Bangladesh can demonstrate its autonomy from Indian domination, especially when India has found it difficult to make significant progress on thorny bilateral issues. Hasina visited China in June 2014 for her second major overseas trip (after Japan) since retaining power in the January 2014 elections, which were marred by an opposition boycott. She signed five deals with China, including one for building a 1,320-megawatt power plant in Patuakhali with Chinese assistance and one for sharing the technology of super hybrid rice with Bangladesh, something that China usually does not do.[5] Given China's growing profile in Bangladesh, the term "all-weather friendship" – usually reserved to describe China's ties with Pakistan – is now also being used to underline the changing nature of the Sino-Bangladesh bilateral relationship.

Domestic politics and the "Other"

A nation's foreign policy is also a function of domestic political institutions. India has emerged as a major factor in domestic Bangladeshi politics. It would not be an exaggeration to say that, in many ways, India is the central issue around which Bangladeshi political parties define their foreign policy agenda. This should not be a surprise given India's geographic, linguistic, and cultural linkages to Bangladesh. Over the years political parties opposing the AL have tended to define themselves in opposition to India, in effect portraying the AL as India's "stooge." Moreover, radical Islamic groups in Bangladesh have tried to buttress their own "Islamic identity" by attacking India.

India realizes that it is perceived in Bangladesh as being close to the AL; consequently New Delhi has made some efforts to rectify this situation. When the BNP-led coalition of Begum Khaleda Zia assumed office in 2001, Indian officials sent a special emissary to Dhaka to assure the new government that New Delhi had no political favorites in Bangladesh and that its internal affairs were not India's concern. But this failed to make any long-term impact on the new political alignment in Bangladesh. Some in India argue that India should separate its relationship with Bangladesh from the latter's domestic politics and pursue greater engagement.[6] However the harsh reality is that political parties in Bangladesh invariably drag India into the nation's domestic politics in order to criticize each other. By visiting India just before 2008 elections and showing that she too can do business with India, Khaleda Zia was hoping to marginalize her long-time rival in Bangladeshi politics, Sheikh Hasina Wajed.

The army in Bangladesh has also made periodic forays into politics, further preventing democratic institutions from consolidating. General Zia-ur-Rahman (Begum Khaleda Zia's husband) seized power in 1975 in the turbulent aftermath of the massacre of ruling AL leaders including Sheikh Mujib-ur-Rahman (Sheikh Hasina Wajed's husband). To give his military regime increased legitimacy, Zia actively wooed domestic Islamist fundamentalists and the Islamic regimes of the Middle East. In essence, he transformed Bangladesh from a secular to an Islamic republic. This transformation continued under his successor, General Hussain Mohammed Ershad, who ruled from 1982 to 1990, thereby ensuring that the military held an entrenched position in Bangladeshi politics. The army's role is less active today but it still remains a powerful force with its own deep-seated interests. Elements in Bangladesh's army continue to hold a strong anti-India outlook, in part because of the military's institutional Pakistani legacy.

The inability of civilian state institutions to govern Bangladesh effectively has not only raised serious concerns about the future viability of democracy there but has also undermined relations with India. In the immediate aftermath of the 2001 elections there were concerted attacks by ruling-party activists against Hindus, who were perceived to be supporters of the opposition AL. The weakness of governmental institutions has emboldened non-state actors such as the radical Islamic groups that are attempting to make Bangladesh into another frontier in their global struggle against the "infidels."[7] Religion has succeeded in so dominating political institutions that *The Economist* called the 2001 parliamentary elections in effect "a vote for Bin Laden," given the overwhelming presence of Osama Bin Laden's visage in campaign posters.[8] By 2005 there were estimated to be around 50,000 Islamist militants belonging to more than forty groups controlling large areas of Bangladesh with the assistance of Jamaat-e-Islami and a section of the BNP.[9] The emergence of Bangladesh as a "weak state with fragile institutions" unable to tackle internal security and governance has also given rise to problems in India–Bangladesh relations on a whole range of issues.[10]

Domestic politics in India has also played a role in shaping bilateral relations. The issue of illegal immigration (or infiltration) into India from Bangladesh has been part of the BJP election manifesto for several years, while the other national political parties tend to avoid this sensitive issue in their agendas. When operating in opposition, Congress Party leaders often criticized the BJP foreign policy toward Bangladesh as being driven by sectarian purposes. In this view, the BJP's anti-Muslim posture in domestic politics largely shapes its antagonistic posture toward Bangladesh. For its part the BJP has argued that Bangladesh maintains a lackadaisical attitude on illegal migration and when dealing with anti-India elements within its borders. The BJP's aggressive foreign policy posture was often considered to be reckless and overbearing by other political parties. They argued that it does not behoove a government to project Bangladesh as a bastion of Islamic fundamentalism when the BJP itself often callously tries to polarize Indian society on communal lines for the purposes of gaining domestic political mileage.

In turn, the BJP, when in opposition, argued that the Congress-led United Progressive Alliance's policy toward Bangladesh and illegal immigration is driven by the need to appease minorities rather than India's own national interests.[11] It jumped upon the Indian Supreme Court's ruling that "there can be no manner of doubt that the state of Assam is facing external aggression and internal disturbance on account of large scale illegal migration of Bangladesh nationals."[12] Instead of addressing illegal immigration in a judicious manner, both Congress and the BJP have ended up making a "political football" of the issue even as the problems it engenders continue to fester and the India–Bangladesh relationship continues to deteriorate.

Bilateral issues between India and Bangladesh

Water concerns
Bangladesh is heavily dependent on India for the flow of water from the fifty-four rivers the two countries share. Bangladesh has complained that its share of river waters, in comparison to India's, remains unfair. The

construction by India of the Farakka Barrage – a low dam in West Bengal Province designed to increase water supply in the Hoogli river – was a major bone of contention between the two countries. India has built a feeder canal at Farakka where the Ganges divides into two branches; this has allowed India to control the flow of Ganges water by re-channeling it on the Indian side of the river. This dispute was resolved in 1996 with the mutual signing of a thirty-year water-sharing agreement for the Ganges. This happened after earlier short-term agreements had lapsed.

But differences between the two countries have re-emerged after India announced a plan to link thirty major international rivers in order to divert the flow of water toward its own drought-prone regions. This has generated concerns in Bangladesh about potential economic and environmental problems emanating from this plan, whereas India continues to insist that its project to integrate the rivers will not harm Bangladeshi interests. India's project, however, is currently aimed only at peninsular rivers and officials have indicated that Bangladesh would be consulted when northern rivers were to be interconnected. As the upper riparian state India clearly dominates the management of water resources. Dhaka's bigger grievance is that although a water-sharing accord exists for the Ganges, similar agreements are needed for the remaining fifty-three shared rivers. Officials in the capital assert that many rivers and canals have dried up because of India's denial of water to Bangladesh. During Sheikh Hasina's visit to New Delhi in January 2010, the two sides decided to resolve the issue of the sharing of the waters of the river Teesta after Bangladesh agreed to joint hydrological observations. The construction by India of the Tipai-mukh Dam across the Barak river has also been addressed.

Migration and its discontents
Another kind of flow has also become a serious bilateral issue: the stream of illegal Bangladeshi immigrants to India. India shares a border with Bangladesh running through the Indian states of West Bengal, Assam, Meghalaya, Tripura, and Mizoram. This border is longer than the one India shares with China. Indian officials have alleged that continued illegal immigration from Bangladesh has altered the demography of India's border areas resulting in ethnic imbalance, electoral irregularity, and loss of employment opportunities for Indian nationals.[13] In fact, in the late twentieth century the massive influx of refugees fleeing persecution in East Pakistan (as Bangladesh was known before independence) was one of the major reasons India assisted the Mukti Bahini guerrillas fighting for liberation from Pakistan. According to some estimates around 15–20 million illegal immigrants from Bangladesh have crossed over to India over the last several decades.

The northeastern states in India are particularly vulnerable to population movement: less than 1 percent of the region's external boundaries are contiguous with the rest of India whereas 99 percent are international boundaries. Bangladesh has complained that the overwhelming numerical superiority of Indian security forces along their long common border has spurred the killing of innocent Bangladeshi nationals by India's paramilitary Border Security Force (BSF). According to some estimates the ratio of Indian to Bangladeshi security forces deployed along the border is 2.5:1. Exchanges of fires between the BSF and its counterpart, the Bangladeshi Rifles, are now a regular feature along the border, often resulting in inhumane treatment of each other's forces. It was only in May 2015 that the land boundary delimitation agreement signed in 1974 between Indira Gandhi and Mujib-ur-Rahman was implemented by the Modi government.

Ineffective border management has also emerged as a major irritant in India–Bangladesh relations because of concerns about smuggling, illegal immigration, trafficking in women and children, and insurgency. India's plan to erect a 2,886-kilometer fence along its border with Bangladesh, with an additional 400 kilometers in the state of Mizoram, is nearing completion. However, there is no evidence that fencing will be effective in checking infiltration in the area, where for historical reasons there are around fifty-seven Bangladeshi enclaves in Indian territory and around 111 Indian enclaves inside Bangladesh. In many ways the border with Bangladesh is more difficult for India to manage than the border with Pakistan. The Indian army has little presence on the eastern border which is patrolled almost exclusively by Indian paramilitary forces.[14] New Delhi's concerns are not only about demographic changes but also about the security threat posed by anti-India radicals and insurgents who sneak in along with economically deprived Bangladeshi migrants. After prolonged negotiations, the Indian parliament, showing rare unanimity, passed the Constitution (119th Amendment) Bill in May 2015 to allow the operationalization of the Land Boundary Agreement between Hasina's father Sheikh Mujibur Rahman and the then Indian Prime Minister Indira Gandhi in 1974. This amendment is likely to ensure a permanent settlement of land boundary with Bangladesh and resolution of long-pending boundary issues.

Bangladeshis, for their part, are apprehensive that India has the resources and inclination to reignite ethnic rebellion in the Chittagong Hill Tracts area of Bangladesh. India had been accused of helping Chakma tribal insurgents there with resources and training from 1975 to 1997, when the Dhaka government finally signed a peace treaty with the Chakmas. Part of this accord allowed for the return to Bangladesh of tribal refugees who had fled to India in the 1980s to escape violence caused by the insurgency. But suspicions about Indian motives and potential political leverage remain strong in Bangladesh.

Islamist fundamentalism

The rise of Islamist fundamentalism in Bangladesh has further aggravated India's relations with its neighbor, with India "concerned" about Bangladesh's role as the "next terror frontier."[15] After independence, Bangladesh not only had declared secularism to be one of its founding principles but it had also banned religious political parties. As the military became a major political force in Bangladesh over the years, it used the country's Islamic identity to give its rule increased legitimacy, whilst mainstream political parties started using Islam for their own partisan purposes as well. As a result religion has come to occupy a central place in Bangladeshi political discourse.[16] Islamist radicals are no longer shy of openly declaring their ambitions. After the US invasion of Afghanistan in 2001 the members of the Islami Oikya Jote – one of the constituents of the then ruling coalition led by the BNP – took to the streets chanting, "We will be the Taliban, and Bangladesh will be Afghanistan."[17]

Bangladesh has the third largest Muslim population in the world; but of its 144 million population, seventy million live on less than $10 a day.[18] This has made the country an easy target for Islamic radical groups with global pretensions believing in the unity of *ummah* (the Islamic community of believers) against the West and other non-believers. Militant groups have percolated into all sections of Bangladeshi society including mosques, seminaries, educational institutions, the judiciary, mass media, and the armed forces. The AL, while in opposition, tried to draw the attention of the international community toward the "Talibanization" of Bangladesh.[19] Not only did anti-India rhetoric reached an all-time high in Bangladesh but Pakistan's ISI had been making full use of growing radical Islam for furthering its own activities against India. The BNP leader Begum Khaleda Zia, while in opposition, had been quoted as saying that the insurgents in India's northeast are "freedom fighters" and that Bangladesh should help them instead of curbing their activities.[20] The BNP also went all out to burnish its Islamic credentials with an eye on the elections. For example, a bridge was even named after Hezbollah by a government minister, who claimed that this was being done "because of our love for the Lebanese resistance group."[21] Indian fears were that "the growing trend of Islamisation in Bangladesh is the fall out of its Pakistanisation, which would ultimately turn it also in the category of a second terrorist state neighbouring India."[22]

There is a consensus in India that Bangladesh cannot continue to deny the anti-India terrorist and insurgent activities that emanate from Bangladeshi territory and that Dhaka should be forced to take concerted, verifiable action against anti-India actors within its borders. Bangladesh, in fact, has long been a willing host to militant outfits operating in northeast India.[23] Even before the emergence of Bangladesh as an independent state, the Chittagong Hill Tracts were used by the Pakistani Army to train and shelter Mizo and Naga insurgents fighting against India. It has been suspected that Bangladesh and Pakistan's ISI has been coordinating anti-India activities along with outfits like the United Liberation Front of Assam, the National

Socialist Council of Nagaland, the National Liberation Front of Tripura, and the All Tripura Tiger Force.

There have been concerns in recent years that as Pakistan comes under increasing scrutiny for its role in sponsoring terrorism, some Pakistan-based terrorist groups have moved their training camps to Bangladesh. Indian intelligence agencies also claimed that the ISI and various militant organizations based in Pakistan had changed their modus operandi and were now using Bangladesh as a transit point for pushing terrorists into India. Bangladeshi nationals who are part of terrorist groups are often asked to illegally enter India and set up bases in different parts of the country. They subsequently provide safe hideouts to more incoming terrorists, and act as couriers of explosives and finance.

The rise of the Jamaat-ul-Mujahideen in Bangladesh is a testament to the country's growing Islamic radicalization. As a consequence, Islam in Bangladesh – which has traditionally been tolerant and syncretic in nature – has come to be dominated by the radical strain in more recent years. Although the Jamaat-ul Mujahideen Bangladesh (JMB) was finally banned by the Dhaka government in early 2005 following threats of withdrawal of aid by the West, the group still managed to set off serial bomb blasts during August 2005 in sixty-three out of the sixty-four districts of Bangladesh.[24]

Suicide bombings have also emerged as another tool in the arsenal of radical Islamists, suggesting that militants in Bangladesh are adopting the tactics and techniques of their counterparts in the Middle East. Bangladesh is now viewed as a safe haven by jihadis, who use its friendly government and infrastructure to regroup and for training purposes. A number of recent terrorist attacks in India have been traced back to Bangladeshi nationals working on behalf of Harkat-ul-Jihad-al-Islami (HuJI), which is suspected of being an Al Qaeda front and also has links with the Jaish-e-Mohammed and Lashkar-e-Toiba jihadi groups based in Pakistan. HuJI is now one of the fastest growing fundamentalist organizations in Bangladesh and has been designated a "terrorist organization" by the US government. Islamist radicals from across Asia including India, Myanmar, Thailand, Indonesia, Afghanistan, and the Philippines gravitated toward Bangladesh for military training and refuge from their home governments, under the protection of HuJI.

It is under the AL government that Dhaka has stepped up its activities against Islamist extremists. It cracked down on the Lashkar-e-Toiba and Jagrata Muslim Janata Bangladesh groups; with the chief of the JMB, Saidur Rahman, being finally arrested in Dhaka in 2010 after a pursuit of three years. The Bangladesh government has also acted to pre-empt cross-border attacks on India and on the Indian establishments in Dhaka, which has effectively curtailed the ability of Pakistan to use Bangladesh as a springboard for terrorism against India.

Weak economic ties
The economic basis of bilateral ties between India and Bangladesh remains weak and lacks any constructive agenda, making it even more difficult for the two states to move forward on other issues. This is despite the fact that India and Bangladesh are members of both SAARC and also the Bay of Bengal Initiative for Multi Sectoral Technical and Economic Cooperation (BIMSTEC). The Indo-Bangladesh Joint Working Group on Trade Issues was established in 2003 and has held regular meetings ever since. Nonetheless, it has failed to reorient economic ties between the two states in a meaningful way. Bilateral trade between India and Bangladesh stood at US$6.6 billion in 2013–14; with illegal trade, amounting to about three-fourths of the regular, being the real winner.[25] India's efforts to secure transit and trans-shipment facilities for accessing northeast states through the territory of Bangladesh have been rebuffed by Dhaka.

The BNP government also reneged on its earlier commitment, via the tripartite agreement, for the transportation of natural gas from Myanmar to India via a pipeline running through Bangladesh. India wants to pursue this project because it is deemed to be its most economical option. The India–Bangladesh–Myanmar pipeline idea was initially seen as a landmark in Indo-Bangladesh relations, in which Bangladesh would have agreed to let its territory be used for the transport of an economic commodity to the Indian market for the first time in thirty years. Although India appeared willing to pay a US$125 million transit fee to Bangladesh, Dhaka also wanted additional concessions before concluding this agreement. These included a transit facility through India for hydroelectric power from Nepal and Bhutan to Bangladesh, a Nepal–Bhutan trade corridor, and measures to reduce the bilateral trade imbalance. The Indian corporate giant the Tata Group has proposed massive investments in Bangladesh to the tune of US$2.5 billion in steel, fertilizer, and power sectors but this agreement has been stuck over differences regarding the price of the natural gas that Bangladesh has insisted be used. The Tata Group finally decided to put its investment plans for Bangladesh on hold, citing Dhaka's insufficient progress in assessing and responding to the firm's revised investment offer.

India has also proposed concluding a FTA with Bangladesh. Many Bangladeshis are asking the government to consider this seriously in the light of Sri Lanka, which has operated a FTA with India since 2001.[26] Concluding an FTA would strengthen the economic basis of bilateral ties between India and Bangladesh and go a long way toward solving the problem of illegal trade. But India's skepticism of Bangladesh's testing procedures for its food exports remains a constraining factor and it has asked for the codes to be harmonized and classifications to be made standard in order to come to a "rules of origin" agreement to give Bangladesh greater access to Indian markets. Many in Bangladesh view this as another sign of India's protectionist tendencies. India has assured Dhaka that it would bring down some of its existing non-tariff barriers to exports from Bangladesh and assist Bangladesh in ensuring that its exports met Indian quality standards. Both countries are working to ensure that long delays experienced by traders on cross-border trade are minimized by trade facilitation measures.

Dhaka has also been asking for unilateral tariff concessions on select items of export interest to help reduce its trade deficit with India. In contrast, India feels that Indian investments in Bangladesh, such as the one proposed by the Tatas, are another way of solving this problem. With India's economic growth at an all-time high, its investments in the region will increase in coming years and there is no reason for Bangladesh to exclude itself from a process that will benefit it immensely. After all, Bangladesh is set to become the second largest economy in South Asia, behind only India. Bangladesh's economic development is also in India's best interests, both to help curb illegal immigration and to make it more difficult for terrorist groups in Bangladesh to find fresh recruits.

India is undertaking actions to meet Bangladesh's immediate energy requirements by selling 250 megawatts of electrical power. Indian companies will find investment opportunities in the development of power infrastructure in Bangladesh as the power deficit in the country is set to increase further in the coming years.

It is clear that India's larger South Asian priorities – including regional free trade, upgrading of the transport and communication infrastructure, and energy cooperation – cannot be fully realized unless India–Bangladesh relations are improved. This is also essential for the integration of the eastern part of the subcontinent, including Nepal and Bhutan, into a regional framework. India realizes that the success of its "Look East" policy depends on Bangladesh acting as an effective bridge between northeast India and Southeast Asia. The need has long been apparent for development of closer transport and communication links between India and Bangladesh in order to achieve the full potential of regional economic integration, but so far progress has only been lacklustre.

By extending a line of credit of US$1 billion for the development of infrastructure, India has cleared the way for its involvement in the development of rail and road communications linking its landlocked northeast with the rest of the country. India is also planning to invest in the development of Chittagong and Mongla ports, which will provide access for goods from Nepal and Bhutan to these ports, furthering regional economic integration.

Conclusion

The present constraints that impinge upon this India–Bangladesh relationship make it imperative for both sides to reduce the mutual "trust deficit" that has crept into their bilateral ties. This is a necessary first step before any meaningful relationship can emerge. India, being the bigger and economically more powerful of the two, can and should take the lead in this process by taking generous and constructive steps to improve relations with Bangladesh.

But Bangladesh also needs to return to the more secular, tolerant traditions of Islam which it used to espouse, and to oppose Islamic radicalism more forcefully. It has been rightly observed that the unchecked rise of religious extremism currently underway in Bangladesh bodes ill for the country, its neighbors, and the world. A weak and fractured Bangladesh is in no one's interest. India will have to take a long-term view and work with Bangladesh to ameliorate its problems, both domestically and in a broader regional context.

Notes

1 "Bangladesh: Elections Scarred by Violence," Human Rights Watch, April 29, 2014, www.hrw.org/news/2014/04/29/bangladesh-elections-scarred-violence.
2 *Ibid.*, p. 161.
3 S. Kapila, "Bangladesh-China Defence Co-operation Agreement's Strategic Implications," *Papers* (SAAG), No. 582, January 14, 2003.
4 R. Maitra, "Prospects Brighten for Kunming Initiative," *Asia Times*, February 12, 2003.
5 Ananth Krishnan, "Hasina Seeks Partnership with China," *The Hindu*, June 11, 2014.
6 See, for example, C. Raja Mohan, "Five Fold Embrace for Khaleda," *Indian Express*, March 20, 2006.
7 M. Hossain, "The Rising Tide of Islamism in Bangladesh," *Current Trends in Islamist Ideology*, Vol. 3 (2006).
8 "A Vote for Bin Laden?" *The Economist*, September 27, 2001.
9 K. Lakshman, "Islamist Extremist Mobilization in Bangladesh," *Terrorism Monitor*, Vol. 13, No. 12 (2005), p. 6.
10 Iftekharuzzaman, "Bangladesh: A Weak State and Power," in M. Alagappa, *Asian Security Practice: Material and Ideational Influences* (Stanford: Stanford University Press, 1998), p. 317.
11 "Bangladeshi Infiltration Deeply Affecting Assam: BJP," *Hindustan Times*, March 27, 2006.
12 "Assam Facing External Aggression. SC," *Indian Express*, July 15, 2005.
13 R. Sengupta, "Why India is Concerned About Bangladesh?" *India Abroad*, December 22, 2005.
14 R. Sengupta, "Bangladesh: Next Terror Frontier?" *India Abroad*, December 19, 2005.
15 Sengupta, "Why India is Concerned About Bangladesh"; "Bangladesh: Next Terror Frontier?".

16 A. Riaz, "God Willing: The Politics and Ideology of Islamism in Bangladesh," *Comparative Studies of South Asia, Africa, and Middle East*, Vol. 23, No. 1/2 (2003), pp. 310–20.
17 E. Griswold, "The Next Islamist Revolution," *New York Times*, January 23, 2005.
18 A. Perry, "Rebuilding Bangladesh," *Time* (Asia), April 3, 2006.
19 See, for example, the seventy-four-page report "Growing Fanaticism and Extremism in Bangladesh: Shades of the Taliban" on the official website of the AL, www.albd.org/aldoc/growing/growing.fanaticism.pdf. Also S. Kapila, "Bangladesh Government in Denial Mode on Country's Talibanisation," Papers (SAAG), No. 1062, July 15, 2004.
20 H. Karlekar, "Cautious Tango," *South Asia Intelligence Review*, Vol. 1, No. 42 (2003).
21 "An Ugly Alliance," *The Economist*, August 12, 2006.
22 R. Upadhyay, "De-Pakistanisation of Bangladesh," *Papers* (SAAG), No. 2199, April 7, 2007.
23 P. Tarapot, *Insurgency Movement in North Eastern India* (New Delhi: Vikas Publishing House, 1993), pp. 127–46.
24 "459 Blasts in 63 Districts in 30 Minutes," *Daily Star*, August 18, 2005.
25 "India-Bangladesh Trade May Almost Double to $10 Billion by 2018: CII," *Economic Times*, June 24, 2014.
26 This view has been articulated very forcefully by a former Foreign Secretary of Bangladesh, Farooq Sobhan. See his paper, "India-Bangladesh Relations: The Way Forward," 2005, www.bei-bd.org. Also World Bank, "India-Bangladesh Bilateral Trade and Potential Free Trade Agreement," *Bangladesh Development Series Paper*, No. 13 (2006).

8

Nepal and Sri Lanka: India struggles to retain its relevance

In an interesting contrast to its predecessors, the Modi government's initial outreach to Nepal managed to hit the right notes, capturing the imagination of Nepalese people and politicians alike. The visits of the Indian Prime Minister, Narendra Modi, and the External Affairs Minister, Sushma Swaraj, to Nepal in 2014 soon after assuming office were significant in recalibrating Indo-Nepalese ties and they have succeeded in doing precisely that. Modi's visit to Nepal in August 2014 was the first bilateral visit to Nepal by an Indian prime minister in seventeen years, an example of Indian foreign policy's skewed priorities. Nepalese polity, cutting across party lines, had welcomed the assumption of power by Modi, with most expressing hope that Nepal would be a beneficiary of Modi's developmental agenda. And Modi reached out to Kathmandu promptly as a sign that he is serious about prioritizing India's South Asia policy.

Nepal, too, reached out to Modi in an unprecedented manner – the Prime Minister of Nepal, Sushil Koirala, breaking protocol and receiving Modi at the airport, giving Modi a nineteen-gun salute on his arrival, the Nepalese parliament inviting Modi for an address, the first by a foreign head of state to that body after 1990, with the people of Nepal giving him a rousing public welcome. Modi's speech at the Nepalese parliament was a graceful reflection on the trials and turbulence that have shaped Indo-Nepalese ties over the last few years with a promise of a change of course in the coming years.[1] Modi's visit saw the conclusion of three MoUs. These included one on the 5,600-MW Pancheshwar project, the first report of which was drafted by India as far back as 2002. The other two were a Rs 69 million grant to Nepal for the supply of iodized salt and cooperation between Nepal Television and Indian state broadcaster, Doordarshan. Modi announced a 10,000 crore (Nepalese rupees) line of concessional credit to Nepal. Most significantly, Modi has promised prompt implementation of Indian projects in Nepal, a cause of needless irritation in this bilateral relationship as delay is seen as symptomatic of India's lack of seriousness by most Nepalese people.

The groundwork for Modi's visit was done during Sushma Swaraj's visit a few days earlier, when she managed to convey the right message by settling a long-pending issue. That is, she promised a review of the 1950 Treaty of Peace and Friendship, on the basis of recommendations from a group of eminent persons from both countries.[2] The Modi government had an opportunity to reshape the contours of New Delhi's relations with Kathmandu at a time when India seemed to be losing ground in Nepal to China. But this bonhomie was not to last long and regional realities soon made their presence felt.

A yam between two rocks

Despite being a tiny landlocked state, Nepal has a pivotal position in the South Asian geo-strategic environment as it shares a border of 1,236 kilometers with China and 1,690 kilometers with India.[3] For both China and India, therefore, Nepal holds great strategic value. "A yam between two rocks" was how the founder of Nepal, Prithvi Narayan Shah, described the kingdom. For China, Nepal's strategic significance lies, first and foremost, in its close proximity to Tibet. Nepal, according to Beijing, constitutes a vital part of an inner security ring that cannot be allowed to be breached by any global or regional power.[4] The Chinese occupation of Tibet in 1950 significantly increased Nepal's strategic importance for China. Ensuring Nepal's neutrality on the issue of Tibet, and securing active Nepali cooperation to prevent Tibetans from launching anti-China activities, was Beijing's primary objective in Nepal.[5]

For India, Nepal remains the principal strategic land barrier between China and its own resource-rich Gangetic Plain. India's strategic stakes in Nepal dramatically increased with the communist victory in China and the country's subsequent occupation of Tibet in 1950. Since the middle of the nineteenth century, Tibet, rather than Nepal, had served as India's buffer with China. The role of buffer passed on to Nepal after the Chinese annexation of Tibet. It became imperative for New Delhi to deny China direct access to Nepal because of the vulnerability of India's Gangetic Plain, which contains critical human and economic resources.[6]

Nepal's strategic importance has led Beijing to focus its policies on preserving and enhancing the Himalayan state's independence and neutrality by trying to reduce its dependence on India in the political, economic, and security arenas. China's policy options, however have been severely circumscribed by the special security relationship between India and Nepal formalized in the 1950 Peace and Friendship Treaty between the two.[7] In the early years of the Cold War, Beijing, wary of an alliance between the United States and India, accepted India's pre-eminent position in Nepal, and followed India's lead in its relations with Nepal. Diplomatic links between China and Nepal were established only in August 1955. China, in deference to India, agreed to handle its relations with Nepal through its embassy in New Delhi. Nonetheless, Beijing continued to engage Nepal by providing economic aid and by strongly supporting Kathmandu in its disputes with New Delhi on issues of trade and transit, thereby increasing its influence among Nepalese elites.

As China's economic and political power increased, it became more assertive in Nepal. By the late 1980s, China's engagement with Nepal had grown substantially. It signed a secret intelligence-sharing agreement with Nepal in 1988 and agreed to supply arms. This arms agreement elicited a strong reaction from India which imposed an economic blockade on Nepal from 1989 to 1990.[8] This did not prevent economic interactions between China and Nepal from gathering momentum in the next decade. Despite its 1950 treaty with India, Nepal began importing Chinese weaponry and sought extensive military cooperation with China in a move to reduce its dependence on India. When the United States, the United Kingdom, and India refused to supply arms to the regime of King Gyanendra, China responded by dispatching arms to Nepal despite the king's anti-Maoist ideological stance. China supported the Nepalese King Gyanendra's anti-democratic measures in the name of political stability, but was nimble enough to shift its support to the Maoists as they gained ascendancy in Nepalese politics. China became the first country to provide military assistance to the new Maoist government.

Over the years, China's policy toward Nepal has been guided by its larger strategic game plan vis-à-vis South Asia. In the initial years of the Cold War when Beijing was worried about a possible alliance between India and the United States, it treated Nepal cautiously so as not to offend India. However, once China gained confidence and international respect, it went all out to increase its influence in Nepal. By supporting Kathmandu's position during most disputes between India and Nepal, Beijing was able to project itself as a benevolent power, in contrast with the supercilious attitude of India toward its smaller neighbors. It was also able to upgrade its military ties with Nepal, despite India's stiff resistance. As ethnic tensions have risen in Tibet in recent times, China has sought to curb the activities of Tibetan refugees in Nepal. China's interest and presence in Nepal, however, has gradually expanded and now goes far beyond the Tibet issue. China is projecting its "soft power" in Nepal by setting up China Study Centers that are being used to promote Chinese values among the Nepalese populace, which is otherwise tied culturally to India. These centers are emerging as effective instruments in promoting Chinese perspectives on key issues concerning Nepal. China is constructing a 770-kilometer railway line to connect the Tibetan capital of Lhasa with the Nepalese town of Khasa, a move that will connect Nepal to China's national rail network. China is also constructing a 17-kilometer road through the Himalayas linking Tibet to the Nepalese town of Syabrunesi which will not only connect Tibet to Nepal, but when completed will also establish the first direct Chinese land route to New Delhi. China views Nepal as a vital bridge toward South Asia. China has increased its aid to Nepal substantially in the last few years and the trade volume between the two is growing, though the trade balance continues to remain heavily in favor of China, something that China is trying to address by providing duty-free access to Nepali goods in China. China's strategy of providing aid without any conditions and support for building infrastructure is enhancing China's role even as Chinese products are flooding the Nepalese market and replacing Indian ones. By painting India as a creator of instability and an undue beneficiary of Nepal's resources, China has used Nepalese sensitivities vis-à-vis Indian influence to good effect, thereby further undercutting Indian influence in Kathmandu. India's overwhelming presence remains a source of resentment toward India in Nepal. China appears attractive because it can claim that unlike India it is not interested in the internal affairs of Nepal.

The success of a democratic Nepal at peace with its neighbors is essential for the entire region, but what is of far greater importance for India is the trajectory of Nepal's foreign policy. India was concerned that the rise of the Maoists in Nepal could marginalize India in the Himalayan kingdom's foreign affairs. The Maoist-led government indeed made a decisive shift toward Beijing when it suggested that Nepal would maintain equidistance from both China and India.[9] The Maoist leader Prachanda, after becoming Prime Minister, broke the long-standing tradition of Nepalese heads of state of making their first foreign trip to India, and decided make China his first destination, ostensibly to attend the opening ceremonies of the 2008 Olympic Games in Beijing. China also pushed the Maoist government to sign a new treaty to replace the 1960 Peace and Friendship Treaty between China and Nepal. The Maoist government made clear its intention to re-negotiate the 1950 treaty with India, but before they could accomplish that objective, the government fell.

While it was the fear of the unknown that haunted India after the victory of the Maoists, it was clear that other political entities in Nepal, the monarchy in particular, had not been particularly well-disposed toward India for the last several years. Nepal under the Maoist regime has been no different than Nepal under its discredited monarch, who did his best to play off China against India to increase his time in power. Recent political developments in Nepal – culminating in the resignation of Maoist Prime Minister Prachanda and the possibility of resumption of conflict between the Maoists and the military – have again created problems for India. Maoists have spoken of there being a "foreign hand" behind recent events, and few Nepalese take this as anything but an allusion to India. The resignation of the Maoist-led government in Nepal has plunged the Himalayan kingdom into crisis and India is being blamed for pulling strings behind the scenes. New Delhi must allay concerns that it is interested in controlling Nepalese politics while quietly nudging Nepalese political parties into forming a stable government and working to counter China's growing influence. As Tibet develops economically and transport links emerge between Nepal and China, China's ability to project power in Nepal will likely increase significantly.

These fears have been exacerbated by turmoil in Indo-Nepal ties the promulgation of a constitution in September 2015 that, according to its critics, discriminates against the Madhesis and the Tharus, who account for 70 percent of the population living in the Terai region bordering India, as well as against the country's indigenous groups, the Janjatis. These groups, making up nearly half of Nepal's population, were marginal to the larger constitution-making process, controlled by upper caste elite. The marginalized protest that their political power is reduced with the redrawing of political subdivisions, and the Indian sympathy they enjoy makes their protest part of a greater geopolitical struggle with China, Nepal's other giant neighbor. Indo-Nepal relations took a nosedive with Kathmandu blaming India for growing fuel shortages, implying that India had imposed an informal blockade by not allowing fuel trucks to cross the border into Nepal. New Delhi blamed this disruption on the mass protests. Nepal imports almost all its oil from India, and road links to China through the Himalayas have been blocked since the April earthquake. As tensions with India mounted, China reopened its border with Nepal in Tibet and stepped in to provide fuel. The disruptions underscore the Himalayan kingdom's profound economic vulnerability, further inflaming anti-India passions. China is likely to be a beneficiary of this turmoil in India's periphery.

India has struggled to retain its relevance in Nepal in recent years but the continuing attempts at the highest levels of the Indian political leadership underscore the importance of Nepal for Indian foreign policy priorities. A new chapter in India–Nepal relations is not possible without frequent and broad-based political engagement, and closer cooperation. It is extremely critical for India to view Nepal as a development partner, and work toward finding viable areas of cooperation.

From Rajapaksa to Sirisena

In a stunning blow to Mahinda Rajapaksa in January 2015, the Sri Lankan voters opted for his former colleague Maithripala Sirisena as the new President to end a decade-long regime that has been increasingly marked by allegations of nepotism, corruption, and authoritarianism. Rajapaksa, after having defeated the Liberation Tigers of Tamil Elam (LTTE), won an overwhelming mandate for himself and his party in the 2010 elections. The LTTE had been fighting since 1983 for an independent homeland for minority ethnic Tamils after decades of discrimination at the hands of the Sinhalese majority.[10] Though the civil war in Sri Lanka, which lasted for more than twenty-five years and claimed over 100,000 lives, ended in 2009, the country still remains bitterly divided and reconciliation efforts have faltered. When the war ended in 2009, there was an opportunity for the ethnic communities to reconcile and the government was expected to implement measures to address the problems faced by the country's minorities, particularly by Tamils. That did not happen.

It was Rajapaksa who had called for elections in January 2015, a full sixteen months ahead of schedule. His confidence stemmed from the fact that under his leadership the civil war ended in 2009, term limits for the presidency were removed in 2010, a wave of infrastructure investment poured in, and the country's economy is experiencing a still-rising peace dividend. The Sri Lankan economy has seen robust annual growth at 6.4 percent over the course of 2003 to 2012, well above its regional peers.[11] Following the end of the civil conflict in May 2009, growth rose initially to 8 percent, largely reflecting a "peace dividend," and underpinned by strong private consumption and investment. While growth was mostly private sector driven, public investment contributed through large infrastructure investment, including postwar reconstruction efforts in the North and Eastern provinces. Growth was around 7 percent in 2013, driven by a rebound in the service sector, which accounts for approximately 60 percent of GDP.[12]

Despite an end to the violent conflict with the LTTE in 2009, social tensions have persisted in Sri Lanka. A predominantly militarized development process imposes a top-down strategy at the expense of incorporating local voices and ideas. Though more discrete than was previously the case, the armed forces are involved in all levels of civilian administration in the North, and development projects must be military-approved. The International Crisis Group has argued that "instead of giving way to a process of inclusive, accountable development, the military is increasing its economic role, controlling land and seemingly establishing itself as a permanent, occupying presence."[13] Sri Lanka has also been witnessing religious tensions between the Sinhala Budhdhists and the Muslims. The anti-Muslim campaign has been triggered by the Bodu Bala Sena (meaning "Buddhist Power Force") over the abolition of the Halaal certification process and banning of the niqab. Bodu Bala Sena was formed in July 2012. Since its formation, it has taken up various anti-Muslim activities – for example, asking people not to buy from Muslim shops.[14] Not surprising, therefore, that the minority Tamils and Muslims appeared to have voted heavily against Rajapaksa.

As a new era began in Sri Lanka, Indian Prime Minister Narendra Modi promptly reached out to Sirisena to congratulate him on his victory and assured him of India's continued solidarity and support to the country's peace and development. In return, President Sirisena traveled to New Delhi in February 2015 on his first state visit abroad. The government of Rajapaksa had become ever more confident of disregarding Indian concerns. India has been emphasizing the need for urgent steps to resettle the internally displaced persons (IDPs) and has urged the Sri Lankan authorities to expedite rehabilitation and reconstruction efforts in northern and eastern Sri Lanka. India has underlined the need for a meaningful devolution package, building on the 13th amendment to the Sri Lankan Constitution that would create the necessary conditions for a lasting political settlement. However, the Rajapaksa government was largely non-committal on most of India's demands. Sirisena's trip to India resulted in a civil nuclear energy cooperation pact even as his government underlined that it would have a "different approach" than the previous Rajapaksa government, which even allowed a Chinese submarine to dock in Colombo in September 2014, raising hackles in New Delhi.[15] The Sirisena government made its desire public to correct Rajapaksa's tilt toward China and made some significant overtures toward India. Risking diplomatic row with is largest trading partner, Sri Lanka suspended a US$1.5 billion Chinese luxury real estate project in Colombo, the biggest of several Chinese investments in Sri Lankan ports and infrastructure. Though the Sri Lankan government suggested that the deal lacked transparency and did not meet environmental standards, India too had expressed its concerns about the project.[16]

Modi's trip to Sri Lanka in March 2015 was the first in twenty-eight years by an Indian prime minister and it resulted in four agreements including ones for visa-exemptions for holders of diplomatic passports, cooperation in mutual assistance in customs, an MoU for youth development, and another for establishing a museum dedicated to Rabindranath Tagore. India also offered a fresh line of credit of US$380 million dollars to Sri Lanka's railway sector. India also committed itself to making Trincomalee a petroleum hub with Sri Lanka's state-run Ceylon Petroleum Corporation and the local subsidiary of Indian Oil Corporation agreeing to develop a strategic oil storage facility in Trincomalee. Modi also became the first Indian Prime Minister and only the second foreign leader after British Prime Minister David Cameron to visit Jaffna in the war-ravaged Northern Province, where he handed over homes built with the help of Indian assistance. Underscoring New Delhi's desire to see the 13th Amendment implemented, Modi assured Colombo that India stands with Sri Lanka "to build future that accommodates all sections, including Tamils, for peace, justice and equality in Sri Lanka."[17] Jettisoning the diffidence of the past, Modi visited the memorial to the Indian Peace Keeping Force outside Colombo that pays homage to the Indian soldiers who lost their lives in the military operation in the late 1980s.

As India's ties with Sri Lanka have entered a turbulent phase in recent years, China's presence in the country has become more significant, posing a serious challenge to Indian policy.[18] Historically, India was the main driver in Sri Lanka's foreign policy, as was reflected in the Sri Lanka government's demand that the British leave their naval base at Trincomalee and air base at Katunayake in 1957. After the Chinese victory in its 1962 war with India, however, Sri Lanka began to court China much more seriously. China, for its part, viewed India's role in Sri Lankan affairs not only as a means to "control" Sri Lanka and achieve "regional hegemony" in South Asia but also to "expel the influence of other countries."[19] The Indo-Sri Lankan agreement of 1987, whereby the two sides agreed that neither would allow its territory to be used against the security interests of other, and Colombo guaranteed that foreign military and intelligence personnel in Sri Lanka would not hurt Indo-Sri Lankan ties, merely confirmed Beijing's suspicions that India wishes to exert control over affairs in Sri Lanka.[20] Sri Lanka's support of China on the question of China's sovereignty over Taiwan and Tibet, and China's support for issues related to Sri Lankan territorial integrity, reinforced the Sino-Sri Lankan bilateral relationship. But given Beijing's inability to effectively project power in South Asia until the early 1990s, it could only be a marginal player in the Indo-Sri Lankan dynamic and was forced to accept India's central role in Sri Lanka, especially as India seemed willing to pursue coercive diplomacy until the late 1980s. It was Sri Lanka's war against the LTTE (also known as the Tamil Tigers) that made India's role contentious both domestically and in Sri Lanka, and allowed China crucial maneuvring space to enhance its profile in the country.

When the Sri Lankan government of Mahinda Rajapaksa decided to launch an all-out offensive against the Tamil rebels, after being humiliated with the discovery of LTTE air prowess, it decided to court China more actively in the defense sphere.[21] When India made it clear that it could not send offensive weapons and weapon systems such as radar and the West decided to suspend military aid on account of human rights concerns, China decided to come to the rescue of the Sri Lankan government. Sri Lanka signed a US$37.6 million deal in 2007 to buy Chinese ammunition and ordnance for its army and navy even as China supplied Sri Lanka fighter jets to counter LTTE's air prowess. Today, China not only supplies military hardware and training, but assists Sri Lanka in gas exploration and the construction of a modern port in the southern town of Hambantota. China's arms transfers include fighter aircraft, armoured personnel carriers, anti-aircraft guns, air surveillance radars, rocket-propelled grenade launchers and missiles, strengthening the position of the Sri Lankan Army against the first terrorist organization to boast of an army, navy, and air force, along with a small submarine force.

Chinese military supplies to Sri Lanka are estimated at US$100 million per year, with China supporting Sri Lankan defense forces in boosting its capabilities for high-technology aerial warfare, and restructuring and reorienting the military. China has encouraged Sri Lanka's participation in multilateral regional military activities, and Sri Lanka was accepted as a Dialogue Partner to the Shanghai Cooperation Organization (SCO) in 2009. China emerged as the largest foreign finance partner of Sri Lanka in 2010, overtaking India and Japan, and its third largest trading partner in 2012.[22] Sri Lanka is also committed to join the Maritime Silk Road initiative of Beijing which is a vital strategic project for China in the Indian Ocean. For China, Sri Lanka is a gateway port up the western coast of India and further west to Iran, an important oil exporter to China.

China's support was crucial for Sri Lanka during the last phase of the war against the LTTE. Chinese support was also invaluable as Sri Lanka was confronted by US-backed resolutions at the UN Human Rights Council (UNHRC). As a result, the two nations now have a declared "strategic co-operation partnership." For China, its ties with Sri Lanka give it a foothold near crucial sea lanes in the Indian Ocean, as well as entry into what India considers its sphere of influence. China is financing more than 85 percent of the Hambantota Development Zone, to be completed over the next decade. This will include an international container port, a bunkering system, an oil refinery, an international airport, and other facilities. The port in Hambantota, deeper than the one at the Sri Lankan capital, Colombo, is to be used as a refuelling and docking station for the Chinese Navy. Although the two sides claim that this is merely a commercial venture, it is viewed in New Delhi as yet another pearl in China's string, which aims to encircle India in the Indian Ocean.

India's political and economic influence in Sri Lanka has shrunk significantly because strong domestic Tamil sentiment against supporting Sri Lanka's counter-insurgency strategy prevented India from playing any meaningful role in the defeat of the LTTE. Colombo turned to Beijing for military supplies after New Delhi refused, and with this India's strategic space in Sri Lanka shrank to an all-time low, despite its geo-strategic advantage and economic clout. China's diplomatic support helped Sri Lanka to deflect Western criticism of its human rights record in defeating the LTTE. India had hoped that with the defeat of the LTTE, it would be able to get back its original clout in the island nation. However, domestic sensitivities on the issue remain very strong. In southern Indian states and especially in Tamil Nadu, anger at the Rajapaksa government's conduct during the war with the LTTE continues to be high.

In March 2013 India voted with twenty-four other states in favor of a controversial UNHRC resolution on human rights violations in Sri Lanka. The main aspect of Indian intervention was the need for the institution of a credible and independent investigation into alleged war crimes and human rights abuses during the final stages of Sri Lanka's civil conflict. In his remarks, India's permanent representative to the UNHRC, Dilip Sinha, referred to the "inadequate progress by Sri Lanka in fulfilling its commitment" to the UN Council, while also urging Sri Lanka to "pursue a lasting political settlement, acceptable to all communities in Sri Lanka, including the Tamils."[23]

One year earlier, in March 2012, the Indian authorities had supported a similar resolution at the UNHRC, provoking considerable attention as this appeared to contravene a traditional Indian policy of abstaining on country-specific UNHRC resolutions. If in 2012 India had tried to amend the US-sponsored resolution to make it less intrusive, more balanced, and more respectful of Sri Lankan sovereignty, in 2013 it was trying to do the opposite: bringing in amendments to make some words in the resolution stronger. It reportedly pushed for seven written amendments to six paragraphs of the resolution.[24] India's stance was widely reported to reflect pressure exerted on the federal government by its political partners in the state of Tamil Nadu. However, if this was aimed at the domestic political landscape, it failed to have any impact as the main regional parties accused the government of "diluting" the resolution against Sri Lanka, with the Tamil Nadu-based Dravida Munnetra Kazhagam withdrawing from the ruling coalition, contending that the Indian authorities had failed to use their influence to secure a more forceful resolution.[25]

As a consequence of this domestic political posturing, India not only marginalized itself in the affairs of Tamils in Sri Lanka but has also ensured that one of its most important neighbors would move further into the arms of China. After previously opposing country-specific resolutions at the UNHCR and other such bodies, India also set a dangerous precedent that might create future foreign policy dilemmas for the Indian authorities. Where India has to balance its domestic sensitivities and strategic interests, China faces no such constraint in developing even stronger ties with Sri Lanka. Sri Lanka matters because the Indian Ocean matters. The "great game" of this century will be played in the waters of the Indian Ocean. Though India's location gives it great operational advantages in the Indian Ocean, it is by no means certain that New Delhi is in a position to hold on to its geographic advantages despite a friendlier government in Colombo. With geography as well as its age-old cultural and ethnic ties to Sri Lanka, India wants to be "first amongst equals" in terms of influence over its island neighbor. And that remains a work in progress for Indian foreign policy.

Notes

1 "Narendra Modi Wins Hearts by Using Nepali in Address Speech," *Indian Express*, August 3, 2014.
2 Utpal Parashar, "India-Nepal Agree to Update 1950 Treaty of Peace," *Hindustan Times*, July 27, 2014.
3 This and other geographical details regarding Nepal can be found at the Central Intelligence Agency's World Factbook, available at www.cia.gov/library/publications/the-world-factbook/geos/np.html.
4 For a detailed discussion on Tibet's strategic importance for China, see Rama Kant, "Nepal's China Policy," *China Report*, Vol. 30, No. 2 (1994), pp. 164–6.
5 Narayan Khadka, "Chinese Foreign Policy Towards Nepal in Cold War Period: An Assessment," *China Report*, Vol. 35, No. 1 (1999), pp. 62–5.
6 John W. Garver, *Protracted Contest: Sino-Indian Rivalry in the Twentieth Century* (Seattle: University of Washington Press, 2001), p. 140.

7 The full text of the 1950 Treaty of Peace and Friendship is available at http://meadev.nic.in/economyibta/volume1/chapter38.htm.

8 For details on the Indian economic blockade of Nepal, see Garver, *Protracted Contest*, pp. 155–62.

9 "Nepal for Equidistant Ties with India, China," *India Abroad*, June 23, 2008.

10 Harsh V. Pant, "End Game in Sri Lanka," *Yale Global*, February 23, 2009, http://yaleglobal.yale.edu/content/end-game-sri-lanka.

11 "Sri Lanka: Overview," The World Bank, March 31, 2014, www.worldbank.org/en/country/srilanka/overview.

12 *Ibid.*

13 "Sri Lanka's North: Rebuilding the Military," International Crisis Group, March 16, 2012, available at www.crisisgroup.org/~/media/Files/asia/south-asia/sri-lanka/220-sri-lankas-north-ii-rebuilding-under-the-military.pdf.

14 Ana Lehmann, "Sri Lanka: Torn between Yesterday and Tomorrow," *Deutsche Welle*, May 15, 2014.

15 Rajat Pandit, "India Suspicious as Chinese Submarine Docks in Sri Lanka," *Times of India*, September 28, 2014.

16 Shihar Aneez, "Sri Lanka Cabinet Suspends Chinese Project on Approval Issue," Reuters, March 5, 2015.

17 "India Seeks a Life of Peace and Dignity for Tamils in Sri Lanka: PM Modi," *Economic Times*, March 13, 2015.

18 Dhirendra Mohan Prasad, *Ceylon's Foreign Policy under the Bandarnaikes (1956–65): A Political Analysis* (New Delhi: S. Chand, 1973), pp. 304–88.

19 Garver, *Protracted Contest*, pp. 308–9.

20 For a detailed examination of this accord, see Shelton U. Kodikara, "Genesis of the Indo-Sri Lankan Agreement of 29 July, 1987," *Contemporary South Asia*, Vol. 4, No. 2 (July 1995), pp. 171–85.

21 For a discussion of the factors responsible for the defeat of the LTTE, see Pant, "End Game in Sri Lanka."

22 For details on China–Sri Lanka economic relations, see S. Kelegama, "China–Sri Lanka Economic Relations: An Overview," *China Report*, Vol. 50, No. 2 (May 2014), pp. 131–49.

23 "UN Human Rights Council Adopts US-Sponsored Resolution against Sri Lanka, India Votes in Favour of the Document," *Daily News and Analysis*, March 21, 2013.

24 *Ibid.*

25 "DMK Withdraws from UPA, but Govt Safe," *Business Standard*, March 20, 2013.

9

India and Afghanistan: a test case for a rising power

Welcoming Afghan President Ashraf Ghani in India in April 2015, Indian Prime Minister Narendra Modi underlined that "the relationship between India and Afghanistan is not just between two countries or governments. It is a timeless link of human hearts."[1] With that spirit Modi made it clear that India would support Afghanistan's security forces and open the Attari checkpoint in Punjab to Afghan trucks in order to increase trade between the two countries. Modi stated: "India will walk shoulder to shoulder with you and the Afghan people in a mission of global importance." In addition to proclaiming India's support for Afghanistan's security forces, Modi announced that India is "prepared to join the successor agreement to Afghan-Pakistan Trade and Transit Agreement" which will "re-establish one of the oldest trading routes of South Asia."[2] For his part, President Ghani signaled his disappointment with Pakistan over its refusal to allow direct trade with India via the Wagah border, and suggested that if the deadlock continues Afghanistan "will not provide equal transit access to Central Asia [for Pakistani trucks]."[3]

But even as the Afghan President was being welcomed in India, there has been a growing sense that New Delhi is fast losing its carefully nurtured decade-old clout in Afghanistan. Compared to his predecessor, Hamid Karzai, Ghani has been lukewarm to India. His visit to New Delhi came long after his outreach to Pakistan and China, both of whom seem more firmly embedded in the peace overtures to the Taliban than India. Ghani's government has also been keen to see China take a more active role in the reconciliation process. India stands isolated with many in the country wondering whatever happened to the much-hyped Delhi–Kabul strategic partnership. This chapter examines the evolution in India–Afghanistan relations over the last few decades, underlining the challenges that India continues to face as it seeks to project its economic and military power in Afghanistan.

The Cold War and beyond

Bilateral ties between India and Afghanistan span centuries, given Afghanistan's close links to the South Asian civilization historically. India

has traditionally maintained strong cultural ties with Afghanistan, resulting in stable relations between the two states. Of course, imperial powers
such as Great Britain and Russia used Afghanistan as a pawn in their "great
game" of colonization, and, given the contested boundary between British
India and Afghanistan, the ties between the two frayed.[4] But after independence, as the problem of the Durand line, a boundary established in the
Hindu Kush in 1893 running through the tribal lands between Afghanistan
and British India, got transferred to Pakistan, India had no reason not to
enjoy good ties with Afghanistan, especially given the adversarial nature of
India–Pakistan relations.

The Cold War also forced the two states to assume roughly similar foreign policy postures. While India was one of the founding members of the
NAM, Afghanistan also tried to follow an independent foreign policy and,
for some time at least, was able to effectively play one superpower against
the other, thereby garnering economic assistance from both sides. But given
the United States' close ties with Pakistan and the Soviet Union's generosity
in providing extensive military and economic aid, Afghanistan gradually fell
into the Soviet orbit of influence, resulting in the Soviet invasion in 1979.
The NAM was divided on this issue, and India was one of the few nations
to support the Soviet invasion and occupation of Afghanistan, thereby damaging severely its prestige and credibility in the international community.[5]
Given India's antagonistic relations with Pakistan, India decided to support
Pakistan's adversaries and ended up supporting whoever was in power in
Kabul with Soviet support. This came to an abrupt end with the victory of
Pakistan-based mujahideen in 1992.[6]

The chaos that resulted in Afghanistan following Soviet occupation and
their ultimate withdrawal in 1989 had far-reaching implications for global
politics as well as Indian foreign policy. As the Cold War ended in the early
1990s, India faced a plethora of challenges on economic and foreign policy fronts. It had little time or inclination to assess what was happening
in Afghanistan, and so when the Taliban, spawned by the chaos and corruption that dominated post-Soviet Afghanistan, came to power in 1996,
India was at a loss to evolve a coherent foreign policy response. India's ties
with Afghanistan hit their nadir through the Taliban's seven-year rule when
India continued to support the Northern Alliance by providing money and
materiel.[7]

Ever since the fall of the Taliban in 2001, India has tried to engage
Afghanistan in a broad-based interaction.[8] This was also a time when Indian
capabilities – political, economic, and military – increased markedly, and
India became increasingly ambitious in defining its foreign policy agenda.[9] In
many ways, Afghanistan became emblematic of such an ambitious course that
India seemed to be charting in its foreign policy since the end of the Cold War.

India's role in Afghanistan can be divided into three distinct phases as it
evolved in response to the changing ground realities in the country.

Phase I: a "soft" engagement

India's engagement with Afghanistan readily became multidimensional after the defeat of the Taliban and the installation of an Interim Authority in 2001. This was reflected in an immediate upgrade of Indian representation in Afghanistan from a liaison office to a full-fledged embassy in 2002. India actively participated in the 2001 Bonn Conference convened to choose the leader of an Afghan Interim Authority and was instrumental in the emergence of post-Taliban governing and political authority in Afghanistan. Since then, India's main focus has been to support the Afghan government and the political process in the country as mandated under the Bonn agreement of 2001.[10] It has continued to pursue a policy of high-level engagement with Afghanistan through extensive and wide-ranging humanitarian, financial, and project assistance, as well as participation in international efforts aimed at political reconciliation and economic rebuilding of Afghanistan. As the second largest recipient of Indian development assistance after Bhutan, Afghanistan stood out as a nation where New Delhi made substantive economic investment so as to secure its strategic interests.

India's relations with Afghanistan steadily improved for a number of reasons. Unlike Pakistan, ties between India and Afghanistan are not hampered by the existence of a contiguous, and contested, border. Its support for the Northern Alliance against the Pakistan-backed Taliban in the 1990s strengthened its position in Kabul after 2001. Many members of the Alliance are members of the government or hold influential provincial posts. India has tried to restore the balance in its engagement with a range of different ethnic groups and political affiliations in Afghanistan. The balance was tilted toward the Tajik-dominated Northern Alliance during the 1990s as a counter to Pakistan-controlled hard-line Pashtun factions, led by the Taliban. India has used its vocal support for Karzai, an ethnic Pashtun educated in India, to demonstrate its keenness to revive its close ties with Pashtuns.

During each of the visits to India by Afghanistan's president, several important bilateral initiatives were announced by the two sides. These included a US$150 million financial commitment by India for the construction of a 215-kilometer Zaranj–Delaram road in the Nimruz province of Afghanistan; a preferential trade agreement between the two states; MoUs of cooperation in the fields of civil aviation, media and information, rural development, standardization, and education; and the establishment of a joint committee at the level of commerce ministers to conclude an EXIM Bank line of credit to the tune of US$50 million to promote business-to-business relations. Afghanistan has also sought Indian aid in agri-technology, which would halt desertification, deforestation, and water wastage.[11]

In consonance with the priorities laid down by Afghanistan's government as outlined in the Afghanistan National Development Strategy, Indian assistance has focused on building human capital and physical infrastructure, improving security, and helping the agricultural and other important sectors of the country's economy such as education, health, transport, telecommunications, civil aviation, irrigation, power generation, industry, and rural development. In the realm of defense, India's support has been limited to supplying defensive military equipment such as armored checkpoints and watch towers to Afghanistan.

India and Afghanistan have a long-standing record of technical and economic cooperation in various fields as, prior to 1979, Afghanistan was the largest partner in India's technical and economic cooperation program.[12] India launched an extensive assistance program in Afghanistan immediately after the fall of the Taliban regime in 2001 and pledged US$750 million toward reconstruction efforts, most of which was unconditional. Of this, more than US$450 million has already been utilized, and the projects range from humanitarian and infrastructure to health and rural development and training of diplomats and bureaucrats. New Delhi has emerged as one of Afghanistan's top six donors, having extended a US$500 million aid package in 2001 and gradually increasing it ever since.

Among the most high-profile of the infrastructure projects undertaken by India was the reconstruction of the 220-kilometer Zaranj–Delaram road at a cost of US$150 million. The road will enable Afghanistan to have access to the sea via Iran and will provide a shorter route for Indian goods to reach Afghanistan. This project was completed in 2008 by India's Border Roads Organization despite stiff resistance from the Taliban. Eleven Indians and 129 Afghans lost their lives during the completion of this project. The security of the Indian workers working on this project was provided by a 300-strong paramilitary force provided by India itself, because of which the project overshot time and monetary deadlines. After its success with the project, India has been asked to help in connecting Afghanistan to its other Central Asian neighbors like Turkmenistan and Tajikistan.[13]

India is also investing in the rebuilding of institutional capacity in Afghanistan by providing training to more than 700 Afghans in various professions, including diplomats, lawyers, judges, doctors, paramedics, women entrepreneurs, teachers, officials in various departments of Afghanistan's government, public officials, and cartographers. Afghanistan's budding public transport system relies on Indian support as India not only provides buses but also training to traffic operators and other personnel related to transport. India gifted 400 buses to Afghanistan initially, followed by 200 minibuses and 105 utility vehicles to lay the groundwork for a modern public transport system in Afghanistan. India also gifted three airbus aircrafts to get Afghanistan's native carrier, Ariana Afghan Airlines, off the ground and continues to train airline officials to develop capacities in this crucial area. The new parliament building in Kabul, constructed with Indian help, is perhaps the most visible sign of India's outreach to Afghanistan as a fellow democracy. India's Bureau of Parliamentary Study and Training provides training to officials of the Afghan National Assembly Secretariat. India's Election Commission has signed an MoU with its Afghan counterpart, leading to mutual visits and regular exchanges for training and study purposes.

India has been providing 500 short- and medium-term training slots annually to Afghan public servants and 500 scholarships to Afghan students studying at the undergraduate and postgraduate levels. Around 5,500 Afghan students are studying in India as of June 2013, of which about 300 are women. Afghans want to come to India because of the low cost of living, scholarships, familiarity with Indian culture, good bilateral relations, easy-to-obtain visas, and the use of English in Indian educational institutions. Of the 2,325 scholarships given annually to international students by the Indian Council for Cultural Relations, 675 are reserved for Afghans, the largest of any nationality.[14] In July 2014, India liberalized its visa policy for Afghan citizens that allows them to stay in India for up to two years and exempts police reporting for senior citizens and children.

India is also funding and executing the Salma Dam Power Project in Herat province, involving a commitment of around US$80 million as well as the 202-kilometer long double circuit transmission line from Pul-e-Khumri to Kabul.[15] India agreed to adopt 100 villages in Afghanistan to promote rural development by introducing solar electrification and rainwater harvesting technologies. Five Indian medical missions have been operating in Kabil, Herat, Jalalabad, Kandahar, and Mazar-e-Sharif, with nearly 3,60,000 poor patients using their services annually. India also worked toward the rehabilitation of the only hospital for children in Afghanistan – the Indira Gandhi Institute for Child Health – and has worked toward upgrading its capacity in various spheres.

Bilateral trade between India and Afghanistan reached US$600 million in 2011 and is expected to should exponentially rise, following the full implementation of the Afghanistan and Pakistan Trade and Transit Agreement (APTTA). The preferential trade agreement signed by India and Afghanistan gives substantial duty concessions to certain categories of Afghan dry fruits when entering India, with Afghanistan allowing reciprocal concessions to Indian products such as sugar, tea, and pharmaceuticals.

The Afghan government has been urging the Indian corporate sector to invest in Afghanistan and has even decided to accord special treatment to Indian investors.[16] A consortium of Indian steel companies, led by the National Mineral Development Corporation, India's largest iron ore miner, made a successful bid to acquire mining rights to Afghanistan's 1.8-billion-tonne Hajigak iron ore mines.[17] This bid is a rare instance of public and private sector companies joining forces to bid for an overseas raw material asset. Indian companies are afraid to venture solo, worried as they are about the safety of their investment because of the Taliban threat. A consortium of Indian companies also went on to bid for mining copper and gold in Afghanistan in 2012 with the help of US technical expertise but was not successful.

India also piloted the move to make Afghanistan a member of the SAARC, with the hope that the entry of Afghanistan would help address issues relating to the transit and free flow of goods across borders in the region, thereby leading to greater economic development of Afghanistan and the region as a whole.

Bollywood remains immensely popular in Afghanistan, which was the biggest market for its films until the early 1990s. Ordinary Afghans have also lapped up Indian television soap operas and Hindi film music, underscoring not only the close cultural links between the two nations but also generating people-to-people affinity. Ordinary Afghans appear to have welcomed Indian involvement in development projects in their country. Almost 74 percent of Afghans hold a favorable view of India compared to only 8 percent who have a positive impression of Pakistan.[18] It has been India's deliberate policy to refrain from giving its support a military dimension and to stick to civilian matters. Western observers, though, tended to view Indian involvement in Afghanistan as problematic as it has worked to undercut Pakistan's influence in the country. The result was that, over time, India's attempt to leverage its "soft power" in Afghanistan became increasingly risky.

Phase II: New Delhi marginalized

As India's profile grew in Afghanistan, its adversaries, intent on ridding Afghanistan of Indian involvement, also upped the ante in an attempt to rupture burgeoning India–Afghanistan relations. This happened as the West got distracted by its war in Iraq, allowing the Taliban, with support from Pakistan, to bounce back and reclaim the strategic space from which it had been ousted. As the balance of power shifted in favor of Pakistan and its proxies, Indian interests, including personnel and projects, emerged as viable targets. In July 2008, the Indian embassy in Kabul was struck by a blast that left sixty dead, including an Indian Foreign Service officer and an embassy defense attaché. In October 2009, a suicide car bombing outside the Indian embassy left at least seventeen dead and scores of others wounded.[19] Investigators soon concluded that the attack was perpetrated by the Pakistan-based Haqqani Network and suggested that Pakistani intelligence had also played a role. The Afghan envoy to the United States underscored the involvement of Pakistani intelligence – the first time that a top Afghan official had openly blamed the ISI for a terrorist attack in his country.[20] India faced a tough road ahead as a perception gained ground that the Taliban was on the rebound with a heightened sense of political uncertainty in Washington about the future of American military presence in Afghanistan.

The return of the Taliban to Afghanistan would pose a major threat to its borders. In the end, the brunt of escalating terrorism would be borne by India as "the sponge that protects" the West. Indian strategists have, for some time, been warning that a hurried US withdrawal, with the Taliban still posing a threat to Afghanistan, would have serious implications for India, not the least of which would be to see Pakistan, its eternal rival, step in more aggressively. To be fair, India's role in Afghanistan should not have been viewed through the eyes of Western observers, who dubbed India's Afghan engagement provocative for fear of offending Pakistan, or through the eyes of Pakistan, which resented its own waning influence. Rather, India's involvement should have been considered through the eyes of the Afghan people, who had arguably benefited from the use of their neighbor's "soft power," whatever its end motivations.

There has been consensus in India that it should not send troops to Afghanistan. Yet, beyond this, there was little agreement about what policy options it had if greater turbulence in the Af-Pak region spilled over into India. The traditional Indian stance had been that while India was happy to help the Afghan government in its reconstruction efforts, it would not be directly engaged in security operations, but this increasingly became harder to sustain. The inability of the Indian government to provide for the security of its private sector operating in Afghanistan led to a paradoxical situation, in which the Indian government's largest contractors in Afghanistan seemed to have participated in projects that might have ended up paying off the Haqqani Network, one of Afghanistan's deadliest and most anti-India insurgent groups.[21] A debate therefore started taking place as to whether India should start supporting its humanitarian endeavors in Afghanistan with a stronger military presence. If Afghanistan was the most important frontier in combating terrorism targeted at India, the critics asked, how long could India continue with its present policy trajectory whereby its civilians were killed in pursuit of its developmental objectives?

It was the sixty-nation London Conference on Afghanistan in January 2010 that advocated talks with the Taliban that jolted India, as New Delhi viewed with alarm its rapidly shrinking strategic space for diplomatic maneuvring. When then Indian External Affairs Minister S.M. Krishna underscored the folly of making a distinction "between a good Taliban and a bad Taliban" at the London Conference, he was completely out of sync with the larger mood at the conference.[22] The US-led Western alliance had made up its mind that it was not a question of if but when and how to exit from Afghanistan, which, to the leaders in Washington and London, was rapidly becoming a quagmire. So when it was decided in London that the time had come to woo the "moderate" section of the Taliban back to share power in Kabul, it was a signal to India that Pakistan had convinced the West that it could play the role of mediator in negotiations with the Taliban, thereby underlining its centrality in the unfolding strategic dynamics in the region. It would be catastrophic for Indian security if remnants of Taliban were to come to power with the backing of the ISI and Pakistan's military.

These changing ground realities forced India to start reconsidering the terms of its involvement in Afghanistan. Pakistan's paranoia about Indian presence in Afghanistan had led the West to underplay India's largely beneficial role in the country, even as Pakistan's every claim about Indian intentions was being taken at face value. The Taliban militants who blew up the Indian embassy in Kabul in 2008 and tried again in 2009 had sent a strong signal that India was part of the evolving security dynamics in Afghanistan despite its reluctance to take on a more active role in military operations. After targeting personnel involved in developmental projects, and emboldened by India's non-response, these terrorists trained their guns directly at the Indian state by attacking its embassy. Moreover, as India's isolation at the London Conference underlined, its role in Afghanistan was not fully appreciated even by the West.

Though the US and Afghan governments insisted that any settlement process should result in an end to Taliban violence and a willingness to conform to the Afghan constitution, the possibility of a Pakistan-sponsored settlement between hard-line elements of the Taliban and the Afghan government became a serious concern for India. As the diplomatic cables released by WikiLeaks – a whistleblower organization – in July 2010 underscored, India was concerned about US plans to exit from Afghanistan and its possible repercussions on India's security. Manmohan Singh expressed his hope to the Obama administration in 2009 that all those engaged in the process of moving toward stability in Afghanistan would "stay on course."[23] But the hope shattered as the United States actively discouraged India from assuming a higher profile in Afghanistan for fear of offending Pakistan.[24] At the same time, it failed in getting Pakistan to take Indian concerns more seriously.

By refusing to meld elements of hard and soft power and to assert its profile more forcefully, India soon made itself irrelevant as the ground realities changed and a divergence emerged between the strategic interests of India and Washington. A United States intent on moving out of Afghanistan managed to signal to Indian adversaries that they could shape the post-American ground realities to serve their own ends. India lost the confidence of its own allies in Afghanistan. India's "soft power" in Afghanistan had only resulted in soft targets for Pakistan-based terror groups, which India has found difficult to protect. If India was unwilling to stand up for its own interests, few saw the benefit of aligning with India. The Indian presence only seemed to get weak with the Obama administration deepening its security dependence on Pakistan in the hope of achieving some semblance of success in Afghanistan.

Phase III: India fights back

To preserve its interests and retain some credibility in a rapidly evolving strategic milieu where New Delhi had been marginalized, India was forced to take a number of policy measures vis-à-vis Afghanistan. These included a decision to step up its role in the training of Afghan forces, achieving greater policy coordination with states like Russia and Iran, and reaching out to all sections of Afghan society.[25]

As the strategic realities in South Asia radically altered in the aftermath of the killing of Osama Bin Laden – Al Qaeda founder and the brain behind 9/11 – then Indian Prime Minister Manmohan Singh lost no time in reaching out to Afghanistan with his two-day visit to Kabul after a six-year absence. He announced a fresh commitment of US$500 million for Afghanistan's development, over and above India's existing aid assistance of around US$1.5 billion.[26] New Delhi and Kabul agreed that the "strategic partnership" between the two neighbors, to be implemented under the framework of a partnership council headed by the foreign ministers of the two nations, will entail cooperation in areas of security, law enforcement, and justice, including an enhanced focus on cooperation in the fight against international terrorism, organized crime, illegal trafficking in narcotics, and money laundering. Most significant of all was Singh's expression of India's support for the Afghan government's plan of national reconciliation involving Taliban insurgents, thereby signaling an end to India's public opposition to a deal with the Taliban and bridging a strategic gap with the United States.[27] Also, shedding its reticence on Afghan security issues, India became more outspoken about its commitment to build the capabilities of the Afghan security forces.[28] New Delhi's review of its regional foreign policy priorities couldn't have come at a more urgent time.

Singh's visit was followed by the signing of a landmark strategic partnership agreement between New Delhi and Kabul during Karzai's visit to New Delhi in October 2011. It committed India to "training, equipping and capacity building" of the Afghan security forces. India pledged to train and equip Afghanistan's army and police force, expanding on the limited training it conducted for the army in India in 2007. India acceded to Afghanistan's request for 150 army officers to receive training at Indian defense and military academies, and India also agreed to begin hosting training sessions for Afghan police officers.[29] This was Afghanistan's first strategic pact with any country, though Karzai later signed such pacts with the United States and NATO to ward off the challenge from Pakistan. As part of the new pact, bilateral dialogue at the level of the national security advisor was institutionalized to focus on enhancing cooperation in security issues. New Delhi hoped that Kabul would take the lead in defining the exact terms of this engagement even as it made it clear that India would "stand by Afghanistan" when foreign troops withdrew from the country in 2014.

New Delhi launched a major effort toward the capability enhancement of the Afghan National Army (ANA) to help it handle the internal security of Afghanistan after the departure of Western forces. The number of ANA personnel being trained in Indian Army institutions jumped from 574 in 2012–13 to well over 1,000 in 2013–14.[30] Meanwhile, as Kabul and Washington decided to make moves toward negotiations with the Taliban, New Delhi also signaled that it was willing to engage with sections of the Taliban. The questions remained, however, if it was possible to differentiate between the so-called "reconcilable" and irreconcilable elements of the insurgents in Afghanistan and if even the reconcilable ones were really interested in negotiations at a time when they seemed to be winning.

Even as New Delhi reached out to Kabul for a strengthened security partnership, it also recognized the need to coordinate more closely with states such as Russia and Iran, with which it shared convergent interests vis-à-vis Afghanistan and Pakistan. None of these states would accept a fundamentalist Sunni-dominated regime in Kabul or the re-emergence of Afghanistan as a base for jihadist terrorism directed at neighboring states. The Indian government reached out to Moscow at the highest political levels, reiterating the two nations' shared positions on Afghanistan and institutionalizing cooperation on this issue.[31]

Highlighting Russia's serious concerns on the evolving situation in Afghanistan after the departure of NATO troops in 2014, its Deputy Prime Minister Dmitry Rogozin suggested in 2012 that India and Russia would have to work together to manage regional security as "thousands of terrorists and fundamentalists will seek refuge in Afghanistan as well as the region around the country" and this would "change the situation drastically around the region and for countries like Tajikistan, Kazakhstan and Central Asia."[32] During Manmohan Singh's visit to Russia in October 2013, the two sides emphasized that Pakistan's attempt to bring back the Taliban into Afghan political structures was an outcome not acceptable to the two states. India and Russia also began working together to revive an arms maintenance factory in Afghanistan in a sign of their stepped-up engagement in Afghan security.[33] Russia has been trying to increase its military and economic ties with Afghanistan even as it has been busy enhancing its military presence in various Central Asian states.

Iran is the other nation India reached out to. The two countries had worked closely when the Taliban was in power in Kabul and continued to cooperate on several infrastructure projects allowing transit facilities for Indian goods. Despite bilateral differences New Delhi revived its partnership with Tehran on Afghanistan, with the two sides deciding to hold "structured and regular consultations" on the issue of Afghanistan.[34] India and Iran signed an agreement to set up a joint working group on terrorism and security, the main purpose of which was to share intelligence on Al Qaeda activities in Afghanistan.

Moreover, India's plan to build a highway linking the southern Afghan city of Kandahar to Zahidan was of concern to Pakistan as it would reduce Afghanistan's dependence on Pakistan to the benefit of Iran. India's building of roads in Afghanistan was seen as particularly worrisome as it would increase the influence of India and Iran and boost Afghanistan's connectivity to the outside world. India also hoped that the road link through Afghanistan and Iran would open up markets for its goods in Afghanistan and beyond in Central Asia.

Despite American pressure, India decided to pump in US$100 million for the upgrade of Chabahar in May 2013, not only to get easier access for Indian goods into Central Asia but also to counter the China–Pakistan axis in the Indian Ocean after Islamabad decided to hand over the operational control of its Gwadar port to China.[35] This would also help in circumventing the problems of Pakistan's continuing denial of access to Indian shipments bound for Afghanistan as well as lower Afghanistan's dependence on Pakistani ports.

Finally, India also realized there was no alternative to direct talks with Pakistan if a regional solution to the Afghanistan conundrum was to be found. New Delhi restarted talks in 2010 with Pakistan, which had been suspended in the aftermath of the terrorist attacks in Mumbai in November 2008, and these included back-channel negotiations with the Pakistani military. While these attempts failed to produce anything concrete, the hope in New Delhi was that they would at least stave off pressure from the United States to engage Islamabad. Therefore, even though negotiations with Pakistan were hugely unpopular at home, the Indian government decided to proceed with them. India hoped that by doing so, it would be viewed as a more productive player in the West's efforts at stabilizing Afghanistan.

For many in the policy establishment in New Delhi, however, the Pakistani military and intelligence establishment is not at all favorably inclined to accept any role for India in Afghanistan.[36] India–Pakistan engagement on Afghanistan remains perfunctory at best. The Pakistani military hopes to dominate Afghanistan through its proxies, but there are groups that have even targeted the Pakistani military. The gap between Pakistan's strategic aspiration to control the internal politics of Afghanistan and its patent inability to pacify some of the groups, such as Tehrik-e-Taliban Pakistan, has grown in recent years. The Nawaz Sharif government, despite the occasional rhetoric, is yet to give a serious indication that it is willing to take a risk in nurturing positive ties with India or that it is willing to take on the "spoilers" – those elements in the Pakistani military and its non-state proxies who remain intent on derailing the Indo-Pak dialogue process. In fact, the day Sharif visited New Delhi for the swearing-in of the Narendra Modi government on May 26, 2014, Pakistani rangers fired at Indian troops on the border, and, days before, the Indian consulate in Herat had come under attack from

Lashkar-e-Toiba operatives in Afghanistan, all intended to create a crisis ahead of the taking over by the new Indian government and to unequivocally underscore that Pakistan's India policy remains firmly under the Pakistani Army's control.

Even though the Modi government is expected to continue with its limited outreach to Islamabad, it is not readily evident if Indian attempts at redefining the terms of its engagement in Pakistan at this very late stage are likely to produce an outcome conducive to protecting and enhancing Indian interests in Afghanistan. This is especially true in a context in which the extant regional environment precludes any possibility of a sustainable outcome for Afghanistan.

Conclusion

A major factor behind India's proactive Afghanistan agenda has been India's attempt to carve out for itself a greater role in regional affairs, more in consonance with its rising economic and military profile. India wants to establish its credentials as a major power in the region that is willing to take responsibility for ensuring stability around its periphery. By emerging as a major donor for Afghanistan, India is trying to project itself as a significant economic power that can provide necessary aid to the needy states in its neighborhood. Moreover, India's long-term ambition to emerge as a "great power" will be assessed by the international community in terms of its strategic capacity to deal with the instability in its own backyard. India is following an ambitious foreign policy agenda vis-à-vis Afghanistan as it tries to shed its inward-looking strategic insularity to carve out a larger regional role for itself. Its success, or lack thereof, will have serious consequences for India's stature in the region and the international system at large.

Notes

1 S.K. Ramachandran, "India Will Walk Shoulder to Shoulder with People of Afghanistan, Says Modi," *The Hindu*, April 28, 2015.

2 *Ibid.*

3 Suhasini Haider, "Pakistan Must Open Wagah for Trade: Ghani," *The Hindu*, April 30, 2015.

4 V. Gregorian, *The Emergence of Modern Afghanistan* (Stanford: Stanford University Press, 1969), pp. 91–128.

5 Partha S. Ghosh and Rajaram Panda, "Domestic Support for Mrs Gandhi's Afghanistan Policy: The Soviet Factor in Indian Politics," *Asian Survey*, Vol. 23, No. 3 (1983), pp. 261–3.

6 Details of Pakistan's ties to the Taliban can be found in Ahmed Rashid, *Taliban* (New Haven: Yale University Press, 2001).

7 Steve Coll, *Ghost Wars: The Secret Story of the CIA, Afghanistan, and Bin Laden, from the Soviet Invasion to September 10, 2001* (New York: Penguin Books, 2004), pp. 463, 513. This has been corroborated by the author's discussions with senior Indian bureaucrats in the Indian Ministry of External Affairs and Ministry of Defense.

8 See the Statement made by the Indian Prime Minister at the end of signing of the first-ever Strategic Partnership Agreement with Afghanistan on October 4, 2011. The text is available at www.thehindu.com/news/resources/article2513967.ece.

9 On the changing priorities of Indian foreign policy in recent years, see Harsh V. Pant, *Contemporary Debates in Indian Foreign and Security Policy: India Negotiates Its Rise in the International System* (New York: Palgrave Macmillan, 2008).

10 Agreement on Provisional Arrangements in Afghanistan Pending the Re-Establishment of Permanent Government Institutions, Bonn Agreement, United Nations, Bonn, Germany, December 5, 2001, available at www.unhcr.org/refworld/docid/3f48f4754.html.

11 "India-Afghanistan Blossom Amidst Turmoil," Press Trust of India, December 27, 2006.

12 A. Baruah, "Karzai Keen on Indian Expertise," *The Hindu*, January 22, 2002.

13 "US Seal on India's Key Role in Rebuilding Afghanistan," *Times of India*, October 20, 2012.

14 Bijoyeta Das, "Afghan Students Flock to India's Universities," *Aljazeera.net*, June 3, 2013.

15 V.K. Nambiar, Statement on the Situation in Afghanistan at the Security Council, April 6, 2004, available at www.un.int/india/2004/ind910.pdf.

16 "Karzai Invites India Inc. to Invest in Afghanistan," *Deccan Herald*, November 10, 2012.

17 Eltaf Najafizada, "Indian Group Wins Rights to Mine in Afghanistan's Hajigak," *Bloomberg*, December 6, 2011.

18 Sanjeev Miglani, "India Stepping Up to the Challenge of Post-2014 Afghanistan," Reuters, November 12, 2012.

19 "India Hints at Pak Link to Kabul Embassy Attack," *Indian Express*, October 10, 2009.

20 "ISI Behind Attack on Indian Embassy: Afghan Envoy to US," *Indian Express*, October 10, 2009.

21 Matthieu Aikins, "Following the Money," *The Caravan Magazine*, September 1, 2011, available at www.caravanmagazine.in/Story/1051/Following-the-Money.html.

22 Ashis Ray, "World Rejects India's Taliban Stand," *Times of India*, January 29, 2010.

23 B. Muralidhar Reddy, "Don't Leave Afghanistan, India told US," *The Hindu*, May 24, 2011.

24 "US Seeks to Balance India's Afghanistan Stake," Reuters, June 1, 2010.

25 Based on the author's private interview with a senior Indian foreign policy official. For details on the changing trajectory of Indian policy in Afghanistan, see Harsh V. Pant, "India's Changing Role in Afghanistan," *Middle East Quarterly*, Vol. 18, No. 2 (Spring 2011), pp. 31–9.

26 "Strategic Ties with Kabul ... India Not Like US, Says PM," *Indian Express*, May 13, 2011.

27 Teresita and Howard Schaffer, "India and the US Moving Closer on Afghanistan?" *The Hindu*, June 1, 2011.

28 "India Committed to Building the Capabilities of Afghan Security Forces," *The Hindu*, June 2, 2011.

29 Tom Wright and Margherita Stancita, "Karzi Sets Closer Ties With India on Visit," *Wall Street Journal*, October 5, 2011.

30 Rajat Pandit, "US Exit: India Steps Up Afghan Army Training," *Times of India*, July 13, 2013.

31 Vladimir Radyuhin, "India, Russia to Step Up Cooperation in Afghanistan," *The Hindu*, August 3, 2010.

32 "Russia Warns of 'New Wave' of Terror, Seeks India's Help," *Times of India*, October 14, 2012.

33 Shubhajit Roy, "India, Russia to Revive Arms Maintenance Factory in Afghanistan," *Indian Express*, December 10, 2013.

34 Harsh V. Pant, "Delhi's Tehran Conundrum," *Wall Street Journal*, September 20, 2010.

35 Amitav Ranjan, "As China Offers Funds to Iran, India Set to Fast-Track Chabahar Pact," *Indian Express*, July 1, 2013.

36 Personal interview with a senior member of the National Security Council, Government of India.

Snapshot 3: India and Bhutan

Indian Prime Minister Narendra Modi embarked on a two-day visit to Bhutan in June 2014 soon after assuming office, his first trip abroad, underscoring the importance India attaches to its ties with Bhutan whose Prime Minister Tshering Tobgay was among the leaders from the neighboring countries to attend the new government's swearing-in in May 2014.

Bhutan, the size of Switzerland and with a population of 750,000, has only recently emerged from centuries of isolation. Its first road was built in 1962 and television and the Internet arrived in 1999. It is the first country to monitor gross national happiness, an alternative to GDP, to balance a tentative embrace of modernity with an effort to preserve traditions. But Bhutan, which made the transition from absolute monarchy to parliamentary democracy in 2008, is struggling with high unemployment and a growing national debt.

It is a tribute to the ham-fisted manner in which Indian foreign policy is managed that even India's relations with Bhutan had seemed in trouble in the last few years. The withdrawal of subsidies to Bhutan on petroleum products in the midst of its 2013 elections was merely a manifestation of how poorly conceived and executed India policies had become, completely disconnected from any strategic thinking. After the elections there was widespread hype in the Indian media that with the coming to power in Thimpu of the former opposition People's Democratic Party, emphasizing strong ties with India, all would be well once again. Trouble in Delhi–Bhutan ties is only beginning to emerge and this process will be accelerated by the onset of real democracy and competitive politics in the Himalayan Kingdom.

The King of Bhutan, Jigme Khesar Namgyal Wangchuk, was the chief guest at the 2013 Republic Day celebrations in New Delhi eight years after his father graced the occasion. As it turned out, however, he was not the first choice of the Indian government. New Delhi wanted the Sultan of Oman to be the chief guest but the great Indian bureaucracy even mishandled this routine invitation. Even though this was a major debacle, New Delhi quickly tried to salvage this situation by turning to its old friend in Bhutan for damage control who agreed to act as a replacement. Though the Bhutanese king was received with due pomp and ceremony in New

Delhi, the cavalier attitude of India toward its smaller neighbors did not go unnoticed.

Bhutan remains the only resolutely pro-India country in South Asia today. At a time when India is rapidly ceding strategic space to China in its vicinity, it should be cultivating its immediate neighbors with greater sensitivity. As it is Bhutan has signaled that it does not want to remain the only country in India's neighborhood without official ties with Beijing. The previous Bhutanese Prime Minister Jigme Thinley made overtures to Beijing, meeting his Chinese counterpart on the sidelines of the UN Conference on Sustainable Development at Rio de Janeiro in 2013 in an attempt to lobby for Bhutan's candidacy for the non-permanent seat in the UN Security Council. He encouraged more countries to open missions in Bhutan and reportedly sought to establish diplomatic relations with China, the United States, Russia, France, and the United Kingdom. Such a foreign policy shift was perceived as being unfavorable to Indian sensitivities. Thinley also reportedly raised the issue of establishing diplomatic ties between the two nations though this was later denied by Thimpu. China's economic engagement with Bhutan is also likely to grow in the future especially as China's infrastructure development leads to greater connectivities between the two states.

What might be most troubling for India is a boundary settlement between China and Bhutan. Besides India, Bhutan is the only country with a land border dispute with China today as the 470-kilometer border between the two nations remains contentious. China's slow encroachment into Bhutanese territory is also making Bhutan eager for an early boundary settlement. And if such a settlement allows China access to disputed areas in the Chumbi Valley, a tri-junction abutting Bhutan, Tibet, and Sikkim, Indian security interests will suffer significantly as the Siliguri corridor connecting India to its northeast will come under direct Chinese threat.

In response India has indeed stepped up its own economic profile in Bhutan. India has remained Bhutan's largest development partner with a large chunk of India's development assistance in the forms of loans, grants, and lines of credit committed to the Himalayan state. With the Treaty of Friendship and Cooperation between the two countries, first signed in 1949, already revised in 2007 to reflect the need for a more symbiotic relationship, India has made efforts to dispel concerns regarding its hegemonic tendencies in its neighborhood. India views Bhutan as a major source of hydropower in the coming years and is seeking greater access for its energy companies. India is hoping to import hydropower from Bhutan and is ramping up its economic aid to Thimpu. Bhutan is set to be a major source of hydropower for India in a few years as India hopes to reap the dividends of its US$1.2 billion investment in the construction of three hydropower projects in Bhutan, with a combined installed capacity of 1,400 megawatts. But the issue is larger than economic assistance and military security. Much like other smaller states in India's neighborhood, Bhutan would also like greater autonomy in its foreign and security policies. And with democracy taking root in the country, India will soon be seen as a nosy external party interfering in

Bhutan's internal affairs. China will then emerge as an effective balancer against India's overweening presence.

Bhutan, the hermit kingdom of South Asia, is opening up to the world. Not only China but other powers too are seeking to engage Thimpu. A fully integrated Bhutan into the world community can only be a good thing for India. The Modi government's focus on Bhutan is significant but New Delhi will have to ensure that Bhutan does not get relegated to the margins once other foreign policy priorities crowd the Indian agenda.

PART III

India's extra-regional outreach

10

India in East and Southeast Asia: "acting" East with an eye on China

While the world has been focusing on China's growing assertiveness in the South China Sea, Beijing and New Delhi are also engaged in a quiet struggle in the contested waters. By putting up for international bidding the same oil block that India had obtained from Vietnam for exploration, China has thrown down a gauntlet.[1] By deciding to stay put in the assigned block, India has indicated that it is ready to take up the Chinese challenge. At stake is Chinese opposition to India's claim to be a regional power.

The conflict between India and China over the South China Sea has been building for quite some time now. India signed an agreement with Vietnam in October 2011 to expand and promote oil exploration in the South China Sea and then reconfirmed its decision to carry on despite the Chinese challenge to the legality of Indian presence.[2]

By accepting the Vietnamese invitation to explore oil and gas in Blocks 127 and 128, India's state-owned oil company ONGC Videsh Ltd (OVL) not only expressed New Delhi's desire to deepen its friendship with Vietnam, but ignored China's warning to stay away. After asking countries "outside the region" to stay away from the South China Sea, China issued a démarche to India in November 2011, underlining that Beijing's permission should be sought for exploration in Blocks 127 and 128 and, without it, OVL's activities would be considered illegal. Vietnam, meanwhile, had underlined the 1982 UN Convention on the Law of the Sea to claim its sovereign rights over the two blocks being explored. India decided to go by Vietnam's claims and ignore China's objections.[3]

China has been objecting to the Indian exploration projects in the region, claiming that the territory comes under its sovereignty. Whereas India continues to maintain that its exploration projects in the region are purely commercial, China has viewed such activities as an issue of sovereign rights. India's moves unsettled China, which views India's growing engagement in East and Southeast Asia with suspicion. India's decision to explore hydrocarbons with Vietnam followed a July 2011 incident during which an unidentified Chinese warship demanded that INS *Airavat*, an amphibious assault vessel, identify itself and explain its presence in the South China Sea after leaving Vietnamese waters.[4] Completing a scheduled port call in Vietnam, the Indian warship was in international waters.

In June 2012, the state-owned China National Offshore Oil Company (CNOOC), opened nine blocks for exploration in waters also claimed by Vietnam.[5] Oil Block 128, which Vietnam argues is inside its 200-nautical mile Exclusive Economic Zone (EEZ) granted under the UN Law of the Sea, is part of the nine blocks offered for global bidding by CNOOC.

By putting up for global bidding a Vietnamese petroleum block under exploration by an Indian oil company, China has forced India into a corner. That India would not be deterred by Chinese maneuvers came during the ASEAN Regional Forum in Phnom Penh in 2012. India made a strong case for supporting not only freedom of navigation but also access to resources in accordance with principles of international law.[6] New Delhi, which so often likes to sit on the margins and avoid taking sides, seems to be realizing that it can no longer afford the luxury of inaction if it wants to preserve credibility as a significant actor in both East Asia and Southeast Asia. This chapter examines India's evolving policy toward East and Southeast Asia, a region where the role of China as a rising power is being most acutely felt.

India fashions a "Look East" policy

Despite its historical and cultural links with East and Southeast Asia, India in its post-independence foreign policy largely tended to ignore the region. The structural constraints of the Cold War proved too formidable despite India's geographic proximity to the East Asian region. It was the end of the Cold War that really brought East Asia back to the forefront of India's foreign policy horizons. The disintegration of the Soviet Union radically transformed the structure of the then prevailing international system and brought to the fore new challenges and opportunities for countries like India. India was forced to reorient its approach toward international affairs in general and toward East Asia in particular. The government of P.V. Narasimha Rao launched its "Look East" policy in the early 1990s explicitly to initiate New Delhi's re-engagement with East Asia.

Indian engagement of East Asia in the post-Cold War era has assumed significant proportions and remains a top foreign policy priority for the Indian leadership. India is now a full dialogue partner of the Association of South East Asian Nations (ASEAN) since 1995, a member of the ASEAN Regional Forum, the regional security forum, since 1996, and is a founder member of the East Asian Summit launched in December 2005. India is also a summit partner of ASEAN on par with China, Japan, and South Korea since 2002. Over the years, India has also come to have extensive economic and trade linkages with various countries in the region even as there has also been a gradual strengthening of security ties. Indian Prime Minister,

Narendra Modi, has made it clear that his government's foreign policy priority will continue to be East and Southeast Asia, which are poised for sustained growth in the twenty-first century.

India's efforts to make itself relevant to the region come at a time of great turmoil in the Asian strategic landscape. Events in recent years have underlined China's aggressive stance against rivals and US allies in Asia, and there may be more tension to come. With its political and economic rise, Beijing has started trying to dictate the boundaries of acceptable behavior to its neighbors. As a result, regional states have already started reassessing their strategies, and a loose anti-China balancing coalition is emerging. India's role becomes critical in such an evolving balance of power. As Singapore's elder-statesman Lee Kuan Yew has argued, he would like India to be "part of the Southeast Asia balance of forces" and "a counterweight [to China] in the Indian Ocean."[7] India's "Look East" policy is part of this larger dynamic. As New Delhi has reached out to its partners in South and Southeast Asia, the regional states have also shown an unprecedented reciprocal interest in Indian foreign policy priorities.

India and Japan: a growing partnership

Both New Delhi and Tokyo have made an effort in recent years to put Indo-Japanese ties into high gear. India's booming economy makes it an attractive trading and business partner for Japan as the latter tries to overcome its long years of economic stagnation. Japan is also reassessing its role as a security provider in the region and beyond, and of all its neighbors, India seems most willing to acknowledge Japan's centrality in shaping the evolving Asia-Pacific security architecture. Moreover, a new generation of political leaders in India and Japan view each other with fresh eyes, allowing for a break from past policies that is changing the trajectory of bilateral relations.

India's ties with Japan have come a long way since May 1998, when Japan imposed sanctions and suspended its overseas development assistance over India's nuclear tests. Since then, the changing strategic environment in the Asia-Pacific region has brought the two countries closer together, culminating in a new roadmap in 2010 to transform a low-key relationship into a major strategic partnership.[8] While China's rise figures into the evolution of Indo-Japanese ties, so, too, does the US attempt to build India into a major balancer in the region. In September 2014, India's newly elected Prime Minister – Narendra Modi – visited Japan, his first foreign visit outside the South Asian region since assuming office in May 2014. Modi described his decision to visit Japan as a "reflection of Japan's importance in India's foreign policy and economic development and her place at the heart of India's Look East Policy."[9] India–Japan ties are expected to get a major boost from the personal camaraderie of Modi and his Japanese counterpart, Prime Minister Shinzo Abe. Both leaders are emblematic of a new, ambitious, and nationalistic Asian landscape. They have decisive mandates to reshape the economic and strategic future of their respective nations and they are already using it with great flourish.

Both Japan and India rely on the security of the sea lanes of communication (SLOC) for their energy security and economic growth. They have a shared interest in guaranteeing the free transit of energy and trade between the Suez Canal and the Western Pacific. With this in mind they are developing maritime capabilities to cooperate with each other and other regional powers. The navies of the two are now exercising regularly, and the interactions between the coastguards are increasing with a view to combat to combat piracy and terrorism, and to cooperate on disaster relief operations. Japan feels that only the Indian Navy in the region can be trusted to secure the sea lanes in the Indian Ocean, vital for Japan's energy security. It is also important for India to join hands with the much larger Japanese Navy, Asia's most powerful, to make sure that no adversarial power controls the regional waterways.

The talks on a civilian nuclear pact, however, seem to be going nowhere at the moment, with the two sides merely agreeing to speed up talks.[10] Japan continues to insist that India sign the Nuclear Non-Proliferation Treaty and the Comprehensive Test Ban Treaty before finalizing such a bilateral agreement, but India has no intention of doing so given its long-standing concerns over what it sees as the discriminatory nature of these treaties. Meanwhile, the new nuclear-liability law in India – which established higher financial liability limits for accidents than the industry standard and allows nuclear operators to sue suppliers – could also make greater civilian nuclear cooperation between the two countries more difficult to accomplish. Nevertheless, the push for an agreement will remain strong, as an India–Japan civil-nuclear pact would reinforce India's return to the global nuclear market, while signaling both countries' desire to build a partnership that reinforces regional stability.

Both India and Japan are well aware of China's not-so-subtle attempts at preventing their rise. It is most clearly reflected in China's opposition to the expansion of the UN Security Council to include India and Japan as permanent members. China's status as a permanent member of the Security Council and as a NWS is something that it would be loath to share with any other state in Asia. India's "Look East" policy of active engagement with the ASEAN and East Asia remains largely predicated upon Japanese support. India's participation in the East Asia Summit was facilitated by Japan and the East Asia Community proposed by Japan to counter China's proposal of an East Asia Free Trade Area also includes India. While China has resisted the inclusion of India, Australia, and New Zealand in the ASEAN, Japan has strongly backed the entry of all three nations.

The massive structural changes taking place in the geopolitical balance of power in Asia-Pacific are driving India and Japan into a relationship that is much closer than many could have anticipated even a few years back.

India and South Korea: newfound convergence

After having long ignored each other, India and South Korea are now beginning to recognize the importance of tighter ties. The resulting courtship was highlighted by South Korean President Lee Myung-Bak's state visit to New Delhi in January 2010, when he was the chief guest at the Republic Day celebrations. During his stay, New Delhi and Seoul decided to elevate their bilateral relationship to a "strategic partnership."[11] The South Korean President Park Geun-hye paid a state visit to India in January 2014, which was reciprocated by the Indian Prime Minister in May 2015.

Despite pursuing a "Look East" policy since the early 1990s, New Delhi failed to generate momentum in ties with South Korea. South Korean businesses did not begin to view India as an important destination for investments until after the 1997 financial crisis. South Korea still remained focused on China as an economic partner and has only recently made India a major economic and political priority. With a renewed push from both sides, things have improved dramatically on the economic front over the past few years.

The visit of former Indian President A.P.J. Abdul Kalam to South Korea in 2006 led to the signing of a Comprehensive Economic Partnership Agreement that came into force in January 2010. Though New Delhi and Seoul have set a target of US$40 billion in 2015, bilateral trade has been falling in recent years. South Korean firms are increasing their brand presence in India, and the Indian Chamber of Commerce has also been established in Korea. Major Korean conglomerates including Samsung, Hyundai Motors, and LG have made significant investments in India, estimated at over US$3 billion, while Indian investments in South Korea too have exceeded the US$2 billion mark. FDI into India from South Korea is worth around US$1.4 billion, still behind the United Kingdom, Japan, the United States, and Germany.[12]

Linkages with the Indian economy can help Korea grow at far higher rates than it is currently experiencing. Among other opportunities, Korean firms are looking to participate in India's plans to develop its infrastructure sector. In the IT sector, too, South Korea's competitive advantage in hardware complements India's software profile. India's dynamic, fast-growing economy makes for a natural economic partner for South Korea, often referred to as the most innovative country in the world, with the focus of cooperation likely to be in high-priority areas like IT, civilian space, knowledge-based industries, high technology, energy, automobiles, and defense.

While economic ties between India and South Korea have been diversifying across various sectors, defense cooperation between the two states has also gathered momentum, reflecting the rapid changes in the

Asia-Pacific region's balance of power caused by China's rise. In 2005, India and South Korea inked a memorandum of understanding on Cooperation in Defense, Industry and Logistics, which was followed in 2006 by another on cooperation between the two countries' coastguards. South Korea is one of the world's leaders in naval ship-building technology, and India would like to tap into South Korean naval capabilities to augment its own. As a result, naval cooperation is rapidly emerging as a central feature of bilateral defense cooperation, with the two navies cooperating in anti-piracy operations in the Indian Ocean region and the Gulf of Aden. Both states also share a strong interest in protecting the SLOC in the Indian Ocean region.

Other sectors of convergence include nuclear energy and space. As a member of the NSG, South Korea supported the waiver granted to India at the group's September 2008 meeting.[13] In 2011, India signed a civil nuclear cooperation deal with South Korea, allowing a framework for Korean companies to participate in atomic power plant projects in the country. India launched South Korea's KITSAT-3 satellite in 1999 and has now invited Seoul to join the Indian expedition to the moon – Chnadrayaan-2.

The China factor in India–South Korea ties cannot be underestimated. India's tensions with China have increased in the past few years, with Beijing aggressively asserting its territorial claims on their shared frontier. At the same time, South Korea, too, is re-evaluating its ties with China. In recent years, China could count on South Korea as a friend in the region – a cultural admirer, with residual memories of the close political and cultural ties that existed in Ming times. For its part, Seoul counted on Beijing to help stabilize the situation on the Korean Peninsula. South Korea has become China's largest trading partner in the region and has been eagerly hospitable to Chinese visits.

Yet Seoul found itself disillusioned with Beijing's shielding of North Korea from the global outrage over the *Cheonan* incident.[14] An international investigation convened by South Korea concluded that the sinking of the warship, which killed forty-six South Korean sailors in March 2010, was likely the result of a torpedo fired by a North Korean submarine. Instead of berating Pyongyang, China watered down a UN Security Council presidential statement that, while condemning the incident, failed to hold North Korea responsible. As a result, no punishment was meted out to North Korea for its brinkmanship.

As they carefully assess the evolving strategic environment in the Asia-Pacific region, New Delhi and Seoul need to advance their political ties so that a mutually beneficial and long-term partnership can evolve between the two sides. The resulting relationship could be as important for greater regional stability as it is for Indian and South Korean national interests.

India's ties with Indonesia, Vietnam, Malaysia, and Burma: deepening engagement

The basis of the India–Indonesia partnership dates back to the founding fathers of these two nations – Jawaharlal Nehru and Sukarno – who offered a distinct foreign policy worldview that drew on their shared colonial experiences. They visualized an Asian region that could challenge the Cold War threat perceptions of the two superpowers. Nehru and Sukarno were among the founder members of the NAM.

In the contemporary context, the rise of China has drawn the two states closer. The last few years have witnessed a new phase in this relationship where the two states have pushed their ties to a historic high with strong emphasis on economic and security issues. India, with its "Look East" policy, decided to substantially enhance its presence in the region while Indonesia took the lead in bringing India closer to the ASEAN. The changing strategic landscape of Asia during the post-Cold War era has broadened the canvas of India's engagement with Indonesia. Both want to seize the opportunities being offered by the landmark economic growth being witnessed by the Asian region.

Economic engagement between the two is growing rapidly and will gain further momentum with the signing of the India–ASEAN FTA in 2014. Indonesia is an important source of energy and raw materials for India. Bilateral trade is expected to breach the US$20 billion benchmark by 2015.[15] Major Indian companies, including the Birla group, the Tatas, Essar, Jindal Steel, and Bajaj Motors, are now operating in Indonesia. Indian investment is spread across a range of ares including banking, mining, oil and gas, iron and steel, aluminium, IT, textiles, and telecommunications. It was in 2005 that the two signed the strategic partnership agreement and in 2006 a defense cooperation agreement was announced. Negotiations on a Comprehensive Economic Cooperation agreement have already begun.

Being the most formidable military power in Southeast Asia, Indonesia can effectively work with India in ensuring safety of the SLOC and tackle non-traditional security challenges in the Indian Ocean. Both have a vested interest in ensuring that China's hegemony in the region does not go uncontested. Their location makes them crucial in the emerging maritime calculus in the region as they together control the entry point from the Indian Ocean to the Bay of Bengal in the north and Malacca Straits to the east. Viewing Indian maritime presence as largely benign, Indonesia has openly invited India to help the littoral states in the region in maintaining security in the Malacca Strait. Jakarta now also views India as a major source of military hardware. Joint naval exercises and patrols as well as regular port calls by their respective navies have been a regular feature of India–Indonesian naval cooperation for some time now.

Cultural links between the two nations have always been significant and they are flourishing. After all, Indonesia's name is derived from the Latin word "Indus," meaning India. As the most populous Islamic nation committed to pluralism and democracy, India has huge stakes in the political and economic success of Indonesia. Indonesia's role has been and will remain critical in supporting India's engagement with its Southeast Asian neighbors. And as the United States tries to project Indonesia as a bastion of moderate Islam and political stability, India will only reinvigorate its ties with Jakarta.

Bilateral ties between India and Vietnam have strengthened in recent years with a focus on regional security issues and trade. Traditionally India has had a favorable presence in Vietnam with its support for Vietnamese independence from France and eventual unification of the country as well as its opposition to the US involvement in the Vietnam War. With the rise of China in recent years, their ties have become strategic in orientation. The signing of the India–ASEAN FTA and India's recognition of Vietnam's market economy status has boosted economic ties. Vietnam has backed a more prominent role for India in the ASEAN as well as India's bid for the permanent membership in the UN Security Council. The two states promulgated a Joint Declaration on Comprehensive Cooperation in 2003 in which they envisaged creating an "Arc of Advantage and Prosperity" in Southeast Asia and have initiated a strategic dialogue since 2009.

Given that Vietnam and India use the same Russian and erstwhile Soviet platforms, there is a significant convergence between the two in the defense sector. Vietnam has sought Indian help in the modernization of its military hardware. India's exploration interests near the Vietnamese coasts have been threatened by China's diplomatic offensive. New Delhi and Hanoi have significant stakes in ensuring sea-lane security and preventing sea piracy while they also share concerns about Chinese access to the Indian Ocean and South China Sea. Indian strategic interests demand that Vietnam emerge as a major regional player and India is well placed to help Hanoi achieve that objective. It has been argued in Indian strategic circles that just as China has used states in India's periphery to contain India, New Delhi should build states like Vietnam as strategic pressure points against China to counter it. A common approach on the emerging balance of power is emerging with India and Vietnam both keen on reorienting their ties with the United States as their concerns about China rise.

Naval cooperation between Vietnam and India remains the focus with Vietnam giving India the right to use its port in the south, Nha Trang, situated close to the strategically significant Cam Ranh Bay. During Sang's visit to India, the two sides reiterated the need to enhance cooperation in ensuring safety and security of the region's sea lanes and launched a security dialogue. To give strong economic foundation to the bilateral ties, bilateral trade has been given a boost and it is expected to touch the US$15 billion mark by 2020.[16]

Relations between Malaysia and India have been traditionally strong, with their historical ambivalence about the United States a strong factor. Malaysia under Mahathir Mohamad took a strong line against Washington and was able to steer the Malaysian economy successfully through the financial crisis of 1997. Malaysia has supported Indian presence in the ASEAN and in 2001 also accepted the Indian position on Kashmir that the issue should be resolved only through bilateral negotiations. An MoU on defense cooperation was signed by the two in 1992 and a close defense relationship has emerged over the years with joint military exercises, training of defense personnel, and trade in military equipment. The two have decided to work together to secure the Malacca Straits and Malaysia has requested Indian help in protecting the channel from emerging non-traditional security threats in the region. China remains a security concern for Malaysia given its claims over the Spratly Islands.

Ethnic Indians comprise 8 percent of the Malaysian population. Most of them were forcibly moved to Malaysia to work as plantation laborers under the British policy of indentured labor. Most recently, the Malaysians of Indian origin have asked the Indian government to terminate all business projects with Malaysia because of grave human rights violations being committed against the Hindu community in Malaysia. New Delhi has, however, taken this issue up informally through back-channels and has tried to underplay this issue so as not to hurt India–Malaysia ties.

The two nations are focused on galvanizing bilateral economic cooperation and liberalizing their respective investment regimes to facilitate greater mutual FDI as well as on strengthening their security partnership, by exploring collaborative defense projects and enhancing cooperation in counter-terrorism through information-sharing and the establishment of a joint working group.

Burma too has made its own overtures to India. President Thein Sein has pursued a range of reforms in the domestic realm that include opening substantive talks with opposition leader Aung San Suu Kyi, declaration of amnesty for political prisoners, and cancellation of the Chinese-funded Myitsone Dam project. These efforts could be viewed as an attempt to seek a rapprochement with the democratic world, and that may be why for his first visit abroad as president of a nominal civilian government, Thein Sein chose India in 2011.[17]

During his visit, Thein Sein sought greater Indian investment in Burma's energy sector even as the two nations agreed to expand cooperation in oil and gas exploration, open border trade, and speed up construction of natural gas pipelines. India, which is investing in the Kaladan multimodal transport system, connecting India's eastern seaboard to its northeastern states through Myanmar, further offered US$500 million in credits for infra-structure projects.

While India is under pressure from the West to demonstrate democratic credentials, its strategic interests have been winning out in relations with Burma in recent years. Due to its strategic priorities, New Delhi had only gently nudged the Burmese junta on the issue of democracy, gradually gaining a sense of trust at the highest echelons of Burma's ruling elite. India had been resisting losing this key relationship. As such, India remained opposed to Western sanctions on the country. Burma's first real democratic election in November 2015 is likely give India a larger strategic space to maneuver and, compared to Beijing, New Delhi will be a more attractive partner for Naypyidaw as it tries to find a modus vivendi with the West.

At the broader regional level, India has continued to make a strong case for its growing relevance in the East Asian regional security and economic architecture. India's FTA with ASEAN, signed in 2009, commits New Delhi to cut import tariffs on 80 percent of the commodities it trades with ASEAN, with the goal of reversing India's growing marginalization in the world's most economically dynamic region. Having signed a FTA for goods in 2010, India and ASEAN finalized the FTA in services and investment in 2014. India's trade with ASEAN is expected to double by 2022 from the US$80 billion level at present.[18]

Conclusion

India is emerging as a serious player in the Asian strategic landscape as smaller states in East Asia reach out to it for trade, diplomacy, and, potentially, as a key regional balancer. The "Look East" policy initiated by one of the most visionary of Indian prime ministers, P.V. Narasimha Rao, is now the cornerstone of India's engagement with the world's most economically dynamic region. States in South and Southeast Asia too remain keen on a more proactive Indian role in the region.

China is too big and too powerful to be ignored by the regional states. But the states in China's vicinity are now seeking to expand their strategic space by reaching out to other regional and global powers. Smaller states in the region are now looking to India to act as a balancer in view of China's growing influence and the United States' anticipated retrenchment from the region in the near future, while larger states see India as an attractive engine for regional growth. To live up to its full potential and meet the region's expectations, India must do a more convincing job of emerging as a credible strategic partner of the region. Neither India nor the regional states in East Asia have incentive to define their relationship in opposition to China. But they are certainly interested in leveraging their ties with other states to gain benefits from China and bring a semblance of equality in their relationships. Great power politics in the region have only just begun.

The rapid rise of China in Asia and beyond is the main pivot even as New Delhi is seeking to expand economic integration and interdependence with the region. India is also developing strong security linkages with the region and trying to actively promote and participate in regional and multilateral initiatives. New Delhi's ambitious policy in East and Southeast Asia is aimed at significantly increasing its regional profile. Smaller states in the region are now looking to India to act as a balancer in view of China's growing influence and America's anticipated retrenchment from the region in the near future, while larger states see it as an attractive engine for regional growth. It remains to be seen if India can indeed live up to its full potential, as well as to the region's expectations.

Notes

1 Pranab Dhal Samanta, "China Puts Indian Oil Block up for Auction," *Indian Express*, July 12, 2012.

2 "India, Vietnam Sign Pact for Oil Exploration in South China Sea," *The Hindu*, October 13, 2011.

3 Rakesh Sharma, "ONGC to Continue Exploration in South China Sea," *Wall Street Journal*, July 19, 2012.

4 Ben Bland and Girija Shivakumar, "China Confronts Indian Navy Vessel," *Financial Times*, August 31, 2011.

5 Samanta, "China Puts Indian Oil Block up for Auction."

6 Prak Chun Thal and Stuart Grudgings, "SE Asia Meeting in Disarray Over Sea Dispute with China," Reuters, July 13, 2012.

7 P.S. Suryanarayana, "China and India Cannot Go to War: Lee Kuan Yew," *The Hindu*, January 24, 2011.

8 P. Vaidyanathan Iyer, "India, Japan Cepa Talks," *Indian Express*, October 26, 2010.

9 Ministry of Foreign Affairs (MOFA), Government of Japan (GOJ), "Tokyo Declaration for Japan-India Special Strategic and Global Partnership," September 1, 2014, p. 1, www.mofa.go.jp/mofaj/files/000050549.pdf.

10 Harsh V. Pant, "The Japan Roadblock to Nuclear Cooperation," *Wall Street Journal*, October 28, 2010.

11 Amitabh Sinha, "Choosing R-Day Chief Guest, Behind the Warm Welcome, a Cold Strategy," *Indian Express*, January 25, 2010.

12 Gabriele Parussini, "Narendra Modi on What India Can Learn From South Korea," *Wall Street Journal*, May 19, 2015.

13 On India's finalization of civilian nuclear energy cooperation pact with the United States, see Harsh V. Pant, *The US-India Nuclear Pact: Policy, Process and Great Power Politics* (Oxford: Oxford University Press, 2011).

14 Choe Sang-Hun, "China Balks at Criticism of South Korea," *New York Times*, May 30, 2010.

15 Veeramalla Anjaiah, "RI, India in 'New Frontier' of Bilateral Ties," *The Jakarta Post*, October 25, 2012.
16 "India, Vietnam Trade to Touch $15 bn by 2020," *Economic Times*, January 21, 2015.
17 Sandeep Dikshit, "India, Myanmar Agree to Resolve Border Issues," *The Hindu*, October 14, 2011.
18 "India-Asean Trade to Touch $100 bn by 2015," *The Hindu*, December 11, 2014.

11

India in Africa and Central Asia: part of the new "Great Game"

India's links with Africa are centuries old, bolstered by trade across the Indian Ocean and a million-strong diaspora across Africa. Shared colonial legacy and post-independence development experience has framed India's relationship with Africa. India's role as a champion of anti-colonialism and anti-racism after its independence in 1947 drew it closer to the African nations. India emerged as one of the most vocal critics of Apartheid in South Africa. New Delhi under its first prime minister, Jawaharlal Nehru, became a votary of strong Asian–African solidarity. Nehru played a key role in convening the first Asian–African Conference in the Indonesian city of Bandung which ultimately gave rise to the NAM. Despite being on the peripheries of global politics during the Cold War, India emerged as one of the strongest proponents of the independence of African states from colonial subjugation and a supporter of South–South cooperation in order to challenge the inequities of global political and economic order. But India's substantive presence in Africa remained marginal as it remained focused on its own periphery through much of the Cold War period and its capabilities remained limited. Since the end of the Cold War and propelled by China's growing profile in Africa, India is reinvigorating its ties with the African continent.

A post-Cold War reimagining

Though India was indeed marginal to the developments in Africa during the Cold War years, its "political commitment to the NAM and its at least rhetorical emphasis on South-South cooperation, especially coupled with its consistent diplomatic support for African nationalist movements, left it well positioned to take up its engagements across the continent and forge new ties."[1] The end of the Cold War presented new opportunities to India to interact with Africa differently. There were new challenges for India that had to be managed. India's rapid economic growth needed new markets and access to resources. As a result, economic engagement with Africa has become central to India's new approach. This is related to India's search for energy security in which Africa is playing an increasingly important role. India is seeking diversification of its oil supplies away from the Middle East and Africa will be playing an important role in India's energy matrix. India's search for oil has taken it to various African states including Nigeria, Sudan, Cote d'Ivoire, Burkina Faso, Ghana, Guinea-Bissau, and Senegal. Africa accounts for about 20 percent of India's oil imports which are likely to grow in the future.

India is now giving sustained attention to Africa, opening diplomatic missions on the continent as well as regular high-level political interactions. India is promising loans on easy terms to those nations willing to trade with India and is contributing toward education, railways, and peacekeeping. India has substantially increased its aid and assistance to Africa. India's partnership with Africa is wide ranging and is now focused on human resources and institutional capacity building. It is building economic and commercial ties with Africa even as it is contributing to the development of African countries through cooperation and technical assistance. It is the third largest contributor of UN peacekeepers to the continent. The Indian Navy is also engaged in dealing with pirates off the coast of Somalia. It has been patrolling the waters of the Indian Ocean and helping countries in Eastern and Southern Africa in tackling piracy and surveillance of the EEZ. India has sought cooperation of African states in the Indian Ocean littoral to establish mechanisms for cooperation in order to deal with threats to regional security including terrorism and piracy.

India's trade with Africa passed the US$40 billion mark in 2010 and continues to grow. While India primarily imports oil, gold, and other metals from Africa, its exports are diversified and include manufactured goods, machinery, transportation equipment, food, and pharmaceutical products. The bilateral India–African Union (AU) trade balance favors the AU members, especially in light of the recent expansion of Indian's oil imports from Nigeria and Angola. This is partly a result of India's duty-free tariff preferential scheme for Least Developed Countries launched in 2008, which has benefitted thirty-three African states. India wants a "developmental partnership" with Africa to be the cornerstone of its economic ties with the region. This also allows India to differentiate itself from the principles on which countries belonging to the Organisation for Economic Cooperation and Development (OECD), the traditional donors of foreign aid, have based their relations with the recipient nations.[2]

Indian private sector remains bullish about investing in Africa. This includes the Tata group and Bharti-Airtel. The Tata group has an extensive presence in the continent over a range of sectors including energy, infrastructure development, hospitality, automobiles, financial services, and communication. Indian pharmaceutical companies provide a range of affordable generic drugs to many African countries, thereby establishing their presence in the continent.

The Indian private sector has a better understanding of the African market compared to China's state-owned enterprises. Indian companies have invested in Africa's infrastructure from rail and road development to power transmission projects. Indian business organizations such as the Confederation of Indian Industry and the Export–Import Bank (EXIM), with full support from the Indian government, have been regularly holding meetings with business delegates from Africa to shore up India–Africa business engagements. India is wooing African countries by viewing them as a long-term investment destination. According to one assessment regarding India's economic engagement with African states, "India has sought to gain a foothold in these countries by writing off debts owed under the Heavily Indebted Poor Countries (HIPC) initiative and restructuring commercial debts. At the same time, the EXIM Bank has extended lines of credit to governments, commercial banks, financial institutions and regional development banks."[3]

India is investing in capacity building, providing more than US$1 billion in technical assistance and training to personnel under Indian Technical and Economic Cooperation program. As a full member of African Capacity Building Foundation (ACBF), India has pledged US$1 million toward the ACBF's sustainable development, poverty alleviation, and capacity building initiative. The Indian pharmaceutical sector is also collaborating with African stakeholders to combat the HIV/AIDS pandemic and other infectious diseases like malaria. India has invested US$100 million in the Pan-African E-Network to bridge the digital divide in Africa, leveraging its strengths in information technology. Indian military academies offer training to military officers from a number of African states. India's wooing of Africa includes aid, technology, and education, such as a center in Uganda to train businesses about global markets, a diamond processing facility in Botswana, and assistance to cotton farmers in four of the continent's poorest countries. India is also involved in Africa's mineral sector including Zambian copper and iron ore mines.

Though India continues to value its close ties with some Eastern African nations, it is also investing diplomatically to reach out to African states in the southern and western region. India has been holding India–Africa summits to reach out to all African nations. The first India–African summit was held in New Delhi in 2008 followed by the second summit in Addis Ababa in 2011. It was, however, the Third Summit in 2015 which saw the participation of more than 1000 delegates from all 54 African countries, with more than 40 countries represented at the level of President, Vice President, Prime Minister and King. The cooperation framework agreed at these summits and the Indian initiatives to scale up investment and aid to Africa have underscored India's aim to foster a robust partnership between New Delhi and the African continent. India would also like the Indian Ocean Rim-Association for Regional Cooperation to play a more prominent role in regional affairs as a significant membership of the organization is drawn from the African continent. India has also used IBSA to increase its profile in Africa by calling for the IBSA Trust Fund to be used for helping the developing countries in Africa. Africa, like India, also wants a more substantive presence at the UN Security Council and this has allowed them to work closely with each other.

The presence in Africa of a large Indian diaspora has given India a significant stake in the continent. They are now considered a significant base for the expansion of trade and commerce. India has its own strengths in its dealings with Africa. Its democratic traditions make it a much more comfortable partner for the West compared to China in cooperating on Africa-related issues. India is viewed as a more productive partner by many in Africa because Indian companies are much better integrated into the African society and encourage technology transfers to its African partners.

The China factor

Despite India's strengths, China has enjoyed a much higher profile in Africa in recent years. It almost seems as if Africa is the new El Dorado given the vigor with which China seems to be pursuing the region. Top Chinese officials have been regularly visiting the continent for the last several years underscoring the solid commitment of the communist leadership to make China the principal external partner of the continent. China organized the China–Africa forum with great fanfare in 2006 that was attended by the political leaders of forty-eight of the fifty-three African countries. It was this that forced India to organize its own India–Africa summit in 2008.

It is not without significance that the superpower-in-waiting is asserting its growing political and economic profile in a continent that has often felt neglected by other major global players. China is the second largest consumer of oil in the world and one-third of China's total crude imports come from Angola, Sudan, Congo, Gabon, Equatorial Guinea, Chad, and Nigeria.[4] Beijing's huge purchases of oil and other resources have made it Africa's third largest partner, after the United States and France. Angola is now the largest oil exporter of oil to China, even sidelining Saudi Arabia.

The structural constraints imposed by the Cold War disappeared in the early 1990s and since then China has gradually tried to increase its clout in Africa more substantively. In a rapidly evolving global strategic environment, cultivating economic and diplomatic ties with the African nations has emerged as a major foreign policy priority for China. China's trade with Africa has grown by an astounding 1,000 per cent during the past decade, faster than with any other region except the Middle East, and touched the US$100 billion mark in 2010, surpassing the US trade with the continent.[5]

Countries like Angola, Namibia, Zambia, and Ethiopia are now heavily dependent on Chinese largesse. China has targeted Africa's oil-producing states to diversify its sources of oil, signing energy deals with Algeria,

Nigeria, Angola, Gabon, and Sudan. Angola is China's second largest trading partner in Africa and its largest exporter of oil since 2006. This remarkable progress in Angola since the end of its civil war has been attributed to China's growing role in the country. China has strengthened its ties with Angola in recent years and the southern African country now sells around half of its 1.7 million barrels per day oil output to Beijing. Beijing has issued several oil-backed loans to Angola dating back to 2003, a year after the African nation emerged from a twenty-seven-year civil war. Prior to this loan, China had lent Angola US$14.5 billion since the war's end.[6] China's state-owned oil company, Sinopec, has a joint venture with Sonangol, operating several large offshore projects. Chinese consumer goods have flooded the markets in Africa and the country's investment in infrastructure projects has made the Chinese presence ubiquitous. China is investing billions and extending easy loans in exchange for access to resources.

The largest China–Africa gathering since the founding of communist China in 1949 was held in 2006, where Chinese and African leaders signed deals worth US$1.9 billion, covering telecommunications, infrastructure, insurance, and mineral resources, amid assurances from China that it would not monopolize Africa's resources. China also agreed to extend US$1.5 billion in loans and credits to Africa, forgive past debts, and double foreign aid to the continent by 2009. China and the participating nations from Africa also declared a strategic partnership and "action plan" that charts cooperation in the economy, international affairs, and social development.[7]

For many African nations, the most attractive aspect of Chinese involvement in their continent is its no-strings-attached aid policy. The aid from the West is often linked to good governance and human rights clauses which the political leaders in Africa find unpalatable and describe as "neo-colonialism," an approach aimed at imposing Western political values on them. China has so far tended to ignore the global lending standards intended to fight corruption in the region. Even the IMF and World Bank see their years of painstaking efforts to arrange conditional debt relief being undermined by China's unrestricted lending. But China has made "non-interference in other states' internal affairs" a central tenet of its foreign policy. This has as much to do with making China an attractive partner for the Africans as it has to do with China's own sensitivities toward interference in its domestic politics. Even as the IMF was negotiating structural reforms with the Angolan government in 2004, China stepped in and offered Angola aid without any preconditions, thereby luring Angola away from much-needed reforms.

China's military presence is also growing on the African continent with Beijing supplying arms to both sides in one of Africa's longest running conflicts, between Ethiopia and Eritrea. China has also supplied arms to Sudan, Congo, Angola, Sierra Leone, and Liberia. China is sending more peacekeeping troops to Africa than ever before, and expanding its military exchanges with various African governments. It is the leading military supplier to

Zimbabwe, even as Robert Mugabe has used this military hardware and training mainly to contain growing domestic opposition against his government. Mugabe's "Look East" policy, initiated in response to his regime's ostracization by the Western governments for his human rights abuses, has had its biggest success in attracting China to Zimbabwe, so much so that China is now Zimbabwe's second largest trading partner.[8] More significant, especially in light of developments in Darfur, China developed a military relationship with the Sudanese government and, despite the UN arms embargo, China's military engagement with Sudan remained undiminished.

China's soft power has also been on the ascendant in Africa. It is being viewed as a land of opportunities and prosperity, replacing the role that the United States and Europe have long played in the consciousness of the people of Africa. African students are going to China in larger numbers than ever before. China is leveraging its soft power – culture, investment, academia, foreign aid, public diplomacy – more effectively than before to influence Africa and other regions in the developing world.[9]

In this context, India's competition with China in Africa has come to the fore. Beijing's policy of using financial and military aid to secure oilfields in Africa has resulted in New Delhi losing out. The fierce competition between China and India for resources, minerals, and food to fuel their economies has been likened to the so-called scramble for Africa among European countries in the nineteenth century.

The fear of lagging behind China in its quest for global influence is forcing India to shape up. But in many ways it might already be too late. Despite India's long-standing cultural and commercial ties with Africa, India now finds itself catching up to China as it ignored the continent during the 1990s. New Delhi has been tardy in seizing new opportunities in Africa and capitalizing on its long history of engagement with the continent. New Delhi's failure to secure backing of African nations for India's permanent membership in the UN Security Council jolted the government out of its slumber, galvanizing it to strengthen its ties with a continent that has often complained of indifference on the part of New Delhi. China nudged the AU into taking a position that demanded not only a permanent representation in the Security Council but also veto power. This led to the collapse of the nascent attempts to expand the Security Council.[10]

India, which had been complacent about its presence in Africa, found that it is not only the West but also China which has challenged Indian profile in Africa in recent years. And Indian diplomatic energies seem to be invested in regaining its traditional influence in the continent.

India's challenge in Central Asia

India's ties with Central Asia are also attaining a new trajectory at a time when major powers are competing for influence in Central Asia, comprising of the five nations of Kazakhstan, Kyrgyzstan, Tajikistan, Turkmenistan, and Uzbekistan. Russia has made its determination to restore some of its historic influence over its former Soviet empire clear. Moscow remains determined to signal to the rest of the world that when it comes to Central Asia, Russia remains the regional hegemon that would decide on how the larger strategic realities shape up in its near abroad. The US presence in Central Asia has been growing since 2001 and there is deep resentment in Moscow about this.

Russia viewed the popular uprising in 2005 in Kyrgyzstan – the Tulip Revolution – that toppled the previous authoritarian regime as part of the US strategy to undermine Russian influence in the region.[11] It has been exerting pressure on Kyrgyzstan to evict the US forces from what it regards as its strategic sphere of influence. Russians tried to use the military base in Manas as a bargaining chip in order to underscore that it might just be willing to support US efforts in Afghanistan if the United States decided to tacitly accept Russian power projection in its neighborhood.[12]

The issue of supply lines to NATO and American forces in Afghanistan emerged as key, with the Taliban controlling the route from Pakistan over the Khyber Pass. Almost 75 percent of US supplies to Afghanistan traveled through Pakistan but increasing attacks on transportation depots and truck convoys in Pakistan raised doubts about its ability to protect vital supply routes. This made alternative supply lines through Central Asia all the more crucial.[13]

Major powers have competed for power and influence in Central Asia since the nineteenth century and that "Great Game" seems to be back with a bang. The importance of the SCO that has evolved into a forum for discussion on regional security and economic issues cannot be overstated in this context. It has become even more important post-9/11, because growing ethnic nationalism and Islamic fundamentalism is a major cause of concern for Russia, China, and Central Asian states. Russia and China have been successful in using the strong aversion of the United States to terrorism after 9/11 for their own ends to tackle Islamic insurgency within their territories. In the post-9/11 environment, the SCO serves as a means to keep control of Central Asia and limit US influence in the region.[14] In fact, the SCO denounced the misuse of the war on terror to target any country and threw its weight behind the UN in an attempt to show its disagreement with the US-led war in Iraq.

Unlike China, which shares a border with Kazakhstan, Kyrgyzstan, and Tajikistan, India's transit to the region lies through Pakistan and Afghanistan, limiting India's reach. Yet India's growing interests in Central Asia are well-recognized. There is a growing convergence between the US and Indian interests, especially their reluctance to see the region fall under the exclusive influence of Russia or China. India was worried in the 1990s when the Russian influence in Central Asia weakened substantially with a commensurate rise in the Chinese influence. This negatively impacted upon Indian threat perceptions which stabilized only after the growing US presence in the region since 2001.

India's ties with the regional states are growing. India views itself as a stabilizer and security provider in the region and with its growing economic clout, an attractive economic power for regional states. India's interest in securing reliable energy supplies and trade through Central Asia remains substantial. Besides oil and gas, energy-hungry India is eyeing imports of uranium from both Kazakhstan and Uzbekistan.

As a consequence, New Delhi has little incentive to support forces that seek destabilization in Afghanistan which will have spill-over effects on the larger Central Asian region. It is with this larger perspective that India opened its air base in Ayni, Tajikistan, in 2002 to guard against growing instability in the region. The moderate Islam of the region also makes it imperative for India to engage the region more substantively. Other powers, barring China, have recognized this reality and have sought to harness India toward achieving common goals. Russia, for example, supports Indian membership in the SCO and has talked about the possibility of India participating in the Collective Security Treaty Organization. In order to upgrade its ties with Central Asia, India launched its "Connect Central Asia" policy in 2012, which calls for intensified diplomatic engagement with the region through a multi-level approach entailing political, security, economic, and cultural connections. This new approach seeks to address New Delhi's regional security concerns vis-à-vis Afghanistan and Pakistan and to position India favorably by leveraging cross-regional economic potential, thereby boosting its status as an emerging power. At the same time this policy will allow India to pursue its plans for the region in the economic, political, education, trade, energy, transit, and military spheres on both bilateral and multilateral bases.[15]

Seeking bilateral partnerships

As the NATO-led Western military forces prepare to withdraw from Afghanistan, all major regional players and global powers are struggling to come to terms with the aftermath. Regional cooperation, time and again, has been declared as the only viable alternative to the festering regional tensions that have plagued Afghanistan for decades. Various South and Central Asian governments, for example, have underscored that they recognize that Afghanistan's problems of terrorism, narcotics trafficking, and corruption affected them all and had to be addressed through cooperative efforts. They adopted the Istanbul Protocol in November 2011 that commits countries as diverse as China, India, Iran, Kazakhstan, Pakistan, and Russia to cooperate in countering terrorism, drug trafficking, and insurgency in Afghanistan and in the neighboring areas.[16] In this context, Afghanistan's traditionally divisive neighbors have pledged to support its efforts to reconcile with insurgent groups and to work together on joint security and economic initiatives to build long-term Afghan stability. The New Silk Road strategy was embraced by the participants at the Istanbul Conference that envisages a dynamic Afghanistan at the heart of South and Central Asian trade and economic relationships.[17] For Afghanistan and the larger Central Asian region, the potential for trading with India, as well as transit through India to reach Southeast Asian markets, is huge and is at the heart of the push to develop a North–South Corridor for trade and transit in Eurasia.

India's geopolitical and security interests in the Central Asian region converge with Russia in so far as religious extremism, terrorism, drug trafficking, smuggling in small arms, and organized crime, emanating largely from Central Asia, threaten both India and Russia equally. As a consequence, Russia has pushed for a full membership of India in the SCO where India holds an observer status. The SCO was established in 1996 as a regional strategy grouping aimed mainly at combating separatist unrest. The group's members, including Russia, China, and most Central Asian states, share intelligence and conduct joint military exercises, even if they fail to coordinate larger policy because of competing interests. The SCO plans to focus more on Afghanistan and Pakistan in the coming years given a rising anxiety among neighboring states that extremist and terrorist forces will find a fresh opportunity to gain traction once the United States and allied forces leave Afghanistan. The SCO membership will allow India greater leverage in shaping the ground realities in Afghanistan once the United States and NATO leave Afghanistan. The SCO could provide the regional framework for the stabilization of Afghanistan as all neighbors of Afghanistan, except Turkmenistan, are members of the SCO in one form or another. The United States itself has started a dialogue process with the SCO. With the United States now set to make its own military retreat from Afghanistan, Russia and India will have to work together to avert a destabilizing power vacuum there if terrorist blowback from the Af-Pak region is to be avoided. Both New Delhi and Moscow agree that the key to resolving Afghanistan is a regional solution where all neighbors ensure that Afghanistan must control its own future and no one should intervene in its internal politics.

New Delhi has repeatedly underscored its desire to seek full member status of the six-nation grouping and made it clear that India remains keen to deepen security-related cooperation with it, particularly with the SCO's Regional Anti-Terrorism Structure. Toward that end, India is willing to sign the Model Protocol of Intent as a demonstration of its commitment.

Given the rapidly evolving security situation in Afghanistan, New Delhi has linked the developments in Afghanistan to the need for a pan-regional effort in managing the negative externalities emerging from there. Underscoring the role of the SCO in offering a credible alternative regional platform to discuss the challenges related to Afghanistan, Indian foreign minister suggested in 2012 that India "strongly believes that Afghanistan can successfully complete the security, political and economic transitions in coming years and regain its historical place as a hub for regional trade and transit routes" but "this presupposes fulfillment of pledges made by the international community for security and civilian assistance to Afghanistan and non-interference in Afghanistan's internal affairs."[18] India has also underscored that the SCO should "step up its engagement in the rebuilding and reconstruction of Afghanistan, through common projects and financial commitments. India would then support the efforts by Russia to craft common SCO positions on Afghanistan."[19]

India has long wanted to play a larger role in the SCO and has been seeking support from individual member states for quite some time. However, New Delhi has not been successful in achieving an upgrade in its observer status. The organization has failed to achieve a consensus on India's role in the grouping. It is not very difficult to see why this should be the case. China was reluctant to see India as a full member of the group despite its official rhetoric that it wants to see India play a larger role in the grouping. China, Kazakhstan, Kyrgyzstan, Russia, and Tajikistan had been members of the Shanghai Five, founded in 1996; after the inclusion of Uzbekistan in 2001, the members renamed the organization. India was admitted as an observer at the 2005 Astana Summit along with Iran and Pakistan. Though the 2010 Tashkent Summit lifted the moratorium on new membership, India's role in the grouping remained a marginal one. With Russian support, India, along with Pakistan, was granted full membership of the SCO beginning in 2016.

Against this backdrop, Indian strategy has focused on developing strong bilateral partnerships in the region. With Uzbekistan, India has signed a pact on the import of over 2,000 tonnes of uranium much like the one India has signed with Kazakhstan. India is also exploring with Uzbekistan the possibility of extending the Friendship Railway Bridge to Herat in western Afghanistan. The requirements of energy security also postulate a continuing positive relationship with Moscow and friendly ties with all the Central Asian states. India must create firm ties among the energy-exporting states of Central Asia, particularly Kazakhstan, Uzbekistan, and, if possible, Turkmenistan.

But India has so far failed to invest the diplomatic capital that the region demands. India tried to open an air facility in Ayni, Tajikistan, in 2002 to guard against growing instability in the region though nothing much happened on that front for long. And in 2010 the Tajik government officially made it clear that Russia is the only country likely to use the airbase in the future. This happened despite India spending around US$70 million between 2002 and 2010 to renovate the Ayni base and extending the Ayni runway to 3,200 meters as well as installing state-of-the-art navigational and air defense equipment there.[20] Meanwhile, China managed to win the competition for the Kashagan oilfield in Kazakhstan and the Dauletabad gas field in

Turkmenistan. The much-hyped Turkmenistan–Afghanistan–Pakistan–India gas pipeline which is supposed to transport gas from Turkmenistan across Afghanistan and Pakistan to India is yet to get off the ground.

With a strategic approach toward Central Asia, China has made significant headway in the region with a US$10 billion grant and aid to SCO members and developments of regional linkages with its western region. China's trade with the Central Asian region reached the US$46 billion mark in 2012 whereas trade between Central Asia and India remains much below potential, struggling to hit the US$800 million mark in 2012–13.[21] India's lack of a direct overland access to the region due to Pakistan's reluctance in allowing Indian goods to pass through its territory has constrained India's trade interests from growing in the Central Asian region and, consequently, trade with the region has only risen slowly from US$115 million to US$738 million from 1996 to 2012.[22]

A great power competition in Central Asia will make it harder for India to pursue its interests in the region. As such, it becomes imperative for Indian diplomacy to work toward major power cooperation to bring some measure of stability to the larger Central Asian region. This region remains critical for India's security and energy needs. With China the largest trading partner of four of the five regional states, India increasingly looks like a pygmy and its imprint will only reduce in the coming years in the absence of a strategic approach to the region. With this in mind, Indian Prime Minister Narendra Modi visited all five states in Central Asia together in July 2015, becoming the first prime minister after Jawaharlal Nehru to undertake a regional outreach.

As India rises in the global inter-state hierarchy, there are not only new opportunities for engagement in regions such as Africa and Central Asia but New Delhi is also having to come to terms with other major powers, in particular China, who are also trying to expand their profiles. How India manages to navigate the choppy waters of major power politics in these regions will determine the extent of its presence in Africa and Central Asia.

Notes

1 J. Peter Pham, India's Expanding Relationship with Africa and their Implications for US Interest," *American Foreign Policy Interests*, Vol. 29 (2007), p. 343.

2 Biswajit Dhar, "An Indian Adventure in Africa," *Mint*, May 23, 2011.

3 Alex Vines, "India's Africa Engagement: Prospects for the 2011 India–Africa Forum," Chatham House, December 2010, available at www.chathamhouse.org/sites/files/chathamhouse/public/Research/Africa/1210vines.pdf.

4 Yaroslav Trofimov, "In Africa, China's Expansion Begins to Stir Resentment," *Wall Street Journal*, February 2, 2007.

5 "Trade with Africa Set to Achieve Record High," *People's Daily*, October 15, 2010.

6 Joe Brock, "China to Loan Angola's Sonangol $2 bln for Oil Projects," Reuters, December 18, 2014.
7 Chen Aizhu and Lindsay Beck, "Chinese-African Summit Yields $1.9 Billion in Deals," *Washington Post*, November 6, 2006.
8 David Smith, "Robert Mugabe Visits China as Critics Condemn 'Desperate' Bid for Investment," *Guardian*, August 26, 2014.
9 On China's reliance on its soft power in its dealings with other states, see Joshua Kurlantzick, *Charm Offensive: How China's Soft Power is Transforming the World* (New Haven: Yale University Press, 2007).
10 James Traub, "The World According to China," *New York Times*, September 3, 2006.
11 A detailed account of Russian response is available in Thomas Ambrosio, *Authoritarian Backlash: Russian Resistance to Democratization in the Former Soviet Union* (Surrey: Ashgate, 2013).
12 Luke Harding, "Kyrgyzstan to Close Key US Military Airbase," *Guardian*, February 4, 2009.
13 Thom Shanker and Richard A. Oppel, "U.S. to Widen Supply Routes in Afghan War," *New York Times*, December 30, 2008.
14 Stephen Aris, "Russian-Chinese Relations Through the Lens of the SCO," Russi. Nei.Visions No. 34, IFRI. September 2008, available at www.ifri.org/sites/default/files/atoms/files/Ifri_RNV_Aris_SCO_Eng.pdf.
15 Roman Muzalevsky, "India's 'Connect Central Asia' Policy Seeks to Compensate for Lost Time," *Eurasia Daily Monitor*, Vol. 9, No. 176 (September 27, 2012).
16 Sebnem Arsu, "Afghanistan Consults Neighbors on Security," *New York Times*, November 3, 2011.
17 *Ibid.*
18 "India Keen to Deepen its Security-Related Cooperation with SCO: Salman Khurshid," *Business Standard*, September 13, 2013.
19 *Ibid.*
20 R. Sharma, "India's Ayni Military Base in Tajikistan is Russia-Locked," *Russia and India Report*, October 26, 2012.
21 Arvind Gupta, "India and Central Asia: Need for a Pro-Active Approach," IDSA Policy Brief, October 14, 2013.
22 Hemant Shivakumar, Persis Taraporevala, Kailash K. Prasad, and Rani D. Mullen, "India – Central Asia Relations: Moving Towards Broader Development Partnerships," India Development Cooperation Research (IDCR) Project, Background Paper No. 4, January 6, 2014. Available at http://idcr.cprindia.org/blog/india-central-asia-backgrounder.

12

India and the Middle East: a fine balance

The visit of the then newly installed and soon to be deposed Egyptian President, Mohamed Morsi, to India in March 2013 brought to focus India's changing role in the larger Middle East where it has significant stakes which are rising by the day. India's relationship with the Middle East as a region today is dramatically different than a generation ago, when from 1947 to 1990, India was too ideological toward the region, as was reflected in its subdued ties with Iran, Saudi Arabia, and Israel.[1] Today, however, it is these three states around which India is developing its new Middle Eastern strategy, with New Delhi taking special care to nurture all these relationships and pursue its substantial regional interests. And now with a post-Arab Spring Middle East going through a tumultuous phase, India is re-negotiating the terms of its engagement with the region.

India's policy toward the Middle East has in recent years been viewed primarily through the prism of Indo-Iranian relations. The international community, and the West in particular, has been obsessed with New Delhi's ties to Tehran, which are actually largely underdeveloped, while missing India's much more substantive simultaneous engagement with Arab Gulf states and Israel. It was this that led to a much more cautious approach from New Delhi to the Arab revolutions in the beginning compared to the West and rapid overtures to new regimes once they emerged. Not only have the political transitions not been easy for the countries affected by the Arab Spring but the great tumult in the Middle East is testing the resolve of the international community in tackling difficult issues in the region. All major global powers are struggling with tough choices as they try to strike a balance between their values and strategic interests in crafting a response to the still-unfolding crisis in the region. India is no exception.

This chapter examines India's role in the Middle East at this time of great tumult. The Arab revolutions and their aftermath seem to have merely confirmed for India that its policy of engaging various stakeholders in the region has been a wise one and, given its immense stakes in the region, it can ill-afford to be more adventurous.

India responds to the Arab revolutions: caution all the way

The so-called "Arab Spring" started when in January 2011 an impoverished Tunisian fruit vendor set himself on fire after being publicly humiliated by a policewoman who tried to confiscate his unlicensed street cart. Within days, protests started across the country, calling upon President Zine El Abidine Ben Ali and his regime to step down. About a month later, he fled. The momentum in Tunisia set off uprisings across the Middle East that became known as the Arab Spring. Yet the initial euphoria that swept the Arab world has since suffered a sharp reality check. The response to uprisings that followed in some other countries has ranged from violent repression in Syria to near civil war in Libya and Yemen: a chilling disincentive to potential protesters elsewhere. The ossified dictatorships in all three countries have proved their readiness to exploit latent sectarian, ethnic, or tribal rivalries in cynical and reckless bids to divide and rule.

In Bahrain and Libya India kept silent by abstaining from the United Nations Security Council (UNSC) resolutions and adopted a "wait and watch" approach. But in Syria, it voted in favor of the UNSC resolution ostensibly on humanitarian grounds while underlining that it does not support regime change. Libya was the first major critical issue for Indian diplomacy as New Delhi assumed non-permanent membership of the UNSC in January 2011. New Delhi supported Security Council Resolution 1970, which imposed sanctions on the Muammar Gaddafi regime: a comprehensive arms embargo designed to prevent the direct or indirect supply, sale, or transfer of arms and military equipment to Libya and the freezing of economic resources "owned or controlled, directly or indirectly" by designated Gaddafi family members. But even this was not an easy choice given the domestic political sensitivities involved.

As the discussion at the UN shifted toward the possibility of imposing a no-fly zone over Libya, New Delhi became more nervous, proclaiming the centrality of the principle of non-intervention in the internal affairs of other nations. When it came to the crunch, India – along with Germany, Brazil, China, and Russia – abstained from voting on the Security Council Resolution that approved a no-fly zone over Libya, and which authorized "all measures necessary" for protecting civilians from Gaddafi's forces. India argued that it could not endorse the drastic steps called for in the Resolution without hearing from the UN Secretary-General's special envoy.[2] It also underlined the AU's attempt to end the crisis in a peaceful manner. India cautioned that "the Resolution that the Council adopted authorizes far-reaching measures under Chapter VII of the UN charter with relatively little credible information on the situation on the ground in Libya."[3] What was worse, India argued, was that there was no clarity in the Resolution about who would enforce it, and how. Responding to reports that a possible solution could be the division of Libya, India insisted that Libyan sovereignty, unity, and territorial integrity should be preserved.

India remained unconvinced that the intervention in Libya would lead to a swift, successful outcome. Concern also emerged that the use of force might not be effective; many in the West held similar views. The Obama administration was reluctant to get involved and only began to seriously consider military intervention when pressure from France and Britain as well as from domestic critics increased. Furthermore, India was also was also discomfited by the precedent-setting parts of the Resolution.

These reservations echoed the standard policies of New Delhi at least since the 1990s if not before. India, much like other major powers in the international system, favors a multipolar world order in which US domination remains constrained by other "poles" in the system. It zealously guards its national sovereignty and remains wary of US attempts to interfere in what it sees as domestic affairs of other states, be it Serbia, Kosovo, or Iraq. It took strong exception to the US air strikes on Iraq in 1998, the US-led air campaign against Yugoslavia in 1999, and the US campaign against Saddam Hussein, arguing that these violated the sovereignty of both countries and undermined the authority of the UN.

The debate on Libya underlined that despite all the hyperbole about the decline of the West and the rise of the rest, the "rest" is not yet ready to take on roles as global powers. The emerging powers like India are yet to articulate a world vision that provides an alternative to the Western-designed global order. They have yet to review the concept of sovereignty in a globally interconnected world where a government's brutal repression of its citizens is instantaneously broadcast around the world, raising questions of moral responsibility for fellow human beings separated by state borders. Opposing every move by the West is easy, and criticizing from the sidelines is even easier. Offering a credible alternative is the real test of global leadership of the rising powers.

And yet there were significant differences too in the approach of these powers. In China's and Russia's case, abstention actually meant a yes as their veto would have killed any UN action. The fact that they abstained meant that they were willing to let the West proceed against Libya, albeit with limits. The actions of states like India and Brazil, however, underline the real challenges of the emerging global order.

After the downfall of Gaddafi regime's, India needed diplomatic agility to renew a relationship with the new government in Tripoli. New Delhi had started interacting with the National Transition Council of Libya long before it gave it formal recognition in November 2011. The new political leadership was familiar with India, with the new Prime Minister Ali Zeiban having studied in India. India conveyed its readiness to extend all possible assistance to Libya in its political transition and offered humanitarian

assistance to the tune of US$2 million. India has offered its help in the draft-
ing of Libyan constitution and provided its expertise in the management of
elections. The two nations have signed an MoU for cooperation in the field
of election conduct and management.

India's trade with Libya today exceeds that during the pre-crisis years
with hydrocarbons, information technology, banking, education, and health
emerging as key priority areas of bilateral cooperation.[4] Indian companies remain keen to resume their stalled projects and to partake in Libya's
post-crisis reconstruction efforts. India oil companies would be major
beneficiaries if the oil sector in Africa's largest oil producer is liberalized.
Major oil companies of India, including ONGV Videsh, Bharat Heavy
Electricals, Punj Lloyd, D.S Construction, and Unitech, all have operated in
Libya before the war started and are looking for new opportunities in the
new Libya.

India's response to the Egyptian crisis too was caution writ large. After
days of silence, the only response to the political crisis in Egypt that the
Indian government could muster was of "closely following" developments
in Egypt and hoping "for an early and peaceful resolution of the situation
without further violence and loss of lives." The Indian government's statement, however, had to concede that the street protests in Cairo against Hosni
Mubarak's regime in early 2011 reflected the people's desire for reform as
New Delhi underlined that the mass protests in Egypt "are an articulation
of the aspirations of the Egyptian people for reform" and that "the current
situation will be resolved in a peaceful manner, in the best interests of the
people of Egypt."[5]

Once the government of Mohamed Morsi took charge in June 2012,
New Delhi reached out to the new regime. As founding members of the
NAM, India and Egypt shared a close relationship under the leadership of
Jawaharlal Nehru and Gamal Abdel Nasser. With the coming to office of
Hosni Mubarak, the relationship petered out. Morsi was trying to reorient
Egyptian foreign policy away from the West and revival of traditional ties
with India was back on the agenda.

India started to pursue an ambitious agenda with Egypt as was underscored by Morsi's visit to New Delhi in March 2013. The focus of his visit
was on economics and trade as he asked India to join the 190-kilometer
Suez Canal corridor project that is aimed at making Egypt into a global
economic hub. Morsi was also pushing for Egypt's inclusion in the BRICS
grouping. But there was also an attempt to move beyond trade, and
defense cooperation might play a significant role in the coming years with
the two states deciding to initiate military exchanges. However, Morsi
was soon toppled with the Egyptian military back in charge leading to
widespread violence. India urged all political forces in Egypt to abjure
violence, respect democratic principles, and engage in a conciliatory
dialogue to address the situation after suspension of constitution by the

army. New Delhi underlined that "as the world's largest democracy, India was amongst the first countries to welcome the January 25 revolution and the promise of genuine democracy in a large and important country like Egypt with which we have traditionally enjoyed close and friendly ties."[6] But beyond that, New Delhi refused to go beyond treating the turmoil as an internal matter of Egypt.

This principle was carried forward in the Syrian case as well. The crisis in Syria continues with the Assad regime showing greater resilience than other regimes. India has been walking a tightrope between the United States and Syria. It voted in favor of sanctions on the Assad regime but later abstained from another vote in the United Nations General Assembly, arguing that it opposed acts that aimed at regime change in Syria. New Delhi has also tried to articulate a common policy with the emerging powers through the BRICS framework. On Syria, the group has argued that "global interests would best be served by dealing with the crisis through peaceful means that encourage broad national dialogues that reflect the legitimate aspirations of all sections of Syrian society and respect Syrian independence, territorial integrity and sovereignty."[7] The BRICS have continued to underline the need for respecting Syrian sovereignty and have refused to support any resolution against the regime of Bashar al-Assad. Before the Durban summit, Assad publicly urged the BRICS leaders to help stop the violence in his country, asking them to call for a peaceful resolution that did not impinge on Syria's sovereignty.[8] In response, the BRICS final communiqué after the Durban summit conveyed "deep concern with the deterioration of the security and humanitarian situation," and "condemned the increasing violations of human rights and of international law" but refrained from taking any sides.[9] At the same time, however, India reached out to the moderate factions among opposition groups in Syria so as not to keep all its eggs in Assad's basket. One important consideration in the Indian response has been a recognition that for all his flaws, Bashar al-Assad runs one of the few secular regimes in the Middle East. India supports Syria's right to the Golan Heights, and in exchange, Syria endorses India's position that Kashmir is a bilateral issue. Such support is rare in the Arab world; while officially the Arab League does not take a stance on Kashmir, it tends to empathize with Pakistan.

New Delhi's response to the Arab Spring has underscored that India, like other emerging powers, is not yet ready to answer the really tough questions about its global priorities. The so-called BRICS have yet to develop a coherent philosophy on citizen's rights and role of sovereign states in an interconnected globalized world. By refraining from offering a credible alternative, the emerging powers have ensured that the responsibility to protect humans from mass atrocities remains a Western, as opposed to a truly international, responsibility. Clearly, this is not an effective approach to deal with issues of human rights and state sovereignty. As such, for all the talk of the rise of new powers on the global stage, they continue to be largely peripheral in shaping global discourse and events. The Arab Spring has been no exception.

The tumult in the Arab street will have enormous implications for India's rapidly growing interests in the region. A new order is unfolding in the region and New Delhi is still struggling to spell out how it wants to engage the new ground realities. Silence may no longer be an option. When a new era unfolds in the Arab world, India would like to be on the right side of history. Yet at the same time it has to ensure that it is engaging all major stakeholders. While the West may have the luxury of taking sides, New Delhi has to be ready to deal with whoever is in power given its immense regional stakes. For example, Egypt has traditionally been one of India's most significant trading partners in the region and even after Morsi was deposed, relations continue to flourish. Bilateral trade grew from US$5.42 billion in 2011–12 to US$5.45 billion in 2012–13. More than fifty Indian companies operate in Egypt, with a total investment of US$2.5 billion, making a diverse range of products from PVC to seeds development. More significantly, no Indian company has left Egypt since the January 25 revolution.

New Delhi has been emphasizing the principle of non-intervention and backed efforts at political reconciliation and the construction of an inclusive constitutional order in various crisis-ridden states in the Middle East. One of the main reasons for India's lackadaisical approach toward the Arab Spring is that for New Delhi this has really been a side-show. The real issue that India faces in the region is in balancing its ties with Iran and Arab Gulf states where it has been focusing its diplomatic energies in recent years.

India and Iran: nothing "strategic" about it

Ever since India and the United States began to transform their ties by changing the global nuclear order to accommodate India with the 2005 framework for the Indo-US civilian nuclear agreement, Iran has become a litmus test that India has occasionally had been asked to pass to satisfy US policy-makers. Nascent Indian–Iranian ties have been categorized as an "axis," a "strategic partnership," or even an "alliance," which some in the US strategic community have suggested could have a potentially damaging impact on US interests in Southwest Asia and the Middle East.[10]

At the same time, the Indian left has also developed a parallel obsession, making Iran an issue emblematic of India's "strategic autonomy" and using the bogey of toeing American line on Iran to coerce New Delhi into following an ideological, independent, anti-American foreign policy. A close examination of the Indian–Iranian relationship, however, reveals an underdeveloped relationship despite all the spin attached to it.

India would like to increase its presence in the Iranian energy sector because of its rapidly rising energy needs, and is rightfully feeling restless about its own marginalization in Iran. Not only has Pakistan signed a pipeline deal with Tehran, but China also is starting to make its presence felt. China is now Iran's largest trading partner and is undertaking massive investments in the country, rapidly occupying the space vacated by Western firms. Where Beijing's economic engagement with Iran is growing, India's presence is shrinking, as firms such as Reliance Industries have, partially under Western pressure, withdrawn from Iran and others have shelved their plans to make investments.[11]

There is little evidence so far that Iran would be a reliable partner in India's search for energy security. A number of important projects with Indian businesses and Indian government have either been rejected by Iran or have yet to be finalized due to last-minute changes in the terms and conditions by Tehran. To date, Iran accounts for only about 8 percent of Indian oil imports. Moreover, both of the major energy deals recently signed with great fanfare, and raising concerns in the West, are now in limbo. India's twenty-five-year, US$22 billion agreement with Iran for the export of LNG has not produced anything since it was signed in 2005, as it requires India to build an LNG plant in Iran. The plant would need American components, which might violate the US Iran–Libya Sanctions Act. The other project – involving the construction of a 1,700-mile, US$7 billion pipeline to carry natural gas from Iran to India via Pakistan – is also stuck. The current Indian government initially viewed the pipeline project as a confidence-building measure between India and Pakistan, but when pressure started mounting, former Indian Prime Minister Manmohan Singh went so far in 2005 as to say that he did not know if any international consortium of bankers would underwrite the project, given uncertainties about Iran. The Indian strategic community has never been in favor of the pipeline proposal anyway, as in their opinion, it gives Pakistan too much leverage over India's energy security.

Both these projects have also made the unreliability of Iran as a trade partner clear to India. The national oil companies of Iran and India disagree about the legal interpretation of the contract for the export of LNG to India. This deal was signed in 2005 before Mahmoud Ahmadinejad was elected president of Iran, and was tied to a relatively low market price for crude oil. India considers the deal final and binding, while Iran has argued that it is not binding because it has not been ratified. Amid the growing global isolation of Iran, sections of the Indian government have suggested that India's participation in the gas pipeline deal might not be strategically advantageous to India, given the very low quantity (thirty million standard cubic meters per day) of gas involved. Moreover, it appears that the Iranian gas is not the lowest-priced option for India today. New Delhi has made it clear that although it remains interested in the pipeline project, it would pay for the gas only after it is received at the Pakistan–India border, it would not pay penalty in case of a delay, and it is opposed to Iran's demand to revise the deal's gas prices every three years.[12] India's interests in the relationship with Iran, however, do not appear to be strictly commercial. After Pakistan and

Iran signed their pipeline deal in 2009, for example, India indicated that it was willing to resume negotiations regarding independently importing natural gas from Iran via sea pipeline, allowing India to get around Pakistan.

The nuclear issue is equally complex for Indian–Iranian relations. New Delhi and Tehran have long held significantly different perceptions of the global nuclear order. Iran was not supportive of the Indian nuclear tests in 1998 and backed the UNSC Resolution asking India and Pakistan to cap their nuclear capabilities by signing the NPT and the Comprehensive Nuclear-Test-Ban Treaty (CTBT). Iran repeatedly has called for universal acceptance of the NPT, much to India's chagrin. Although Iran has claimed that this was directed at Israel, the implications of such a move are far-reaching for India. With the conclusion of the US–India nuclear deal, Iran warned that the pact had endangered the NPT and would trigger new "crises" for the international community.[13]

Iran's position on several other issues crucial to India has run counter to Indian interests. Tehran has been critical of Indian government on its handling of Kashmir protests earlier this year and the Indian government was forced to issue a démarche, protesting against Iranian interference in Indian domestic issues.[14] India's position on the Iranian nuclear question is relatively straightforward. Although India believes that Iran has the right to pursue civilian nuclear energy, it has insisted that Iran should clarify the doubts raised by the IAEA regarding Iran's compliance with the NPT. India has long maintained that it does not see further nuclear proliferation as being in its interests. This position has as much to do with India's desire to project itself as a responsible nuclear state as with the very real danger that further proliferation in its extended neighborhood could endanger its security. India has continued to affirm its commitment to enforce all sanctions against Iran as mandated since 2006 by the UNSC, when the first set of sanctions was imposed. However, much like Beijing and Moscow, New Delhi has argued that such sanctions should not hurt the Iranian populace and has expressed its disapproval of sanctions by individual countries that restrict investments by third countries in Iran's energy sector.[15]

Despite hype about growing defense ties between India and Iran, India has a more substantive defense relationship with the Arab world. Iran has joined the Indian Navy's annual initiative, the Indian Ocean Naval Symposium, which provides a forum for the navies of the Indian Ocean littoral states to engage each other and plans are afoot for greater maritime cooperation. This defense relationship, however, remains not only sporadic and tentative, but also circumscribed by India's growing defense linkages with Israel.

The crucial regional issue where India and Iran need each other is the evolving security situation in Afghanistan. Against the backdrop of the withdrawal of Western forces from Afghanistan, India has reached out to Iran about Afghanistan, and the two sides are now involved in "structured and regular consultations" on the issue.[16] Both New Delhi and Tehran are unlikely to accept a political regime in Kabul which serves as a springboard to project Pakistan's military interests. Following the Geneva interim deal in November 2013, and the partial ease of sanctions against Iran, India announced that it was ready to pay US$1.5 billion to Iran for its oil imports. India owes Tehran nearly US$5.3 billion for its oil imports. India is hoping that Iran's rapprochement with the West after the 2015 nuclear accord will allow it to have a more purposeful engagement with Iran.

The underlying reality is that India has far more significant interests to preserve in the Arab Gulf, and as tensions rise between the Sunni Arab regimes and Iran, India's larger stakes in the Gulf might lessen the possibility of healthy Indian–Iranian ties. At the same time, New Delhi's outreach to Tehran will remain circumscribed by the internal power struggle within Iran, growing tensions between Iran and its Arab neighbors, and Iran's continued defiance of the global nuclear order.

India and the Arab Gulf: something "strategic" about it

India's engagements with the Arab states in the Middle East have gained momentum in the last few years, even as Iran continues to hog the limelight. India wants to secure energy supplies and consolidate economic and trade relations with the Gulf states, while these states (Bahrain, Kuwait, Oman, Qatar, Saudi Arabia, and the UAE, or the members of the Gulf Cooperation Council) have adopted a "Look East" policy which has allowed them to carve out a much more substantive relationship with India than in the past.

In January 2006, Saudi King Abdullah bin Abdul-Aziz al-Saud visited India (along with China) on his first trip outside the Middle East since taking the throne in August 2005. Some commentators, noting the trip's significance, labeled it as "a strategic shift" in Saudi foreign policy and reflective of "a new era" for the kingdom.[17] Indian Prime Minister Singh reciprocated by visiting Riyadh in 2010, twenty-eight years since the last Indian premier visited the Saudi kingdom, and promptly elevated the Indo-Saudi relationship to a "strategic partnership." With his visit to Saudi Arabia, the Prime Minister re-emphasized that, when it comes to the Gulf, Iran will not be the focus of Indian foreign policy.

Although India is not a Muslim-majority country, it still hosts the second largest Muslim population in the world, a constituency which remains interested in Saudi Arabia given the holy shrines at Mecca and Medina. There is already significant cultural interchange between the two countries, with approximately 1.5 million Indian workers constituting the largest expatriate community in the Saudi kingdom.[18]

Riyadh is the chief supplier of oil to India's booming economy, and India is now the fourth largest recipient of Saudi oil after China, the United

States, and Japan.[19] India's crude oil imports from the Saudi kingdom will likely double in the next twenty years.[20] During his visit to India, the Saudi king emphasized his country's commitment to uninterrupted supplies to a friendly country such as India regardless of global price trends.[21] As with Saudi Arabia and China, energy infrastructure investment is a major component in developing Saudi–Indian relations. India's Reliance has invested in a refinery and a petrochemicals project in Saudi Arabia, and India's state-owned energy firm, Oil and Energy Gas Corporation, is engaging Saudi Arabia as its equity partner for a refinery project in the Indian state of Andhra Pradesh.

King Abdullah and Prime Minister Singh signed an Indo-Saudi "Delhi Declaration" during the Saudi king's 2006 visit which calls for a wide-ranging partnership, including putting energy and economic cooperation in overdrive and cooperating against terrorism.[22] According to some reports, the king waived off Saudi bureaucratic concerns about unwanted precedents or concerns the declaration might create with India's neighbors, especially Pakistan, by calling India a "special case."[23] A Saudi–Indian Joint Business Council is providing an institutional framework to expand bilateral economic ties. Saudi authorities hope that such a channel can tap Indian expertise and help Saudi Arabia to diversify its economy in fields ranging from information technology and biotechnology to education and small-business development.

New Delhi is also cultivating Riyadh for strategic reasons. To Indian strategists, any ally that can act as a counterweight to Pakistan in the Islamic world is significant. Initially, New Delhi sought to cultivate Tehran, but such efforts stumbled in recent years as the Islamic Republic has adopted an increasingly aggressive anti-Western posture.[24] India hopes Saudi Arabia might fill that gap. Indeed, Iranian nuclear ambitions have helped to draw New Delhi and Riyadh closer together.

The Saudi government has its own reasons for cultivating Indian ties. Saudi Arabia and Iran have long competed for power and influence in the Gulf. The 1979 Islamic Revolution in Iran added a new edge to the rivalry, as Iranian ayatollahs increasingly sought to challenge Saudi officials on religious matters, such as the rules and regulations surrounding the hajj, or pilgrimage to Mecca. The fact that about 40 percent of Saudi Arabia's oil-producing eastern province is Shi'ite, and resents Wahhabi rule, worries Riyadh.[25] The anxiety is mutual; in 1994, the Iranian intelligence ministry designated Salafi terrorism as the primary threat to Iranian national security.[26]

During his visit to Riyadh, Prime Minister Singh joined King Abdullah in asking Tehran "to remove regional and international doubts about its nuclear weapons program."[27] As the regional balance of power between Arabia and Persia threatens to unravel in Iran's favor, Singh's visit underlined India's desire to see the extant balance of power in the region stabilize.

Given India's growing stakes in the Gulf, it is not surprising that this should be the case.

The Saudi king's 2006 visit to India was also a signal to the broader Gulf Cooperation Council (GCC) community to build a stronger partnership with India. In an attempt to have a structured exchange on bilateral and collective security issues, the Indian–GCC dialogue previously held annually on the margins of the UN General Assembly is now being held in a GCC country or in New Delhi for a dedicated forum.

The economic dimension of India's Gulf policy has become more pronounced in recent years. As a group, the GCC is India's second largest trading partner, the largest single origin of imports into India, and the second largest destination for exports from India. Bilateral trade between India and the GCC is expected to rise to more than US$130 billion by 2013–14 from a low base of US$5.6 billion in 2001.[28] The UAE by itself is among India's five largest trading partners as well as India's top trading partner in the entire Middle East, accounting for 75 percent of India's exports to GCC countries and 6 percent of India's global exports.[29] The global financial meltdown and the specter of recession in the United States and Europe are further prompting India to turn to Gulf states which are sitting on huge resources and looking for investment opportunities.

The GCC countries remain a major destination for Indian investment, even as India is making a concerted attempt to encourage GCC investment in India. India hopes that major GCC states such as Saudi Arabia, the UAE, and Oman would participate in India's planned infrastructure expansion. With a rising demand for infrastructure development, India is looking for large investments from the Gulf, which is flush with funds due to the recent surge in oil prices. The Gulf states meanwhile are interested in human resources from India in order to develop sectors as varied as information technology, construction, transportation, and services.

Energy is clearly the driving force in Gulf–Indian relations. The GCC countries supply 45 percent of India's petroleum; the Saudis are responsible for a quarter of those supplies, and Kuwait, Oman, and the UAE are other major suppliers. Qatar remains India's exclusive supplier of natural gas, annually supplying five million tons of LNG to India. The Iranian government's decision to renege on some oil supply commitments, after India's vote against Iran at the IAEA, has also spurred New Delhi to diversify suppliers.

India's trade and energy security is inextricably linked to the security of the Straits of Hormuz and Bab el-Mandeb. With this in mind, the Indian Navy regularly visits Gulf ports and trains with states in the region. The Indian Navy has undertaken a series of naval exercises with a number of Gulf states in recent years, thereby lending its hand to Indian diplomacy in expanding India's reach in the region. Indian naval warships have also been deployed in the Gulf of Aden to carry out anti-piracy patrols on the route usually followed by Indian commercial vessels between Salalah (Oman) and

Aden (Yemen). The Gulf of Aden is a strategic choke-point in the Indian Ocean and provides access to the Suez Canal, through which a sizeable portion of India's trade flows.

India has cultivated close security ties with major GCC countries such as the UAE, Qatar, Oman, and Bahrain. The defense cooperation agreements that India has with these states are similar to the ones it has with the United States, the United Kingdom, France, Germany, Australia, and Japan. India and the UAE have decided to streamline their defense relationship, which has been largely dominated by naval ship visits and training exchange programs. Now, the focus is shifting to possibly joint development and manufacture of sophisticated military hardware. UAE authorities have captured and swiftly extradited to India a number of high-profile terror suspects. Though India and the UAE do have an extradition treaty in place, several deportations have taken place without invoking the treaty, showing a high level of mutual understanding between the two states.[30] Defense cooperation between India and Qatar is also extensive and involves training military personnel, joint exercises, and service-to-service information sharing. Consultations are under way between India and Oman for the sultanate possibly to provide berthing facilities for Indian warships deployed in the region.

Indians are the largest expatriate community in the GCC states, numbering between four and five million. Indian expatriate labor constitutes around 30 percent of the total population of the UAE, and Indians have a significant presence in Bahrain, Oman, and Qatar. India receives remittances worth around US$6 billion annually from its Gulf expatriates. These remittances have contributed significantly to India's economic resurgence, even as there have been growing concerns in recent years about the living and working conditions in the host countries. India is pursuing manpower and labor agreements with the Gulf states to help Indian workers in the region.

The security consequences of a rising Iran are as significant for other Arab Gulf states as they are for Saudi Arabia. Tehran's nuclear drive, its interference in neighboring Iraq, and growing Shia–Sunni sectarian polarization the region has raised anxieties in Arab states about a resurgent Iran, forcing them to reorient their diplomacy accordingly. Reaching out to emerging powers such as India is one way to preserve the balance of power in the region.

New partners in the region: Israel and Iraq

India's efforts to improve its relations in the region are not limited to Iran and the Gulf states. There has been a steady strengthening of its relationship with Israel ever since the two established full diplomatic relations in 1992, despite New Delhi's attempts to keep the flourishing bilateral relationship out of public view. In contrast to the back-channel security ties that existed before the normalization of bilateral relations, India is now more willing than ever to carve out a mutually beneficial bilateral relationship with Israel, including deepening military ties and countering the threat terrorism poses to the two societies. Before 1992, India had made the normalization of relations with Israel contingent upon the resolution of the Palestinian issue. In 1992, India decided to delink the two, making it clear that it was not prepared to make an independent Palestinian state a precondition for improving its relations with Israel. This was in tune with the policy much of the world was already following.

The ballast for Indo-Israeli bilateral ties is provided by the defense cooperation between the two states, with India emerging as Israel's largest arms market, displacing Turkey. Israel's military sales to India in the last five years have topped US$5 billion.[31] Israel has adopted a pragmatic attitude with respect to weapon sales to India, contrary to other developed states which have looked at weapons sales to India from the perspective of the balance of power in South Asia. Israel was willing to continue and even step up its arms sales to India after other major states curbed their technological exports following India's May 1998 nuclear tests. Israel provided India much-needed imagery about Pakistani positions using its Unmanned Aerial Vehicles during the Kargil War with Pakistan in 1999 that was instrumental in turning the war around for India.[32]

Though cooperation in defense and anti-terrorism have driven India and Israel closer, the two states are also making concerted attempts to diversify their relationship. The emergence of India and Israel as industrialized and technologically advanced states makes their cooperation on a range of issues meaningful and mutually beneficial. India's trade with Israel has increased by a factor of six in the last decade, with India becoming Israel's second largest trading partner in Asia in non-military goods and services.

India has also started to engage Iraq seriously. Since the 2003 US invasion of Iraq, New Delhi has been ignoring the country and refused to seriously engage with the democratic process in Baghdad. Even as Iraq needed external support to rebuild its war-ravaged economy, India remained reluctant for fear of getting entangled in Iraq's domestic sectarian turmoil. Though India shares strong cultural and historical ties with Iraq and Indian businesses had a strong presence in the country in the 1990s, New Delhi's recent hands-off approach has made it a marginal player in the country with the clout of China, in particular, rising significantly in recent years. At a time when firms from the West, Turkey, South Korea, and China have sought to win major government contracts in Iraq as Baghdad looks to restore its war-battered infrastructure and dilapidated economy, Indian companies have been noticeably absent.

Recognizing its marginalization, New Delhi has taken steps to regain the initiative. Even with all the problems it faces, Iraq has the potential to emerge as a major factor in shaping the regional balance of power in the Middle East along with Iran, Saudi Arabia, Egypt, and Turkey. Indian External Affairs Minister, Salman Khurshid, became the first to visit Iraq in twenty-three years in June 2013 and underscored India's commitment "to participate in rebuilding the infrastructure in Iraq." He went on to suggest that New Delhi wants "to look beyond all sectors" and that the priority India is giving to Iraq "will become more intense and stronger" in the coming years. Though Iraq remains mired in sectarian and terror violence, Baghdad was keen to attract India with the Iraqi Foreign Minister, Hoshyar Zebari, inviting Indian companies to invest in Iraq, underlining that "there are many places in the country which are peaceful and stable." Iraq is keen to revive bilateral ties with India and is seeking Indian investment to take the relationship beyond that of buyer and seller of oil.

With the world's third largest proven oil reserves, Iraq has replaced Iran as India's second largest crude oil supplier after Saudi Arabia. Iraq is working toward doubling its output of 3.15 million barrels a day of crude by 2020 and is planning to increase its oil exports to Asian economies from the present 50 percent to around 80 percent by 2030. During the 2012–13 fiscal year, Iraq accounted for about 13 percent of India's total crude oil imports.

Then Prime Minister of Iraq Nouri al-Maliki visited India in August 2013 leading a seventeen-member business delegation and seeking investments from the Indian private sector in a variety of fields including energy exploration and production, refineries, fertilizer plants, affordable housing, health, and education. The two also decided to focus on enhancing cooperation in energy security, in particular, through joint efforts to develop capacities to maximize the utilization of energy resources, through joint ventures in oil exploration, petrochemical complexes, and fertilizer plants. Baghdad has expressed interest in investing in the upcoming 15mmt oil refinery at Paradip in India and the two sides have decided to work together to arrive at a mutually beneficial model for such investment. These high-level exchanges indicate that Iraq views India as a serious regional and global interlocutor. This is a time when there is turmoil in West Asia with issues in Syria, Egypt, Turkey, and Palestine all needing regional and global attention. New Delhi and Baghdad are both keen to see stability return to this strategically crucial region.

Conclusion

Despite being the largest democracy in the world, India has largely watched recent events unfold in the Middle East in silence. In many ways, this reticence is understandable; it remains a highly unpredictable situation and New Delhi has been taking its time thinking through the possible implications. Moreover, for New Delhi to comment on events occurring in the region would be hypocritical, given how seriously India takes the principle of non-interference in the internal affairs of other states.

Yet, India claims to be a rising global power. Now in the spotlight, India is finding its actions on important global issues are subject to close and critical scrutiny. India's decision to "sit on the fence" with regard to the churning in the Middle East may perhaps arouse the suspicion that India remains unwilling to contribute to the management of global order. Moreover, the cleavage between India's much-touted democratic credentials at home and its lack of leadership on democracy abroad seems to be widening. The world is taking note, especially as democracy is something Indian leadership often underlines in making a distinction with China's rise.

Developments in the Middle East will have a great bearing on the future of India's ties with the region. Indian policy seems to be favoring the status quo as regional stability is essential for Indian interests in the region. The rivalry between Saudi Arabia and Iran for regional leadership is likely to intensify along sectarian lines in the coming years. Given India's growing stakes in the Gulf, it will be forced to maintain a delicate balance between these two regional rivals. India's cautious response to the Arab Spring and its aftermath is a testament to India's belief that its policy of engaging various stakeholders in the region is the only one that helps New Delhi in preserving and enhancing its interests in the short to medium term.

Notes

1 P.R. Mudiam, *India and the Middle East* (London: British Academic Press, 1994).
2 www.indianexpress.com/news/india-abstains-wary-of-force-unsure-of-whats-on-the-ground/764635/0.
3 www.indianexpress.com/news/india-abstains-on-resolution-authorising-use-of-force-in-libya/764343/.
4 Huma Siddiqui, "India-Libya Trade Better Than Before," *Indian Express*, March 31, 2013.
5 India, Ministry of External Affairs, *Press Release*, at http://meaindia.nic.in/mystart.php?id=530217128.
6 "India Urges Peaceful Resolution to Egyptian Crisis," *Business Standard*, July 4, 2013.
7 "BRICS Summit: Delhi Declaration," Council on Foreign Relations, March 20, 2012, www.cfr.org/brazil/brics-summit-delhi-declaration/p27805.
8 Rama Lakshmi, "In India, Syrian Regime Courts BRIC Countries," *Washington Post*, March 8, 2013.
9 "Joint Statement of the Fifth BRICS Summit in Durban," Council on Foreign Relations, March 27, 2013, www.cfr.org/emerging-markets/joint-statement-fifth-brics-summit-durban-march-2013/p30341.
10 See, for example, "Headlines Over the Horizon," *The Atlantic Monthly*, Vol. 292, No. 1 (July–August 2003), p. 87.

11 Pranab Dhal Samanta, "India Feels the Distance as China Steps into Iran Gap," *Indian Express*, May 10, 2010, www.indianexpress.com/news/india-feels-the-distance-as-china-steps-into-iran-gap/616636/.

12 Amitav Ranjan, "India to Step Up Pressure for Iran Gas Line," *Indian Express*, November 1, 2008, www.indianexpress.com/news/india-to-step-up-pressure-for-iran-gas-line/379947/.

13 "Deal will Trigger New Crises, Says Iran," *The Hindu*, October 6, 2008, www.hindu.com/2008/10/06/stories/2008100655711300.htm.

14 Pranab Dhal Samanta, "Iran Slams India Over J&K Protests, India Hits Back, Issues Demarche," *Indian Express*, October 2, 2010.

15 Sandeep Dikshit, "Unilateral Sanctions on Iran will Hurt India: Nirupama Rao," *The Hindu*, July 6, 2010.

16 "India, Iran Inching Closer on Afghanistan," *Hindustan Times*, August 2, 2010.

17 Anand Giridharadas, "Saudi Arabia Pursues a 'Look-East Policy'," *International Herald Tribune*, January 26, 2006.

18 Divya Pakkiasamy, "Saudi Arabia's Plan for Changing Its Workforce," *Migration Information Service*, November 1, 2004, www.migrationinformation.org/USfocus/display.cfm?ID=264.

19 John Sfakianakis, "Saudi Arabia, India Poised to Play Bigger Role in World Economy," Arab News, February 28, 2010.

20 *Ibid.*

21 The details of the "Delhi Declaration" signed by Saudi Arabia's King and the Indian Prime Minister can be found at http://meaindia.nic.in.

22 Indian Ministry of External Affairs, "Delhi Declaration," Joint Declarations and Statements, January 27, 2006.

23 "Saudi King Took Initiative on Delhi Declaration," *The Tribune* (Chandigarh), January 28, 2006.

24 On the reasons behind Indian–Iranian convergence since the end of the Cold War, see Harsh V. Pant, *Contemporary Debates in Indian Foreign and Security Policy: India Negotiates Its Rise in the International System* (New York: Palgrave Macmillan, 2008), pp. 113–29.

25 Anthony H. Cordesman, *Saudi Arabia Enters the Twenty-First Century: The Political, Foreign Policy, and Energy Dimensions* (London: Praeger, 2003), p. 206.

26 Mahan Abedin, "The Iranian Intelligence Services and the War on Terror," *Terrorism Monitor*, Vol. 2, No. 10 (May 19, 2004), www.jamestown.org/single/?no_cache=1&tx_ttnews[tt_news]=26537.

27 "India, S. Arabia for Peaceful Resolution of Iran's N-Issue," *Press Trust of India*, March 1, 2010.

28 "India- Gulf Trade to Cross $130 bn by 2014," *Indo-Asian News Service*, August 24, 2010.

29 "India–UAE Ties in Trade, Commerce Below Potential," *The Hindu Business Line*, May 29, 2007, www.thehindubusinessline.com/2007/05/29/stories/2007052905101000.htm.

30 Vinay Kumar, "A Milestone in India–UAE Ties," *The Hindu*, December 10, 2002, www.hinduonnet.com/2002/12/10/stories/2002121004251200.htm.
31 Sujan Dutta, "Israel Defense Links Grow," *The Telegraph* (Kolkata), December 22, 2009, www.telegraphindia.com/1091222/jsp/nation/story_11895025.jsp.
32 Vishal Thapar, "How Israel Helped India Win the Kargil War," *CNN-IBN*, July 30, 2007, available at http://ibnlive.in.com/news/how-israel-helped-india-win-the-kargil-war/45840–2.html.

13

India in the Indian Ocean: colliding ambitions with China

It emerged in December 2011 that China will be setting up its first military base abroad in the Seychelles to "seek supplies and recuperate" facilities for its navy. The Indian Ocean island nation defended its decision by suggesting that it had invited China to set up a military base to tackle piracy off its coast and Beijing played it down by underlining that it was standard global practice for naval fleets to resupply at the closest port of a nearby state during long-distance missions.[1] But there was no ambiguity for the rest of the world: Chinese footprint in the Indian Ocean was getting bigger and will continue to expand even further in the future.

The Indian Ocean is increasingly playing an important role in Chinese efforts to establish a position as a leading maritime power in the region. And this is resulting in Sino-Indian competition for influence in the Indian Ocean and beyond. The very steps that China is taking to protect and enhance its interests in the Indian Ocean region are generating apprehensions in Indian strategic circles, thereby engendering a classic security dilemma between the two Asian giants. And it is India's fears and perceptions of China's growing naval prowess in the Indian Ocean that is driving Indian naval posture. This chapter examines this budding maritime rivalry in the Indian Ocean between Asia two rising powers and argues that unless managed carefully, the potential for this maritime rivalry turning serious in the future remains high, especially as Sino-Indian naval competition is likely to intensify with the Indian and Chinese navies operating far from their shores.

The Indian Ocean has long been the hub of great power rivalry and the struggle for its domination has been a perennial feature of global politics. It is third largest of the world's five oceans and straddles Asia in the north, Africa in the west, Indo-china in the east, and Antarctica in the south. Home to four critical access waterways – the Suez Canal, Bab-el Mandeb, Strait of Hormuz, and Strait of Malacca – the Indian Ocean connects the Middle East, Africa, and East Asia with Europe and the Americas. Given its crucial geographical role, major powers have long vied with each other for its control though it was only in the nineteenth century that Great Britain was able to enjoy an overwhelming dominance in the region. With the decline in Britain's relative power and the emergence of two superpowers during the Cold War, the Indian Ocean region became another arena where the United States and the former Soviet Union struggled to expand their power and influence. The United States, however, has remained the most significant player in the region for the last several years.

Given the rise of major economic powers in the Asia-Pacific that rely on energy imports to sustain their economic growth, the Indian Ocean region has assumed a new importance as various powers are once again vying for the control of the waves in this part of the world. It has been rightly observed that "the Indian Ocean would be the world's single most important region in the next 20 years because of the dependence on oil as the primary energy source, the competitive pressures arising from the economic growth of many countries along its rim, and the traditional rivalries that have built volatile relations."[2] Nearly half of the world's seaborne trade is through the Indian Ocean and approximately 20 percent of this trade consists of energy resources. It has also been estimated that around 40 percent of the world's offshore oil production comes from the Indian Ocean, while 65 percent of the world's oil and 35 percent of its gas reserves are found in the littoral states of this ocean.[3] The persistent instability in the Middle East has increased concerns about the security of the regional SLOCs and the rise of Islamist terrorism in the littoral nations has further aggravated global concerns about energy security.

The rest of the world is heavily dependent on oil supplies from the Persian Gulf and so the significance of Indian Ocean SLOCs cannot be overestimated. Unlike the Pacific and Atlantic oceans, almost three-quarters of trade traversing through the Indian Ocean, primarily in the form of oil and gas, belongs to the states external to the region. Free and uninterrupted flow of oil and goods through the Indian Ocean's SLOCs is deemed vital for the global economy and so all major states have a stake in a stable Indian Ocean region. It is for this reason that during the Cold War years when US–Soviet rivalry was at its height, the states bordering the Indian Ocean sought to declare the region as a "zone of peace" to allow for free trade and commerce across the lanes of the Indian Ocean. Today, the reliance is on the United States for the provision of a "collective good": a stable Indian Ocean region.

The Indian Ocean: India's backyard?

As India's global economic and political profile has risen in recent years, it has also, not surprisingly, tried to define its strategic interests in increasingly expansive terms. The Indian Ocean remains a hugely important region for India, the only nation in the world that has an entire ocean named after it. Like other globalizing economies, India's economic growth is heavily reliant on the free flow of goods through the Indian Ocean SLOCs, especially as around 90 percent of India's trade is reliant on merchant shipping. Given

India's growing reliance on imported sources of energy, any disruption in the Indian Ocean can have a potentially catastrophic impact for Indian economic and societal stability. India's EEZ in the Indian Ocean, that according to the Law of the Seas runs 200 nautical miles contiguous to its coastline and its islands, covers around 30 percent of the resource-abundant Indian Ocean region.

Any disruption in shipping across the important trade routes in the Indian Ocean, especially those passing through the "choke-points" in the Strait of Hormuz, the Gulf of Aden, the Suez Canal, and the Strait of Malacca, can lead to serious consequences for not only Indian but global economic prospects. Unhindered trade and shipping traffic flow is a sine qua non for the implementation of India's developmental process. The non-traditional threats in the form of organized crime, piracy, and transnational terrorist networks also make it imperative for India to exert its control in the region.

Indian strategic thinkers have historically viewed the Indian Ocean as India's backyard and so have emphasized the need for India to play a greater role in underwriting its security and stability. Indian strategic elites have often drawn inspiration from a quote attributed to Alfred Mahan: "Whoever controls the Indian Ocean dominates Asia. The ocean is the key to seven seas. In the 21st century, the destiny of the world will be decided on its waters." This quote, though apparently fictitious, has been highly influential in shaping the way Indian naval thinkers have looked at the role of the Indian Ocean for Indian security.[4] While sections of the Indian foreign policy establishment considered India the legatee of the British rule for providing peace and stability in the Indian Ocean, India's neighbors remain concerned about India's "hegemonistic" designs in the region.

Underlining the importance of Indian Ocean for India, K.M. Pannikar, a diplomat-historian, called for the Indian Ocean to remain "truly Indian." He argued that "to other countries the Indian Ocean could only be one of the important oceanic areas, but to India it is a vital sea because its lifelines are concentrated in that area, its freedom is dependent on the freedom of that coastal surface."[5] Pannikar was strongly in favor of Indian dominance of the Indian Ocean region much in the same way as several British and Indian strategists viewed India's predominance of the Indian Ocean as virtually inevitable.[6] It has also been suggested that given the role of "status and symbolism" in Indian strategic thinking, India's purported greatness would be reason enough for Indian admirals to demand a powerful navy.[7]

In view of this intellectual consensus, it is surprising that India's civilian leadership was able to resist naval expansion in the early years after independence. India took its time after independence to accept its role as the pre-eminent maritime power in the Indian Ocean region and for long remained diffident about shouldering the responsibilities that come with such an acknowledgment. The focus remained on Pakistan and China and

the overarching continental mindset continued to dictate the defense priorities of the nation with some complaining that the Indian Navy was being
relegated to the background as the most neglected branch of the armed services.[8] As the great powers got involved in the Indian Ocean during the Cold
War years, India's ability to shape the developments in the region got further
marginalized. India continued to lag behind in its ability to project power
across the Indian Ocean through the early 1990s, primarily due to resource
constraints and a lack of a definable strategy. It was rightly observed that
"if the Indian Navy seriously contemplates power projection missions in the
Indian Ocean, [the then Indian naval fleet] is inadequate ... it has neither
the balance nor the required offensive punch to maintain zones of influence."[9] India, for its part, continued to demand, without much success, that
"extra regional navies" should withdraw from the Indian Ocean, which
met with hostility from the major powers and generated apprehensions in
India's neighborhood that India would like to dominate the strategic landscape of the Indian Ocean. India's larger non-aligned foreign policy posture
also ensured that Indian maritime intentions remained shrouded in mystery
for the rest of the world.

It is only since the late 1990s that India has started to reassert itself in
the Indian Ocean and beyond. This has been driven by various factors –
the high rates of economic growth that India has enjoyed since the early
1990s have allowed the country to invest greater resources into naval
expansion; the growing threat from non-state actors has forced India to
adopt a more proactive naval posture; and, a growing realization that
China is rapidly expanding its influence in the Indian Ocean region, something that many in the Indian strategic community feel would be detri-
mental to Indian interests in the long term. Various terrorist organizations
from Al Qaeda to Jemmah Islamiah use maritime routes around India in
the Indian Ocean region for narcotics and arms trafficking through which
they finance their operations. Indian intelligence agencies have warned
the government that India might face seaborne attacks by terrorist groups
against the nation's oil rigs, involving both production and support platforms, along both the coasts of India.[10] Piracy in various parts of the
Indian Ocean such as the Malacca Straits and Horn of Africa is rampant,
requiring a strong Indian maritime presence. In line with this perception,
the Indian maritime doctrine states: "The Indian maritime vision for the
twenty-first century must look at the arc from the Persian Gulf to the
Straits of Malacca, as a legitimate area of interest."[11] India has a pivotal
position in the Indian Ocean as unlike other nations in the region with
blue-water capabilities, such as Australia and South Africa, India is at
the center and dominates the SLOCs across the ocean in both directions.
There are now signs that India is making a concerted attempt to enhance
its capabilities to back up its aspiration to play an enhanced naval role in
the Indian Ocean.

China's foray in the Indian Ocean

China has emerged as the biggest military spender in the Asia-Pacific since 2006 when it overtook Japan, and now has the fourth largest defense expenditure in the world. The official figures of the Chinese government do not include the cost of new weapon purchases, research, or other big-ticket items for China's highly secretive military. From Washington to Tokyo, from Brussels to Canberra, calls are rising for China to be more open about the intentions behind this dramatic pace of spending increase and scope of its military capabilities. The Chinese Defense White Paper of 2006, its first ever, made it clear that major procurement programs as well as a desire to pursue the Chinese version of "revolution in military affairs" remain at the heart of this massive increase.[12] The Chinese Navy, according to the Defense White Paper of 2006, will be aiming at a "gradual extension of the strategic depth for offshore defensive operations and enhancing its capabilities in integrated maritime operations and nuclear counter-attacks."[13] Chinese President, Xi Jinping, has emerged as a strong supporter of the Chinese naval power, suggesting that the oceans would play an increasingly important role in China's economic development.[14]

China's navy is now considered the third largest in the world behind only the United States and Russia, and superior to the Indian Navy in both qualitative and quantitative terms.[15] With seventy-nine surface ships and fifty-five submarines, the Chinese Navy is now the biggest in Asia. The PLA Navy has traditionally been a coastal force and China has had a continental outlook to security. But with a rise in its economic might since the 1980s, Chinese interests have expanded and have acquired a maritime orientation with an intent to project power into the Indian Ocean. China is investing far greater resources in the modernization of its armed forces in general and its navy in particular than India seems either willing to undertake or capable of sustaining at present. China's increasingly sophisticated submarine fleet could eventually be one of the world's largest and with a rapid accretion in its capabilities, including submarines, ballistic missiles, and GPS-blocking technology, some are suggesting that China will increasingly have the capacity to challenge the United States.[16] In 2012, China commissioned its first aircraft carrier, *Liaoning*, a refurbished vessel purchased from Ukraine in 1998, underscoring a shift away from devoting the bulk of the PLA's modernization drive to the goal of capturing Taiwan.

With a rise in China's economic and political prowess, there has also been a commensurate growth in its profile in the Indian Ocean region. Chinese interests in the region are also expanding and it would like to see a stable Indian Ocean region with its own presence more significant than before. China is acquiring naval facilities along the crucial choke-points in the Indian Ocean not only to serve its economic interests but also to enhance its strategic presence in the region. China realizes that its maritime strength will give it the strategic leverage that it needs to emerge as the regional hegemon and a potential superpower and there is enough evidence to suggest that China is comprehensively building up its maritime power in all dimensions.[17] It is China's growing dependence on maritime space and resources that is reflected in the Chinese aspiration to expand its influence and to ultimately dominate the strategic environment of the Indian Ocean region. China's growing reliance on facilities across the Indian Ocean region is a response to its perceived vulnerability, given the logistical constraints that it faces due to the distance of the Indian Ocean waters from its own area of operation. Yet, China is consolidating power over the South China Sea and the Indian Ocean with an eye on India, something that comes out clearly in a secret memorandum issued by the Director of the General Logistic Department of the PLA: "We can no longer accept the Indian Ocean as only an ocean of the Indians ... We are taking armed conflicts in the region into account."[18] The Chinese military has underscored that India should stop regarding the Indian Ocean as its backyard although it has an important role to play in ensuring peace and stability in the Indian Ocean region.[19]

China has deployed its Jin class submarines at a submarine base near Sanya in the southern tip of Hainan Island in the South China Sea, raising alarm in India as the base is merely 1,200 nautical miles from the Malacca Strait and will be its closest access point to the Indian Ocean. The base also has an underground facility that can hide the movement of submarines, making them difficult to detect.[20] The concentration of strategic naval forces at Sanya will further propel China toward a consolidation of its control over the surrounding Indian Ocean region. The presence of access tunnels at the mouth of the deep water base is particularly troubling for India as it will have strategic implications in the Indian Ocean region, allowing China to interdict shipping at the three crucial choke-points in the Indian Ocean. As the ability of China's navy to project power in the Indian Ocean region grows, India is likely to feel even more vulnerable despite enjoying distinct geographical advantages in the region. China's growing naval presence in and around the Indian Ocean region is troubling for India as it restricts India's freedom to manoeuvre in the region. Of particular note is what has been termed as China's "string of pearls" strategy that has significantly expanded China's strategic depth in India's backyard. China is building strategic relationships and setting up bases along the sea lanes from the Middle East to the South China Sea not simply to protect China's growing energy interests but also to enhance its broader strategic objectives.[21]

This "string of pearls" strategy of bases and diplomatic ties include the Gwadar port in Pakistan, naval bases in Burma, electronic intelligence-gathering facilities on islands in the Bay of Bengal, funding construction of a canal across the Kra Isthmus in Thailand, a military agreement with Cambodia and building up of forces in the South China Sea.[22] Some of these claims are exaggerated as has been the case with the Chinese naval presence in Burma. The Indian government, for example, had to concede in 2005 that such reports of China turning the Coco Islands in Burma into a naval base were incorrect and that there were indeed no naval bases in Burma.[23] Yet the Chinese thrust into the Indian Ocean is gradually becoming more pronounced than before. The Chinese may not have a naval base in Burma but they are involved in the upgradation of infrastructure in the Coco Islands and may be providing some limited technical assistance to Burma. Given that almost 80 percent of China's oil passes through the Strait of Malacca, it is reluctant to rely on US naval power for unhindered access to energy and so has decided to build up its naval power at "choke-points" along the sea routes from the Persian Gulf to the South China Sea. China is also courting other states in South Asia by building container ports in Bangladesh at Chittagong and in Sri Lanka at Hambantota. Consolidating its access to the Indian Ocean, China has signed an agreement with Sri Lanka to finance the development of the Hambantota Development Zone which includes a container port, a bunker system, and an oil refinery. It is possible that the construction of these ports and facilities around India's periphery by China can be explained away on purely economic and commercial grounds but for India this looks like a policy of containment by other means.

China's diplomatic and military efforts in the Indian Ocean seem to exhibit a desire to project power vis-à-vis competing powers in the region such as the United States and India. China's presence in the Bay of Bengal via roads and ports in Burma and in the Arabian Sea via the Chinese built port of Gwadar in Pakistan has been a cause of concern for India. With access to crucial port facilities in Egypt, Iran, and Pakistan, China is well-poised to secure its interests in the region. China's involvement in the construction of the deep-sea port of Gwadar has attracted a lot of attention due to its strategic location, about 70 kilometers from the Iranian border and 400 kilometers east of the Strait of Hormuz, a major oil supply route. It has been suggested that it will provide China with a "listening post" from where it can "monitor US naval activity in the Persian Gulf, Indian activity in the Arabian Sea, and future US-Indian maritime cooperation in the Indian Ocean."[24] Though Pakistan's naval capabilities do not, on their own, pose any challenge to India, the combination of Chinese and Pakistani naval forces can indeed be formidable for India to counter. In recent years, Chinese submarines have been regularly docking in various South Asian states, including Pakistan and Sri Lanka, much to India's consternation.

It has been suggested that the Chinese government appears "to have a very clear vision of the future importance of the sea and a sense of the strategic leadership needed to develop maritime interest."[25] This is reflected in the attempts that China has made in recent years to build up all aspects of its maritime economy and to create one of the world's largest merchant fleets with a port, transport, and ship-building infrastructure to match. In this respect, the Indian Ocean has an important role to play in the Chinese efforts toward establishing its predominance as the main maritime power in the region.

Yet, the notion that China aspires to naval domination of the Indian Ocean remains a bit far-fetched. China would certainly like to play a greater role in the region, protect and advance its interests, especially Chinese commerce, as well as counter India. But given the immense geographical advantages that Indian enjoys in the Indian Ocean, China will have great difficulty in exerting as much sway as easily in the Indian Ocean as India possibly can. But all the steps that China is taking to protect and enhance its interests in the Indian Ocean region are generating apprehensions in Indian strategic circles about her real intentions, thereby engendering a classic security dilemma between the two Asian giants. And it is India's fears and perceptions of the growing naval prowess of China in the Indian Ocean that is driving Indian naval posture.

India responds to the Chinese challenge

The augmentation of China's power projection capabilities in the Indian Ocean has alarmed India and has galvanized it into taking ameliorative measures. Underscoring India's discomfort with China's "string of pearls" strategy, a former Indian naval chief had argued that "each pearl in the string is a link in a chain of the Chinese maritime presence" and had expressed concern that naval forces operating out of ports established by the Chinese could "take control over the world energy jugular."[26] India views Chinese naval strategy as expansionist and intent on encircling India strategically. The current Indian naval strategy is being driven by the idea "that the vast Indian Ocean is its mare nostrum ... that the entire triangle of the Indian Ocean is their nation's rightful and exclusive sphere of interest."[27] Just as the PLA Navy seems to be concentrating on anti-access warfare so as to prevent the US Navy from entering into a cross-Straits conflict, the Indian Navy is also working toward acquiring the ability to deny China access through the Indian Ocean.[28] While the Indian Maritime Doctrine of 2004 underlined "attempts by China to strategically encircle India," the Indian Maritime Strategy released three years later emphasized attempts by the Chinese Navy to emerge as a blue-water force by pursuing an ambitious modernization program, "along with attempts to gain a strategic toe-hold in the Indian Ocean Rim."[29]

India's projection of naval power into the Indian Ocean and beyond is an outcome of India's increasingly outward-looking foreign policy posture in line with its growing economic prowess. Through joint exercises, port visits, and disaster relief missions, the Indian Navy has dramatically raised its profile in the Indian Ocean region in the last few years. India's rapid response to the December 2004 tsunami was the largest ever relief mobilization by its naval forces and underlined India's growing role in the Indian Ocean as well as its ability to be a net provider of security in the region. India was one of the few nations affected by the tragedy that was able to respond relatively effectively and also lend a helping hand to neighboring countries by sending its naval ships and personnel. The Indian Navy also demonstrated its rapid response capability when it evacuated a large number of Indians and other nationals from Lebanon during the 2006 Israel–Lebanon conflict.[30]

Diplomatic initiatives

India is using its naval forces to advance its diplomatic initiatives overseas and in particular toward shaping the strategic environment in and around the Indian Ocean. Indian interests converge with those of the United States in the Indian Ocean region and it is trying to use the present upswing in US–India ties to create a more favorable strategic environment for itself in the region despite its historical sensitivities to the presence of US forces in the Indian Ocean. The United States has also recognized the importance of India's role in the region, as was evident in Colin Powell's contention that it was important for the United States to support India's role in maintaining peace and stability in the Indian Ocean and its vast periphery.[31] The US and Indian navies have stepped up their joint exercises and the United States has sold India its warship, the USS *Trenton* (renamed INS *Jalashwa*), the first of its class to be inducted into the Indian Navy and marking a milestone in the US–India bilateral ties. The United States would like India to join its Container Security Initiative (CSI) and Proliferation Security Initiative (PSI) but India remains reluctant. PSI is viewed as a US-led initiative outside the United Nations mandate while the CSI would result in the presence of US inspectors in Indian ports, making it politically radioactive. However, India has indicated that it would be willing to join the US-proposed 1,000-ship navy effort to combat illegal activities on the high seas, given the informal nature of the arrangement.[32] India is seen a balancer in the Asia-Pacific where the United States' influence has waned relatively as China's has risen. India's ties with Japan have also assumed a new dynamic with some even mooting a "concert of democracies" proposal involving the democratic states of the Asia-Pacific working toward their common goals of a stable Asia-Pacific region.[33] While such a proposal has little chance of evolving into anything concrete in the near term, especially given China's sensitivities, India's decision to develop natural gas with Japan in the Andaman Sea and recent military exercises involving the United States, Japan, India, and Australia does give a sense of India's emerging priorities.[34] India and Australia have also agreed to work together toward providing maritime security in the Asia-Pacific region. India has been watching China's aggressive posturing in the South and East China Seas with concern. India has no territorial claims there per se, but the South China Sea could be viewed "as the antechamber of the Indian Ocean," given the flow of maritime traffic. New Delhi is nervous about Beijing's threat to the freedom of navigation, leading it to strengthen its defense ties with the island nations in the Indian Ocean such as the Maldives, Mauritius, and the Seychelles.

India's decision to establish its Far Eastern Command in the Andaman and Nicobar Islands in the Bay of Bengal is aimed at countering China's growing presence in the region by complicating China's access to the region through the Strait of Malacca, the main bottleneck of oil transit to China. India has launched Project Seabird, consisting of India's third operational naval base in Karwar on the nation's western seaboard, an air force station, a naval armament depot, and missile silos, aimed at securing the nation's maritime routes in the Arabian Sea.[35] India is also set to establish a monitoring station in Madagascar, its first in another country, as it is deemed vital to guard against the terrorist threat emanating from East Africa as well as to keep an eye on China's plan in the region. India also has its eyes on Mauritius for developing a monitoring facility at an atoll and has strengthened its naval contacts with Mozambique and the Seychelles. India responded to then Chinese President Hu Jintao's offer of military assistance to the Seychelles by donating one of its patrol aircrafts to the Seychelles Navy. India's support in the building of Chahbahar port in Iran as well as the road connecting it to Afghanistan is an answer to the Chinese-funded Gwadar port in Pakistan.

Competition between China and India is also increasing for influence in Burma as the Andaman Sea off Burma's coast is viewed as a crucial energy lifeline for China while India also needs Burma for meeting its energy requirements. India will be rebuilding Burma's western Sittwe port and is one of the main suppliers of military hardware to the ruling junta. India is looking to improve connectivity between Indian ports on the eastern seaboard and Sittwe port in Burma in an effort to provide an alternative route for transport of goods to the northeastern regions of the country as well as providing connectivity between India and Burma. China's growing penetration of Burma is one of the main reasons India is reluctant to cease its economic and military engagement with the Burmese junta despite attracting widespread criticism from both outside and within India.

India's "Look East" policy, originally aimed at strengthening economic ties with India's Southeast Asian neighborhood, has now led to naval exercises with Singapore, Thailand, and Indonesia. The ASEAN member states have joined the Indian Navy in policing the Indian Ocean region to check piracy, trafficking, and other threats to sea lanes. India has also accelerated its naval engagement with a number of Persian Gulf states, making port calls and conducting exercises with the navies of Kuwait, Oman, Bahrain, Saudi Arabia, Qatar, United Arab Emirates, and Djibouti as well as engaging with the navies of other major powers in the region such as the United States, the United Kingdom, and France. It has also been suggested that to more effectively counter Chinese presence in the Indian Ocean and to protect its trade routes, India will have to seek access to the Vietnamese, Taiwanese, and Japanese ports for the forward deployment of its naval assets.[36] India is already emerging as an exclusive "defense service provider" for smaller states with growing economies that seek to strengthen their military capabilities in Southeast Asia and West Asia, such as Vietnam, Indonesia, Malaysia, Singapore, Qatar, and Oman, providing it access to ports along the Arabian coast, Indian Ocean, and South China Sea.[37]

Naval platforms and doctrine

The Indian Navy is aiming for a total fleet of 140–145 vessels over the next decade, built around two carrier battle groups: *Admiral Gorshkov*, which was commissioned into the Indian Navy as INS *Vikramaditya* in November 2013 and the indigenous carrier, INS *Vikrant*, likely to be completed by 2018. The Indian government has given approval for the eventual construction of its largest-ever warship, the 65,000-ton aircraft carrier, INS *Vishal*. India's ambition to equip its navy with two or more aircraft carriers over the next decade as well as its decision to launch its first indigenous nuclear submarine is seen as crucial for power projection and to achieve a semblance of strategic autonomy.

India's emerging capability to put a carrier task force as far as the South China Sea and the Persian Gulf has given boost to Indian Navy's blue-water aspirations and India hopes to induct a third aircraft carrier by 2018, ensuring that the Indian Navy has two operational carriers at any given point.[38] The deployment of the Jin class submarine at Hainan by China also pushed India to speed up its indigenous nuclear submarine project that has been in the making for more than a decade with the Indian Navy, rather ambitiously, aiming at the induction of five indigenous ATV (Advanced Technology Vehicle) nuclear submarines. A submarine-based nuclear arsenal is considered critical by Indian strategists to retain a second-strike capability. Indian naval planners have long argued that if it is to maintain continuous operational readiness in the Indian Ocean, protect sea lanes in the Gulf and monitor Chinese activities in the Bay of Bengal, it needs at least three carriers and five nuclear submarines.

Both China and India would most certainly like to acquire the potential to project power and operate independently far from their shores. Yet, it is China that as of now seems more willing to actually commit to the expense of building up its fleet with a clear strategic agenda as to how its wants to utilize its naval assets. The ability of Indian policy-makers to think strategically on national security and defense issues has been questionable at best. Ad hoc decision-making has been the norm leading to a situation where long-time observers of India argue that it's likely that "India will be among the medium powers … a country of great economic capabilities but limited cultural and military influence."[39] With policy-makers in New Delhi far removed from the nation's sea frontiers, there is even less understanding of maritime issues. This political apathy has led to the three services operating in a strategic void. The Indian Navy's attempt to come up with its own strategy and doctrine, though welcome in many respects, has little meaning in the absence of a national security strategy from the Indian government.

Despite the fact that some in India would like their nation to achieve preponderance in the Indian Ocean region, it remains an unrealistic aspiration as other major powers have significant stakes in the region and so will continue to operate and shape its strategic environment. A rising India is beginning to discover that major global powers have stakes in far-flung corners of the world and this realization has allowed India to shun its fundamentally flawed original argument about the need for "extra-regional navies" to withdraw from the Indian Ocean region. India's bilateral and multilateral naval exercises with major naval powers have helped in reducing the misperceptions about India's maritime intentions and have brought the Indian Navy's capacity to contribute to peace and stability in the Indian Ocean littoral to the forefront. India, therefore, will look toward cooperating with other major powers in the region to secure common interests that include safeguarding the SLOCs, energy security, and countering extremist and terrorist groups.

However, Asia is witnessing the rise of two giants, China and India, simultaneously and this will cause some inevitable complications. It has been suggested that much like the Japanese–American rivalry in the Pacific during the first half of the twentieth century over overlapping SLOCs, a similar degree of mutual suspicion and insecurity haunts Sino-Indian relations in the Indian Ocean.[40] Tensions are inherent in such an evolving strategic relationship as was underlined in an incident in January 2009 when an Indian Kilo class submarine and Chinese warships, on their way to the Gulf of Aden to patrol the pirate-infested waters, reportedly engaged in rounds of maneuvring as they tried to test for weaknesses in each other's sonar system. The Chinese media reported that its warships forced the Indian submarine to the surface, which was strongly denied by the Indian Navy.[41] Unless managed carefully, the potential for such incidents turning serious in the future remains high, especially as the Sino-Indian naval competition is likely to intensify with the Indian and Chinese navies operating far from their shores. While the costs of not cooperating will be too high for both China and India, the struggle for power and influence between the Asian giants will continue to shape India's naval posture as well as the strategic environment of the Indian Ocean region in the coming years.

Notes

1 "China to Open its First Military Base Abroad in Indian Ocean," *Times of India*, December 12, 2011.

2 John F. Morton, "US Contribution to the Security of the Indian Ocean," *Asian Defence Journal*, Vol. 7 (1993), p. 17.

3 P.K. Das, "Maritime Dimensions of India's Security," *Indian Defence Review*, Vol. 18, No. 2 (2005), pp. 43–7.

4 Rahul Roy-Chaudhury, *Sea Power and India's Security* (London: Brassey's, 1995), p. 199.

5 K.M. Pannikar, *India and the Indian Ocean: An Essay in the Influence of Sea Power on Indian History* (London: George Allen & Unwin, 1945), p. 45.

6 David Scott, "India's 'Grand Strategy' for the Indian Ocean: Mahanian Visions," *Asia-Pacific Review*, Vol. 13, No. 2 (2006), pp. 98–101.

7 George Tanham, *Securing India* (New Delhi: Manohar Publishers, 1996), p. 59.

8 N. Palmer, "South Asia and the Indian Ocean," in A. Cottrell and R. Burrell (eds.), *The Indian Ocean: Its Political, Economic, and Military Importance* (New York: Praeger, 1972), p. 237.

9 Ashley Tellis, "Demanding Tasks for the Indian Navy," *Asian Survey*, Vol. 25, No. 12 (December 1985), p. 1204.

10 Arun Kumar Singh, "The Next Terror Attack Could Be from the Sea," *Asian Age*, May 18, 2008.

11 "Indian Maritime Doctrine," Integrated Headquarters, Ministry of Defence (Navy), 2009, p. 56.

12 China's Defense White Paper, 2006 is available at www.china.org.cn/english/features/book/194421.htm.

13 *Ibid.*

14 David Lague, "The Chinese Navy 'Dismembers' Japan," Reuters, December 27, 2013.

15 Anthony H. Cordesman and Martin Kleiber, *The Asian Conventional Military Balance in 2006* (The Centre for Strategic and International Studies, June 2006), p. 32.

16 Robert D. Kaplan, "Lost at Sea," *New York Times*, September 21, 2007.

17 Thomas Kane, *Chinese Grand Strategy and Maritime Power* (London: Frank Cass, 2002), p. 139.

18 Youssef Bodansky, "The PRC Surge for the Strait of Malacca and Spratly Confronts India and the US," *Defense and Foreign Affairs Strategic Policy* (Washington, DC, September 30, 1995), pp. 6–13.

19 Saibal Dasgupta, "China Says India Must Not Think of Indian Ocean as its Backyard," *Times of India*, July 1, 2015.

20 Manu Pubby, "China's New N-Submarine Base Sets Off Alarm Bells," *Indian Express*, May 3, 2008.

21 Bill Gertz, "China Builds Up Strategic Sea Lanes," *Washington Times*, January 18, 2005.

22 For a detailed explication of the security ramifications of the Chinese "string of pearls" strategy, see Gurpreet Khurana, "China's 'String of Pearls' in the Indian Ocean and Its Security Implications," *Strategic Analysis*, Vol. 32, No. 1 (January 2008), pp. 1–22.

23 For a nuanced analysis of this, see Andrew Selth, "Chinese Military Bases in Burma: The Explosion of a Myth," *Griffith Asia Institute Regional Outlook Paper*, No. 10 (2007).

24 Ziad Haider, "Oil Fuels Beijing's New Power Game," *Yale Global Online*, available at http://yaleglobal.yale.edu/display.article?id=5411.

25 Geoffrey Till, *Seapower: A Guide for the Twenty-First Century* (London: Frank Cass, 2004), p. 102.

26 Quoted in Gavin Rabinowitz, "India, China Jostle for Influence in Indian Ocean," The Associated Press, June 7, 2008.

27 E. Margolis, "India Rules the Waves," *Proceedings*, US Naval Institute, Vol. 131, No. 3 (March 2005), p. 70.

28 Sam J. Tangredi, "The Future of Maritime Power," in Andrew T.H. Tan (ed.), *The Politics of Maritime Power: A Survey* (London: Routledge, 2007), pp. 143–4.

29 "Freedom to Use the Seas: India's Maritime Military Strategy," Integrated Headquarters, Ministry of Defence (Navy) (2007), p. 41.

30 The details of this Operation can be found at http://pib.nic.in/release/release.asp?relid=20224.

31 Colin Powell, "US Looks to its Allies for Stability in Asia and the Pacific," *International Herald Tribune*, January 27, 2001.

32 Sandeep Dikshit, "Join Global Policing of Sea Lanes, US asks India," *The Hindu*, April 19, 2007.

33 On India–Japan maritime cooperation, see Gurpreet Khurana, "Security of Sea-Lanes: Prospects for India-Japan Cooperation," *Strategic Analysis*, Vol. 31, No. 1 (January 2007), pp. 139–50.

34 On India's strategic priorities in the Asia-Pacific, see Harsh V. Pant, "India in the Asia-Pacific: Rising Ambitions with an Eye on China," *Asia-Pacific Review*, Vol. 14, No. 1 (May 2007), pp. 54–71.

35 Yevgeny Bendersky and Federico Bordonaro, "India's Project Seabird and the Indian Ocean's Balance of Power," *Power and Interest News Report*, July 20, 2005.

36 Mohan Malik, "Chinese Strategy of Containing India," *Power and Interest News Report*, February 6, 2006.

37 Pranab Dhal Samanta, "Start Getting Used to DSP: Defence Services Provider," *Indian Express*, January 1, 2008.

38 Manu Pubby, "3rd Aircraft Carrier to be Inducted by 2017: Antony," *Indian Express*, May 17, 2007.

39 See Stephen Cohen's interview with Pragati, available at http://pragati.nationalinterest.in/wp-content/uploads/2008/06/pragati-issue15-jun2008-communityed.pdf.

40 John W. Garver, *Protracted Contest: Sino-Indian Rivalry in the 20th Century* (Seattle: University of Washington Press, 1989), p. 285.

41 Manu Pubby, "Indian Submarine, Chinese Warship Test Each Other in Pirate Waters," *Indian Express*, February 5, 2009.

Snapshot 4: India and Latin America

India's relations with South America are spread across strategic, economic, and cultural issues. For India, it is the world's "emerging growth pole." With a combined GDP of US$4.9 trillion and FDI inflow of US$179 billion, South America provides India unique economic opportunities. In fact, the importance of South America in Indian diplomacy is established by the fact that the Ministry of External Affairs holds Foreign Office Consultations with almost all South American countries and these negotiations have been firmly institutionalized. India's relations with South American countries are, therefore, marked by "enhanced levels of landmark high level visits, conclusions of bilateral agreements, developmental projects and cultural events" which have helped in "further strengthening relations between India and the region." 2014 was a particularly eventful year for Indian diplomacy in South America. Not only did India's newly elected Prime Minister visit the continent but also held an interactive session with the leaders of South America in Brazil in July 2014 on the sidelines of the BRICS summit. This was the first instance where an Indian prime minister met almost a dozen leaders of South American countries at one place.

Though India has had cordial diplomatic relations with almost all Latin American states, some of these partnerships have attained important strategic value for Indian foreign policy. One of the most important bilateral relationships is with Brazil. India and Brazil share strong convergence in the current state of global politics: both are rising powers looking forward to assume leadership roles in their respective regions; both aspire for high level of economic growth while struggling to bring a huge swathe of their populations out of poverty, both are committed to multilateralism in formulating strategies to confront global challenges evident in their membership of forums such as BRICS, IBSA, and G-20 and, lastly, both wish to have a bigger voice on issues of global governance including permanent membership in the UNSC.

With Prime Minister Modi's visit to Brasilia in July 2014, this "multifaceted relationship" has been further intensified. Brazil and India's commitment to multilateralism was bolstered by the final agreement on the BRICS Bank. On the other hand, bilateral meetings with President Dilma Roussef resulted in three important agreements including those of "Cooperation in the Field of Environment, Space for implementing arrangement establishing cooperation in augmentation of a Brazilian earth station for receiving and processing data from Indian Remote Sensing (IRS) satellites and Establishment of a consultation mechanism on mobility and consular issues." Economic cooperation between the two countries has been steadily rising, with bilateral trade amounting to a total of US$9.3 billion. If in 2013, Brazil was India's twelfth largest trading partner, 2014 saw it move up to eighth position. The trade surplus, though a minuscule US$1.7 billion, is in India's favor.

The current Argentinian government under President Christina Fernandez Kirchner also treats the relationship with India as "strategic" in nature. For India, Argentinian support in the WTO negotiations on agriculture has been crucial and both states have come to similar understandings on issues concerning public stockholding, food procurement and distribution. In 2014, the two countries were able to reach two major breakthroughs which would provide a serious boost to bilateral trade and economic relations. Through a rare presidential decree, India was included in Argentina's pharmaceutical Annex II of countries by which imports of finished formulations of pharmaceuticals are allowed in September 2014. Second, exports of apples, pears, and fruits from Argentina to India are now permitted following the phytosanitary negotiations in November 2014.

India's relations with Guyana "continue to be warm and friendly." President Donald Ramotar and the Indian Prime Minister had a bilateral meeting in Brasilia at the sidelines of the BRICS summit. India has now agreed to provide Guyana with a line of credit amounting to US$4 million for development of irrigation facilities and of US$19 million for the setting up of a super specialty hospital in Guyana. Later in the year, the President of Guyana visited India on an official visit where he was also the Chief Guest of the Pravasi Bhartiya Diwas celebrations.

India's relations with Chile have also continued to prosper. The sixth round of Foreign Office Consultations between India and Chile were held in New Delhi in October 2014. An Indian goodwill parliamentary delegation visited Chile in November 2014. The bilateral trade between the two countries has now reached a figure of US$1.9 billion. The fifth round of Foreign Office Consultations with Colombia were held in Bogota in November 2014. During these consultations, an MoU on sports was signed. The double taxation avoidance agreement between the two countries also came into force in July 2014 after ratification by the Colombian government.

These bilateral relationships and dialogues notwithstanding, India is equally keen to the engage the region as a whole. In 2012, New Delhi had initiated its maiden dialogue with the Community of Latin American and Caribbean Countries (CELAC). This initiative has now been gaining momentum and, in 2014, the Indian External Affairs Minister met the "CELAC quartet" comprising of foreign ministers of Costa Rica, Ecuador, Antigua and Barbuda, and Cuba at the sidelines of the UN General Assembly. This new initiative could possibly result in an India–CELAC dialogue forum replicating the success of the India–Africa Forum Summits that began in 2008. This urge to engage the region as a whole can also be gleaned from the ongoing negotiations to institutionalize cooperation agreements with regional organizations such as Mercosur (comprising of Argentina, Brazil, Paraguay, Uruguay, and Venezuela) and the Andean community (comprising Bolivia, Colombia, Ecuador, and Peru).

Despite these developments, India has a long way to go before it can match up to the profile of other extra-regional powers in South America.

PART IV

India and the global order

14

India as a regional security provider: from activism to forced diffidence

India's economic rise and concomitant expansion of its military capabilities has engendered calls for New Delhi to assume greater responsibility in the management of regional security, especially in its immediate vicinity. Indian policy-makers have asserted that India is willing to take on this role. The Indian Prime Minister, for example, has asserted that India is all "set to emerge as a net provider of regional security."[1] The Indian Defense Minister too has underlined that the Indian Navy has been "mandated to be a net security provider in the Indian Ocean region."[2] The rest of the world has also taken note. The 2014 US Quadrennial Defence Review underlines that as India's "military capabilities grow, India will contribute to Asia as a net provider of security in the Indian Ocean and beyond."[3]

But while India's growing role as a security provider in East and Southeast Asia as well as in the larger Indian Ocean region is garnering a lot of attention, it is in India's immediate neighborhood that New Delhi finds itself constrained to an unprecedented degree. This chapter examines India's role as a regional security provider by looking into four categories of security governance (assurance, prevention, protection, and compellence). It argues that India's role as a regional security provider will remain circumscribed by the peculiar regional constraints India faces.

Threats and security policy

The rapidly evolving security environment facing India continues to pose significant challenges to the nation's policy-makers. A combination of internal and external as well as state and non-state based threats have emerged that have complicated Indian security.[4] Internally, Indian security is challenged by a plethora of insurgencies which are a product of a range of factors including a desire for greater autonomy and resentment over inequality and injustice. Externally, India's immediate neighborhood continues to be the theater of the most serious challenges.

Scholars of Indian security have for the most part focused on India's external threats, especially from China and Pakistan. A rapidly rising China may pose the greatest military threat to India if relations with it do not continue to improve and if, in the long run, the two countries cannot come to an agreement on the border, on the future of Tibet, and the sharing of river waters. In addition, as their economies grow, the two Asian giants could find themselves in competition over international status and over key resources including food and energy.[5] With Pakistan, India has already fought four wars (1948, 1965, 1971, 1999) and has been involved in a series of crises (1986–87, 1990, 2001–02, 2008) under the shadow of nuclear weapons. The quarrel over Kashmir remains live, the two countries are increasingly worried about the sharing of river waters, there are unresolved conflicts over Siachen, Sir Creek, and India's water projects on the Indus river, and Pakistan continues to be a haven for terrorists who want to attack India.[6]

The other significant challenge externally is the turmoil around India's periphery. Instabilities within Afghanistan, Pakistan, Nepal, Bangladesh, Burma, and Sri Lanka impinge on India's security. India's strategic community recognizes that India must engage its immediate neighborhood more meaningfully and become a net provider of security. How this is to be done, on the other hand, is less clear. Over the past two decades, as India's economy has grown and as the country has invigorated its relations with the United States, Southeast and East Asia, Africa, and even Latin America, it has neglected South Asia – a neglect that could come back to haunt it.

However, the most vital threats to Indian unity, stability, and well-being are internal. Internally, the Indian state is witnessing a gradual collapse in its authority and control. New Delhi has to deal with at least three challenges. The first is right-wing Islamic and now Hindu terrorism. The second is left-wing Maoist revolutionary violence in central and eastern India, especially in the states of Andhra Pradesh, Chattisgarh, Jharkhand, Madhya Pradesh, Orissa, and West Bengal. The third is separatism in India's borderlands. While Sikh separatism in the Punjab was stamped out by the mid-1990s, Kashmir and various states in northeastern India continue to be sites of separatist violence led by well-armed and elusive insurgent groups.

India has been a target for Islamist extremism for the past decade, with some estimates suggesting that at the height of insurgent activity in Iraq from 2006 to 2008, India was second only to that unhappy country in the number of lives lost to terrorism.[7] In the initial years after the events of 9/11, the Indian government and the Indian media had claimed that no Indians were linked to Al Qaeda or to any other Islamic groups plotting terror. This myth was soon exposed with the revelation that every major Islamist urban terror cell in India since 1993 has had a preponderance of Indian nationals. India is clearly both a target and a recruitment base for organizations like Al Qaeda and the Islamic State.

Much like Al Qaeda, the most prominent terrorist group in India today, the Indian Mujahideen, is a loose coalition of jihadists bound together by ideological affiliations and personal linkages, with its infrastructure and top leadership scattered across India. Indian security forces are increasingly focused on terrorists operating in the major cities. India's fight against religious extremists has also become considerably complicated by the rise of shadowy right-wing Hindu terrorist groups. The threat of the Islamic State is also rearing its head though New Delhi claims that fewer than 20 Indians have joined Islamic State, some from overseas, while only 30 have been arrested trying to get abroad. As Islamic State marched through Iraq in 2014, it published recruiting materials in Hindi, Urdu, Tamil and other languages spoken in India.[8]

The Maoist insurgency too has spread from a marginal, containable threat to one that has been identified by the former Prime Minister Manmohan Singh as the "greatest internal security threat" facing the nation.[9] The Maoists – aka Naxalites – have taken the fight to the vast hinterland of impoverished villages in central and eastern India. The Indian Home Ministry lists more than 150 districts as being "Naxalite-affected" and the combined force of the Maoist insurgents has been estimated as somewhere between 10,000 and 20,000 armed fighters plus at least 50,000 active supporters. The Indian government has made some significant gains in the military fight against the Maoists but is still struggling to come up with a comprehensive response.

The third great internal challenge is separatism, and here the insurgency in Kashmir still stands as the biggest threat to Indian unity. The Kashmir problem, from the point of view of India's security managers, has risen and fallen. But the ground situation in Kashmir keeps the Indian government perpetually on guard as no Indian government is in a position to allow Kashmir's secession from India for fear of triggering further separatism in a multiethnic, multilingual nation and for fear that Hindu–Muslim relations in the rest of India would be dealt a body blow. Indeed, Indian democracy, beset as it is with various ills and weaknesses, could hardly survive the conflagration that might result from Kashmir's secession. The situation in Kashmir therefore continues to be an uneasy stalemate.

The problems of India's northeast also continue to be stalemated. Insurgencies and violence continue to disrupt daily life and governance, particularly in Assam, Manipur, and Nagaland in spite of both counter-insurgency operations and negotiations. As in Kashmir, alienation from the rest of India culturally, a feeling of neglect economically, political resentment, malgovernance at various levels, sub-ethnic conflict within states (with local majorities and minorities in contention), and of course the collateral and sometime direct violence associated with the military's counter-insurgency operations, all continue to bedevil the northeastern states. Insurgency is helped by administration that does not penetrate the countryside, by terrain, by easy access to small arms, and by refuge in neighboring countries.

The continuing turmoil in Kashmir and the northeast underscore the fragility of India. The Indian media and elite prefer to focus on India's rise, ignoring the parlous state of the domestic realm given the growing threat of Islamist (and now also Hindu) extremism, Maoism, and separatist insurgency. So overall, the security challenges that India faces are growing increasingly complex at a time when India's material capabilities are certainly at an all-time high.

India's sources of power

India's economy is one of the fastest growing in the world; it is a NWS, a status that is being grudgingly accepted by the world; its armed forces are highly professional, on the way toward rapid modernization; and its vibrant democratic institutions, with the world's second largest Muslim population, are attracting global attention at a time when democracy promotion is being viewed as a remedy for much of what is wrong with a large part of the globe. However, the most significant attribute of today's India is an attempt to carve out a foreign policy that is much more confident of Indian's rising stature in the international system.

While some were proclaiming the end of history with the fall of the Berlin Wall, in many ways it was the beginning of history for Indian foreign policy, free as it was from the structural constraints of a bipolar world order. It lost its political, diplomatic, and military ally with the demise of the Soviet Union and its economy was on the threshold of bankruptcy. There was domestic political uncertainty with weak governments unable to last for a full five-year term as a plethora of internal security challenges were becoming more prominent. The ignominy of having to physically lift bullion to obtain credit pushed India against the ropes and the national psyche was at its most vulnerable. It was against this background that the minority government of the late P.V. Narasimha Rao had to formulate its economic and foreign policy to preserve Indian interests in a radically new global environment. And slowly, but surely, the process began that continues to unfold as India has tried to redefine its place in the international system in consonance with its existing and potential power capabilities.

Both India and the international system are undergoing profound changes, complicating the interplay of the two. With India's rise, there are new demands for it to play a larger role in regional and global governance. While traditionally India always tried to be cautious in carving out a role for itself on issues of global governance, on regional security issues India has, more often than not, been an assertive player.

Security governance policies

Assurance policies

The non-intervention principle has always been one of the main official strands of Indian foreign policy. Historically, even as it berated the West for interfering in what it perceived to be internal matters of other sovereign states, New Delhi has never been shy of intervening in what it considered its own "sphere of influence." In justifying the use of force to evict Portugal from Goa in 1961, India's first Prime Minister Jawaharlal Nehru underlined that "any attempt by a foreign power to interfere in any way with India is a thing which India cannot tolerate, and which, subject to her strength, she will oppose."[10] It has been suggested that though the Indian version of the Monroe Doctrine, involving spheres of influence, has not been fully successful in the past, "it has been an article of faith for many in the Indian strategic community."[11]

Indian policy-makers have often suggested that New Delhi has a special responsibility to maintain peace and order in the subcontinent. This, not surprisingly, shaped the perception of India's immediate neighbors in South Asia about India's commitment to the principle of non-intervention as most of them have found themselves at the receiving end of Indian interventions. Two most notable examples include sending troops into East Pakistan to liberate Bangladesh in 1971 and keeping peace in Sri Lanka in 1987.

As India's economic resources have increased since the early 1990s, it has tried to play a larger role in foreign economic reconstruction. The most significant of these regional endeavors is India's economic outreach to Afghanistan.[12] India launched an extensive assistance program in Afghanistan immediately after the fall of the Taliban regime in 2001 and pledged US$750 million toward reconstruction efforts, most of which was unconditional. Out of this more than US$450 million has already been utilized and the projects range from humanitarian and infrastructure to health and rural development, training of diplomats and bureaucrats. India is today the fifth largest provider of development assistance to Afghanistan and Afghanistan has been the second largest recipient of Indian development assistance, with its official US$2 billion dollar commitment exceeding Indian help to any other country except Bhutan.[13]

Sri Lanka has been another regional state where India has tried to play a role in the reconstruction of the war-ravaged nation. The conclusion of the armed conflict saw the emergence of a major humanitarian challenge, with nearly 300,000 Tamil civilians housed in camps for IDPs. In 2009, India announced a grant of more than US$80 million for relief and rehabilitation in Sri Lanka. India has initiated a well-organized program of assistance to help these IDPs return to normal life as quickly as possible and has been advocating the need for them to be resettled to their original habitations. Even as the anti-Sri Lanka mood in the Indian state of Tamil Nadu is getting more belligerent, the Indian government at the center has increased its annual grant to the island nation in its budget. The allocation has gone up to more than US$80 million from around US$30 million in 2011–12.[14]

New Delhi has also been actively assisting with economic reconstruction in areas which are affected by natural disasters. Although India itself had suffered great damage in the 2004 Indian Ocean tsunami, it declined foreign aid offers and itself extended considerable assistance – sixteen naval vessels, twenty-one helicopters, and a total of 1,800 troops to Sri Lanka, the Maldives, and Indonesia. India also joined the international military assistance core group led by the United States. This was an attempt to impress on the international community its desire to get involved in the affairs of East Asia as a major player by its willingness to bear responsibility for the stability of the region. Ahead of the 2006 Israeli–Hizbollah War, the Indian Navy evacuated 2,280 Indian, Sri Lankan, and Nepalese civilians from Lebanon, once again becoming a provider of regional public goods in South Asia.

Prevention policies

Prevention policies encompass issues such as democratization, mediation of conflicts, and immigration. India holds the principle of non-interference in other states' internal affairs dear and so has been reluctant to make democracy promotion as a core strand in its foreign policy despite being the largest democracy in the world.[15] Given India's regional dominance, India tends to become a factor in domestic politics of the regional states. There is also a sense that any attempt by New Delhi to overtly talk of democracy promotion would alienate sections in regional states, further jeopardizing democratic consolidation.

As discussed in Chapter 7, it would not be an exaggeration to say that, in many ways, India is the central issue around which Bangladeshi political parties define their foreign policy agenda. This should not be a surprise given India's geographic, linguistic, and cultural linkages to Bangladesh. Over the years political parties opposing the AL have tended to define themselves in opposition to India, in effect portraying the AL as India's "stooge." Moreover, radical Islamist groups in Bangladesh have tried to buttress their own "Islamic identity" by attacking India.

India realizes that it is perceived in Bangladesh as being close to the AL; consequently New Delhi has made some efforts to rectify this situation. When the BNP-led coalition of Begum Khaleda Zia assumed office in 2001, Indian officials sent a special emissary to Dhaka to assure the new government that New Delhi had no political favorites in Bangladesh and that its internal affairs were not India's concern. But this failed to make any long-term impact on the new political alignment in Bangladesh. The same is true of Nepal where New Delhi is perceived as being closer to the Nepali Congress. As a result, India has avoided taking sides in Nepal's politics and reached out to all political groupings, including the Maoists.

India has bilateral disputes with most regional states and has tried to use bilateral platforms for their negotiated settlement, not encouraging third-party mediation. Taking this principle forward, India has resisted being a party to disputes among regional states though it has officially always been in favor of negotiated settlements. Yet, in the case of Afghanistan–Pakistan bilateral disputes, India has been very vocal in favor of Afghanistan as the issues that concern Kabul about the use of terror as an instrument of policy by the Pakistani military also impinge directly on Indian security.[16]

India shares a border with Bangladesh running through the Indian states of West Bengal, Assam, Meghalaya, Tripura, and Mizoram. This border is longer than the one India shares with China. Indian officials have alleged that continued illegal immigration from Bangladesh has altered the demography of India's border areas resulting in ethnic imbalance, electoral irregularity, and loss of employment opportunities for Indian nationals. In fact, in the late twentieth century the massive influx of refugees fleeing persecution in East Pakistan (as Bangladesh was known before independence) was one of the major reasons India assisted the Mukti Bahini guerrillas fighting for liberation from Pakistan. According to some estimates around 15–20 million illegal immigrants from Bangladesh have crossed over to India over the last several decades.

The northeastern states in India are particularly vulnerable to population movement: less than 1 percent of the region's external boundaries are contiguous with the rest of India whereas 99 percent are international boundaries. Bangladesh has complained that the overwhelming numerical superiority of Indian security forces along their long common border has spurred the killing of innocent Bangladeshi nationals by India's paramilitary BSF. According to some estimates the ratio of Indian to Bangladeshi security forces deployed along the border is 2.5:1. Exchanges of fires between the BSF and its counterpart, the Bangladeshi Rifles, are now a regular feature along the border, often resulting in inhumane treatment of each other's forces.

Ineffective border management has also emerged as a major irritant in India–Bangladesh relations because of concerns about smuggling, illegal immigration, trafficking in women and children, and insurgency. India's plan to erect a 2,886-kilometer fence along its border with Bangladesh, with an additional 400 kilometers in the state of Mizoram, is nearing completion. However, there is no evidence that fencing will be effective in checking infiltration in the area, where for historical reasons there are around fifty-seven Bangladeshi enclaves in Indian territory and around 111 Indian enclaves inside Bangladesh. In many ways the border with Bangladesh is more difficult for India to manage than the border with Pakistan. The Indian Army has little presence on the eastern border which is patrolled almost exclusively by Indian paramilitary forces. New Delhi's concerns are not only about demographic changes but also about the security threat posed by anti-India radicals and insurgents who sneak in along with economically deprived Bangladeshi migrants. India is trying to come to a bilateral settlement of the issue and a Land Boundary pact has been agreed by the two sides in principle.

The border between Nepal and China is largely sealed and as such the border inhabitants among the two countries have not been able to obtain adequate benefit at the local level. India has been trying to develop linkages along its regions bordering Nepal. A transport agreement was signed between Nepal and India in 2004 for the regulation of passenger vehicular traffic through five border crossing points, including Mahendranagar, Nepalgunj, Bhairahawa, Birgunj, and Kakarbhitta. In order to connect the different border districts of Nepal with Indian cities like New Delhi, Kolkata, Patna, and Varanasi, a provision was made for plying fifty-three buses on the agreed routes from each side. The nationals of Nepal and India had expected to be able to travel freely and unhindered either way on vehicles for specific purposes such as to get married, attend religious functions, go on pilgrimages, and participate in study tours.[17] The agreement was expected to bring a new dimension to relations between the two countries, but that scheme has not worked satisfactorily.

New Delhi has agreed to help Kathmandu in increasing the capacity of Nepal's Armed Police Force and expand India's BSF to control criminal activities along the open border. In addition, India offered technical and material assistance to strengthen the immigration set-up along the border should Nepal request such assistance. India has been requesting Nepal to sign the Mutual Legal Assistance Treaty and a revised Extradition Treaty, which the Nepali side is keen to defer because of the ongoing political flux.[18]

Protection policies

Protection policies include a number of areas including health, organized crime, terrorism, and environmental degradation. India has been a long-standing victim of terrorism. India faces a structural problem given its location in one of the world's most dangerous neighborhoods – South Asia – which is now the epicenter of Islamist radicalism with India's neighbors harboring terrorist networks and using them as instruments of state policy. Pakistan has long backed separatists in Jammu and Kashmir in the name of self-determination and India has over the years been a major victim of the radicalization of Islamist forces in Kashmir which have been successful in expanding their network across India.[19] Any breeding ground of radical Islamists under the aegis of Pakistan has a direct impact on the security of India, resulting in a rise in infiltration of terrorists across borders as well attacks. This has had an impact on the India–Pakistan rivalry in Afghanistan as well. It is vital for both India and Afghanistan that the latter should never again emerge as a safe haven for terrorism and extremism. A friendly Afghanistan where religious extremism continues to flourish is seen by Pakistan as essential to keep the pressure on India in Kashmir by providing a base where militants could be trained for fighting against the Indian forces. The mujahideen fighting in Kashmir have not only drawn inspiration from the Afghan resistance against the Soviets but have also drawn resources and materiel support from Pakistan. Kashmiri militants were among the thousands of "volunteers" from various Islamic countries that participated in the war against the Soviet forces. They went back indoctrinated in a version of Islam that destined their victory over the "infidels" as well as with important knowledge of guerrilla warfare. India rightly perceived that the victors of mujahideen against the Soviet Union would fundamentally alter the direction of Islamic extremism as Afghanistan would end up playing a crucial role in the shaping of an Islamic geopolitics, sitting as it does astride the Islamic heartland involving South and Central Asia as well as Middle East.

As discussed in Chapter 9, while India would like to ensure that Afghanistan does not become a springboard for terrorism directed against India once again, the resurgence of the Taliban and Pakistan's ambivalent approach toward this growing menace remains a major headache for India. In recent times, the pattern of medieval Islamist ideology challenging the writ of the state is more evident along the Pakistan–Afghanistan border where the resurgence of the Taliban is manifest in myriad ways. The Taliban forces have attacked Indian nationals working in reconstruction and development projects in different parts of Afghanistan in an effort to intimidate the Indian government. There is significant evidence that training camps of various militant groups continue to operate in different parts of Pakistan.[20] The terror strikes in Mumbai in November 2008 only confirmed Indian suspicions that sections of the Pakistani political and military establishment have no interest in renouncing terrorism as an instrument of their foreign policy.

India has been supportive of all efforts, particularly in the UN, to combat terrorism and has played a leading role in shaping international opinion and urging the international community to prioritize the fight against terror. It is signatory to all the thirteen UN Sectoral Conventions on Terrorism. It has been supportive of all measures within the UN General Assembly, the sixth Committee and the UNSC. It has supported UNSC Resolutions 1269 and 1368, which clearly identify terrorism as a threat to international peace and security. In addition, India has supported and fully implemented Resolutions 1267, 1333, and 1363 relating to terrorism by the Taliban regime in Afghanistan. It has piloted the comprehensive Convention on International Terrorism (CCIT) in the UN with the objective of providing a comprehensive legal framework to combat terrorism. At the regional level, India is a party to the SAARC Regional Convention on Suppression of Terrorism 1987 and has enacted the enabling legislation in the form of the SAARC Conventions (Suppression of Terrorism Act) 1993.[21] India has also criminalized terrorist financing in accordance with international standards, as a member of the Financial Action Task Force, the Eurasian Group on Combating Money Laundering and Terrorist Financing and the Asia-Pacific Group on Money Laundering.[22]

India is one of the most vulnerable countries in respect of the effects of climate change and therefore has an enormous stake in a global accord. It has been suggested that India was one of the earliest to draw attention to the relationship between environmental protection and development, arguing that economic development for the vast mass of humanity was vital if the environment was to be protected and that the industrial powers had historically been the greatest cause of environmental distress.[23] India has been ranked at a low 155th position by the 2014 Environmental Performance Index (EPI) in a global list of 178 countries ranked on how well they perform on high-priority environmental issues.[24]

In the climate change debate, India has chalked out a position consistent with the stance it took in the 1972 Stockholm conference on human environment, namely, the responsibility of the industrial, chiefly Western, powers in creating environmental problems. Since then, in successive conferences on climate change, India has defended the position that there must be differentiated responsibilities in controlling carbon emissions, that those who created the problem must commit themselves to verifiable reductions in emissions, and that the rich must also provide technology and funding for the poorer countries if the latter are to reduce their carbon dependence. New Delhi has worked with others in the developing world, including China, as well as with non-governmental organizations in the developed world to sustain its case. At the regional level, India has used SAARC to underscore the need to strengthen and intensify regional cooperation to preserve, protect, and manage the diverse and fragile ecosystems of the region including the need to address the challenges posed by climate change and natural disasters. India along with other South Asian states adopted the Delhi Statement on Cooperation in Environment in 2009 which identifies many critical areas that need to be addressed and reaffirms the commitment of member states toward enhancing regional cooperation in the area of environment and climate change.

Public health remains another area of policies of protection. India has tried to work with its neighbors in tackling some of the challenges emanating on this front with limited success. After the outbreak of Severe Acute Respiratory Syndrome (SARS) in 2003, India along with member states of SAARC made a commitment to strengthen cooperation in dealing with the pandemic. It signed the 2005 Islamabad Declaration on Health and Population which proposed the creation of a SAARC Disease Surveillance Centre and Rapid Deployment of Health Response System. However, because of bureaucratic inertia and resource crunch, these initiatives have not been fully implemented.[25] Though a regional strategy on HIV and AIDS was enunciated by India as part of the regional grouping in 2006, the region has failed to implement it effectively as well. The SAARC members have also decided to set up a surveillance center at the New Delhi-based National Institute of Communicable Disease to monitor the spread of avian flu in South Asia.

Compellence policies

By contributing nearly 100,000 military, police, and civilian personnel as part of more than forty-five operations so far, India has played a vital role in UN peacekeeping activities. Along with Bangladesh and Pakistan, India has been one of the top three sources of peacekeeping contributions. Many important UN operations like those in Democratic Republic of Congo, Eritrea–Ethiopia, Kosovo, Liberia, Sierra Leone, and Sudan have had the presence of Indian troops and police personnel. This is despite significant domestic demands on Indian security forces to tackle insurgencies in different parts of the country. Like other contributing states, India has also faced the dilemma of using force when the ground situation warranted without undermining the neutrality of the UN blue helmets. While not shying away from undertaking robust measures, India has, as a matter of principle, emphasized the danger of mixing traditional features of peacekeeping – like non-use of force and non-partisanship – with peace enforcement and peacemaking as tended to happen during the post-Cold War phase.[26]

While India has been a great votary of the UN globally, within South Asia it has tended to resist external intervention. Instead, it has relied more heavily on the use of force. Until the 1980s, New Delhi was forceful in asserting its pre-eminence in South Asia even with military interventions and firmly rejected any extra-regional interference. It viewed Western intervention in the region as inimical to its interests, though it could not keep great powers out of its periphery. India's regional security doctrine has been summed up aptly by Hagerty: "India strongly opposes outside interventional in the domestic affairs of other South Asian nations, especially by outside powers whose goals are perceived to be inimical to Indian interests. Therefore, no South Asian government should ask for outside assistance, it should seek it from India. A failure to do so will be considered anti India."[27]

In consonance with this worldview, India has used coercive policies in its own vicinity to assert its regional supremacy. New Delhi's failed counter insurgency campaign in Sri Lanka from 1983 to 1990, its 1988 deployment of special forces to prevent an attempted coup by mercenaries in the Maldives and the 1989–90 trade blockade of Nepal after Kathmandu's decision to buy weapons from China underscore this tendency.

With over 1.3 million men and women in uniform, and an additional one million in reserve, the Indian armed forces constitute the third largest volunteer war-fighting force in the world. Sustained rates of high economic growth over the last decade have given India greater resources to devote to its defense requirements. India has emerged as one of the largest arms buyers in the global market in the last few years.[28] In the initial years after independence in 1947, India's defense expenditure as a percentage of the GDP hovered around 1.8 percent. This changed with the 1962 war with China in which India had to suffer a humiliating defeat due to its lack of defense preparedness and Indian defense expenditure came to stabilize around 3 percent of GDP for the next twenty-five years. Over the past two decades, the military expenditure of India has been around 2.75 percent but since India has been experiencing significantly higher rates of economic growth over the last decade compared to any other time in its history, the overall resources that it has been able to allocate to its defense needs has grown significantly. The armed forces for long have been asking for an allocation of 3 percent of the nation's GDP. This has received broad political support in recent years though this ambition is still far from being realized.

India has asserted its military profile in the past decade, setting up military facilities abroad and patrolling the Indian Ocean to counter piracy and protect lines of communication. As its strategic horizons become broader, military acquisition is shifting from land-based systems to airborne refueling systems, long-range missiles and other means of power projection with all three services articulating the need to be able to operate beyond India's borders.

Yet fundamental vulnerabilities continue to ail Indian defense policy.[29] So while the Indian Army is suggesting that it is 50 percent short of attaining full capability and will need around twenty years to gain full defense preparedness, naval analysts are pointing out that India's naval power is actually declining. During the 1999 Kargil conflict, operations were hampered by a lack of adequate equipment. Only because the conflict remained largely confined to the 150-kilometer front in Kargil sector did India manage to get an upper hand, ejecting Pakistani forces from its side of the LoC. India lacked the ability to impose significant military costs on Pakistan not only during the 2001–02 Operation Parakram – the military mobilization against Pakistan after the December 2001 terrorist attack on the Indian parliament – but even after the Mumbai terror attacks of November 2008 because of the unavailability of suitable weaponry and night vision equipment needed to carry out swift surgical strikes. The Indian public continues to be proud of its military but is skeptical about the political will to use it effectively.

Conclusion

Until the late 1980s, even though India had limited material capabilities, it asserted its pre-eminence within the subcontinent by primarily relying on compellence to manage regional security. New Delhi was keen to control the internal affairs of its neighbors to further its regional security interests and pursued a highly interventionist policy, despite its aversion to a policy of external intervention by other global powers.

Paradoxically since the 1990s, with its economic rise and as its capabilities have grown, constraints have also increased on India's interventionist approach. Smaller states in the region have managed to constrain India's ability to emerge as an effective regional security provider. For long, the dominant narrative with regards to South Asia has been how the India–Pakistan rivalry has constrained Indian foreign policy options in the region and prevented the region from attaining its full potential. That is now rapidly losing its salience with China's growing dominance of the South Asian landscape. The country's rising profile in South Asia has been evident for some time now. As discussed in Part II of this volume, this quiet assertion of China has allowed various smaller countries of South Asia to play the country off against India. Pakistan's "all-weather" friendship with China is well known, but the reach of China in other South Asian states has been extraordinary. Bangladesh and Sri Lanka view India as more interested in creating barriers against their exports than in spurring regional economic integration. Instead of India emerging as facilitator of socio-economic development in Sri Lanka, Nepal, and Bhutan, it is China's developmental assistance that is having a larger impact.

As a consequence, despite being the predominant regional power, India is no longer capable of setting the regional agenda. Given this predicament, India today seems more comfortable to share the burden of regional security management with external actors, in particular the United States. On most regional issues ranging from terrorism emanating from Pakistan, political decay in Nepal and Bangladesh as well as domestic strife in Sri Lanka, New Delhi is much more comfortable with the idea of working with the United States and other Western powers than it has ever been before. There is recognition that India can no longer pursue a unilateral policy of compellence as in the past because of structural and domestic political reasons. Sharing the burden of managing the regional security environment provides India the best means of retaining some leverage on regional issues.

Notes

1 Rajat Pandit, "India Set to Become Net Provider of Security in Region: PM Manmohan Singh," *Times of India*, May 23, 2013.

2 Rajat Pandit, "Def Minister A K Antony Says Indian Navy Has Been Mandated to be a Net Security Provider to Island Nations in the Indian Ocean Region," *Times of India*, October 12, 2011.

3 Quadrennial Defense Review Report, 2010, Department of Defense, United States of America, March. Available at http://archive.defense.gov/pubs/2014_Quadrennial_Defense_Review.pdf.

4 Kanti Bajpai and Harsh V. Pant, *India's National Security: A Reader* (Oxford: Oxford University Press, 2013), pp. 1–15.

5 Harsh V. Pant, *The Rise of China: Implications for India* (New Delhi: Cambridge University Press, 2012).

6 Stephen P. Cohen, *Shooting for a Century: The India-Pakistan Conundrum* (Washington, DC: Brookings Institution Press, 2013).

7 Somini Sengupta, "Terrorist Attacks Unsettling India," *New York Times*, July 29, 2008.

8 'Keeping Islamic State Out of India,' Wall Street Journal, September 10, 2015, http://www.wsj.com/articles/keeping-islamic-state-out-of-india-1441931550 [accessed 4 November 2015].

9 Vinay Kumar, "Manmohan Wants Naxal Forces Crippled," *The Hindu*, December 21, 2007.

10 Jawaharlal Nehru, *India's Foreign Policy: Selected Speeches, September 1946–April 1961* (Delhi: Government of India, 1961), pp. 113–15.

11 C. Raja Mohan, "What If Pakistan Fails? India Isn't Worried ... Yet," *Washington Quarterly*, Vol. 28, No. 1 (Winter 2004/05), p. 127.

12 Harsh V. Pant, "India in Afghanistan: A Test Case for a Rising Power," *Contemporary South Asia*, Vol. 18, No. 2 (2010), pp. 133–53.

13 Rani D. Mullen, "India Development Cooperation Research (IDCR) Project," Bilateral Brief no. 2, May 2013. Available at http://idcr.cprindia.org/blog/india-afghanistan-partnership.

14 S. Karthick, "India Increases Aid to Sri Lanka," *Times of India*, March 2, 2013.

15 Jan Cartwright, "India's Regional and International Support for Democracy: Rhetoric or Reality?" *Asian Survey*, Vol. 49, No. 3 (2009), pp 403–28.

16 For details on India's approach vis-à-vis Pakistan with regard to its Afghanistan policy, see Harsh V. Pant, *India's Afghan Muddle: A Lost Opportunity* (New Delhi: HarperCollins, 2014).

17 Hari Bansh Jha, "Nepal's Border Relations with India and China," *Eurasia Border Review*, Vol. 4, No. 1 (2013).

18 Gyanu Adhikari, "Nepal-India Agree to Find Missing Border Pillars, Enhance Security," *The Hindu*, June 3, 2013.

19 Praveen Swami, *India, Pakistan and the Secret Jihad in Kashmir: The Covert War in Kashmir, 1947–2004* (London: Routledge, 2006).

20 Carlotta Gall, *The Wrong Enemy: America in Afghanistan, 2001–2014* (New York: Houghton Mifflin Harcourt, 2014).

21 D.K. Pathak, Country Report: India. 132nd International Senior Seminar: Strengthening the Legal Regime for Combating Terrorism, The United Nations Asia and Far East Institute for the Prevention of Crime and the Treatment of Offenders (UNAFEI), 2007.

22 N. Lakshman, "US Criticises India's Counter-Terror Infrastructure," *The Hindu*, May 1, 2014.

23 Sandeep Sengupta, "Defending 'Differentiation': India's Foreign Policy on Climate Change from Rio to Copenhagen," in Kanti Bajpai and Harsh V. Pant (eds.), *India's Foreign Policy: A Reader* (Oxford: Oxford University Press, 2013), pp. 389–414.

24 "India Ranked 155th in Global Environment Performance List," *Times of India*, January 25, 2014.

25 Zahid Shahab Ahmed, *Regionalism and Regional Security in South Asia: The Role of SAARC* (Surrey: Ashgate, 2013), p. 84.
26 C.S.R. Murthy, "Assessing India at the United Nations in the Changing Context," *International Studies*, Vol. 47, No. 2 (2010), pp. 214–16.
27 Devin T. Hagerty, "India's Regional Security Doctrine," *Asian Survey*, Vol. 31, No. 4 (1991), p. 351.
28 "Know Your Own Strength," *The Economist*, May 30, 2015.
29 For a detailed examination of Indian defence policy, see Harsh V. Pant (ed), *Handbook of Indian Defence Policy: Themes, Structures, and Doctrines* (London: Routledge, 2015).

15

India and the global nuclear order: a quiet assimilation

Indian nuclear tests of 1998 altered the contours of the security architecture constructed during the Cold War. No doubt, with the end of the Cold War, this security environment was under stress, but Indian nuclear tests were the first open challenge, by a "responsible" as opposed to a "rogue" member of the international community, to this system. Some might argue that surreptitious Chinese nuclear and missile proliferation and clandestine nuclear programs of states such as India, Pakistan, and Israel had begun to undercut the arms control regime long before the 1998 Indian nuclear tests. But India's open defiance of the global nuclear order marked the real beginning of the end of the non-proliferation regime, the bedrock of Cold War international security, and the consequences for global security have been nothing less than revolutionary. Forced by India's open challenge to the global arms control and disarmament framework in May 1998, major powers in the international system have been re-evaluating their orientation toward global arms control and non-proliferation. This chapter examines the evolution in India's role in the global nuclear order – from being a pariah to one at the center of its reformulation.

A historical legacy

India has tried to harmonize its national security interests with its concerns for universal nuclear disarmament right since independence. It has viewed nuclear weapons as instruments of coercion, thereby posing a threat to international peace and security. India nuclear diplomacy, therefore, has focused on the creation of a nuclear weapon free world by eliminating all nuclear weapons through a multilaterally negotiated, effective, and verifiable treaty.

As a consequence, India has steadfastly rejected any move short of universal disarmament since the beginning of multilateral nuclear diplomacy. India had hoped that the 1963 Partial Test Ban Treaty would not only halt the spiraling arms race between the superpowers but would also be a first step toward a comprehensive test ban. But the outcome of the treaty was underground testing rather than any movement toward a comprehensive test ban.

It rejected the 1968 NPT, as the treaty institutionalized the nuclear hierarchy, thereby discriminating between the "nuclear haves" and the "have-nots."[1]

India's diplomatic posture is all the more significant in view of its long and sophisticated nuclear weapons program. The civilian nuclear program was laid down in 1948 with the aim of winning for India all the status, respect, and economic benefits associated with being a nuclear power, including the option of military use of nuclear technology. China's detonation of its first nuclear device in 1964 transformed the strategic environment for India, forcing India to conduct a "peaceful nuclear explosion" in 1974.

This test signaled India's resolve to preserve its strategic autonomy even though the test by itself was inadequate for building and deploying a nuclear arsenal. While India strongly resisted any attempt to cap its nuclear weapons program, it was also not very willing to emerge as a full-fledged NWS because of what it perceived to be significant diplomatic and economic costs associated with a "nuclear" status.[2] It has been argued that this posture of "strategic ambiguity" helped India to harmonize its national security imperatives with its disarmament objectives by reflecting India's moral aversion to nuclear weapons, its emphasis on global nuclear disarmament, and its preference to concentrate resources on economic development. First, because of its very opaqueness and uncertainty, it offered an existential deterrent against China. Second, it pre-empted Pakistan from overtly seeking countervailing nuclear capability. Third, it implicitly avoided any direct confrontation with the global non-proliferation regime led by the nuclear powers. Lastly, it helped India to continue with its efforts toward universal nuclear disarmament.[3]

One of the most important initiatives by India, as part of its endeavor to bring the issue of universal nuclear disarmament to the center stage of international politics, was the Rajiv Gandhi Action Plan on Disarmament in 1988 which presented a time-bound framework of twenty-two years aimed at total elimination of all nuclear weapons.[4]

During the negotiations on the CTBT in the Conference on Disarmament (CD) in Geneva, India participated actively and constructively, putting forward its proposals, in keeping with its long-standing position. For India, a CTBT should have marked the first definitive and irreversible step in the process of nuclear disarmament. However, it was the indefinite extension of an unequal NPT by the NPT Review and Extension Conference in 1995 that made India realize that the US-led "discriminatory" non-proliferation regime was marching forward, forcing India to make some difficult choices with regard to the CTBT. This Conference missed the historic chance to fundamentally reassess the NPT and to make an essential shift toward a more rational and constructive direction. Focusing on the procedural aspects of the NPT extension, the NWS drew attention away from the crucial problems related to existing nuclear weapon arsenals and the global use of nuclear technology. Not only was the NPT extended indefinitely but also no real balance was struck between the unequal set of obligations imposed upon the NWS and the non-NWS. The indefinite and unconditional extension meant, in practice, the indefinite postponement of complete nuclear disarmament as promised in the NPT. It was amply clear that the test ban treaty would be used as a means of drawing non-signatories, including India, into the NPT fold, ensuring control by and dominance of the NWS indefinitely.

India's main concern during the CTBT negotiations was that a test ban treaty should be securely anchored in the disarmament context in order to be effective. The mandate given to the Nuclear Test Ban Committee, which was concerned with the drafting of the treaty, clearly reflected this concern. But the final treaty that emerged did not do justice to this negotiating mandate as it lacked a definitive commitment to nuclear disarmament. Finally, India was forced to reject the CTBT on various grounds. First, India argued that the CTBT that had emerged was an unequal treaty, which did not promise much by way of global security. The NWS failed to give a clear commitment for nuclear disarmament within a time-bound framework. The CTBT, therefore, was merely an extension of the exercise to limit horizontal proliferation, sanctioning, in effect, the possession of nuclear weapons by some countries for their security while ignoring the security concerns of others.[5]

The second key issue related to the scope of the CTBT. India argued that the CTBT would not contribute to nuclear disarmament because it only banned nuclear explosive testing, but not other activities related to nuclear weapons, such as sub-critical (non-nuclear explosive) experiments or computer simulations. The prohibition on explosive testing was considered acceptable by the NWS, as they had already completed their program of explosive testing. They were well-placed to exploit the lessons learned through their extensive testing programs, through more sophisticated and non-explosive technologies.

During the negotiations, treaty language that would have signified an end to the qualitative development and upgradation of nuclear weapons, thus curbing vertical proliferation, was categorically rejected by the NWS. Clearly, for the NWS the CTBT was but one of the means to preserve their nuclear hegemony. The decision of the United States to share the data collected from its sub-critical experiments with the United Kingdom and France should also be seen as part of this larger dynamic.[6]

Third, India asserted that it would not sign the CTBT as it wanted to maintain its strategic flexibility in view of its national security considerations. This was the first time that security vis-à-vis neighbors was directly raised as an issue by India in the context of disarmament negotiations as indirect references were made to China and Pakistan's nuclear programs. During the CTBT debate, Ambassador Prakash Shah, India's permanent representative to the UN, stated that India "cannot permit [its] option to be constrained as long as countries around [it] continue their weapons programs either openly or in a clandestine manner" and as long as "NWS remain unwilling to accept the obligation to eliminate their nuclear arsenals."[7]

Fourth, India also objected to the CTBT's provision for Entry into Force. This provision, Article XIV of the CTBT requires the signature and ratification of forty-four states (those listed by the IAEA as having research or power reactors and that were also members of the CD as of June 18, 1996) for the CTBT to come into effect. This provision also required that if the treaty had not entered into force three years after being opened for signature, a Conference of the states who had ratified it should decide what measures could be taken to expedite Entry into Force. India argued that Article XIV not only disregarded its position but was also contrary to the fundamental norms of international law as it was introduced after India had clearly stated that it was not in a position to subscribe to the CTBT in its present form. Article XIV was, therefore, aimed at imposing obligations on India and placing it in a position in which it did not wish to be.[8]

Finally, India expressed its reservations on the use of national technical means, including satellites and humint, for verification, arguing that the highly intrusive nature of the CTBT's verification regime adversely impinges on the security and autonomy of the less developed states.[9]

The post-Pokharan phase

The Indian position on the CTBT, however, came full circle after it conducted nuclear tests in May 1998. After declaring itself as a NWS in May 1998, India took its first major step of converting that rhetoric into reality in January 2003 when it made explicit its nuclear doctrine and the nature of its command and control over its nuclear arsenal. The Cabinet Committee on Security of the Indian government, composed of the Prime Minister, the Minister of Home Affairs, Defense, Finance, and External Affairs, decided to share with the Indian public and the world some major aspects of the Indian nuclear weapons doctrine and operational arrangements governing India's nuclear assets.

It is important to recognize that the salient aspects of the Indian nuclear doctrine had been enunciated immediately by the Indian government after it conducted its nuclear tests in May 1998.[10] India decided to adopt a no-first-use (NFU) policy and declared that it would never use nuclear weapons against a non-nuclear state. India also made clear its intention of working consistently toward the goal of universal nuclear disarmament. India was also engaged in high-level arms control negotiations with the United States that were trying to define the broad contours of the Indo-US relationship post-Pokharan II.[11] While India had voluntarily declared a moratorium on further nuclear testing, the United States was also pressing India to accept a moratorium on fissile material production and to participate in the Fissile Material Cut-off Treaty (FMCT) negotiations, strengthen its export control system, and engage in a security dialogue with Pakistan.

Even as the debate on India's draft nuclear doctrine continued in India and abroad, India came up with a limited-war doctrine in January 2000.[12] It was a result of the lessons learned from the Kargil conflict of May–June 1999. Kargil was the first crisis situation between India and Pakistan in an openly nuclearized regional environment. While the US role in restraining Pakistan during this crisis and thereby bringing it to an early end is well accepted, several other operational factors have also been cited as tilting the conflict in India's favor. These include an effective use of air power on the Indian side of the LoC, the overwhelming superiority of Indian land forces, and use of massive concentrations of artillery.[13]

As a consequence, in the aftermath of the Kargil conflict, it was argued that the changed strategic milieu in South Asia, because of the nucleariza-tion of India and Pakistan, makes it imperative for India to be able to fight a limited conventional war, thereby disabusing Pakistan of the belief that India would be deterred in any war imposed on it and would not fight back. This was a fairly specific example of efforts to achieve escalation domi-nance as it was argued that in a war with limited political and military objectives "the escalatory ladder can be climbed in a carefully controlled ascent wherein politico-diplomatic factors would play an important role."[14] Despite skepticism in the West and in some sections of the Indian security establishment about the ability of India and Pakistan to keep their conflicts below the nuclear threshold, for India the Kargil crisis was a demonstration of its ability to fight and win a limited war.

The real test for these changing doctrinal assumptions came during the crisis that erupted between India and Pakistan after India's parliament was attacked by terrorists in December 2001. India came under considerable pressure from the West to spell out its official policy on the use of nuclear weapons during this crisis, as India and Pakistan seemed to be on the brink of war. It has also been argued that it was the failure of Operation Parakram, the 2002 army mobilization on the border, that forced the Indian political leadership to explicate the Nuclear Command Authority (NCA) and pro-vide an outline of the nuclear doctrine.[15] A major factor in the failure was that India lacked the capacity, conventional and nuclear, to bend Pakistan to its will. The top political leadership failed to make clear to the armed forces the objectives that India wanted to achieve through the mobiliza-tion of its army. The threat to use nuclear weapons by Pakistan prevented India from undertaking a military offensive, even a limited one. In fact, the Pakistani Army claimed that the Indian Army's "redeployment" or with-drawal was their "victory." However, not everyone agrees that Operation Parakram was a failure and a debate still continues in Indian policy circles on its ramifications.

A speech by General Pervez Musharraf, Pakistan's President, to Pakistani Air Force officers in December 2002 brought South Asia under further international scrutiny. Musharraf asserted that it was Pakistan's threat to use "unconventional tactics" that prevented India from launching a full-scale war against Pakistan in 2002.[16] India chose to interpret the general's words as a threat and reacted vigorously, warning Pakistan that a nuclear strike against India would be met with "massive retaliation." Musharraf's speech was a signal for India to take stock and to respond to what many see as constant nuclear blackmail from across the border.

It was in the midst of this war of words that India, after more than four-and-a-half years, unveiled a final set of political principles and administrative arrangements to manage its arsenal of nuclear weapons. The main elements of the Indian nuclear doctrine are:

- building and maintaining a credible minimum deterrent;
- a posture of NFU;
- retaliatory attacks only to be authorized by the civilian political leadership through the NCA;
- non-use of nuclear weapons against non-nuclear weapons states;
- India to retain the option of retaliating with nuclear weapons in the event of a major attack against India or Indian forces anywhere, by biological or chemical weapons;
- a continuance of controls on export of nuclear and missile related materials and technologies, participation in the FMCT negotiations, observance of the moratorium on nuclear tests, and working toward the goal of universal nuclear disarmament.[17]

The formal declaration of its nuclear doctrine and creation of the NCA by India brought into effect a long-standing requirement, thereby formalizing what was essentially a set of unstructured arrangements among senior members of the politico-military-scientific establishment. It was India's attempt at setting to rest some doubts over nuclear issues while reiterating the promises it made to the international community. The new framework accorded the necessary doctrinal underpinning to India's evolving nuclear posture and the sanctity of government approval for the use of nuclear weapons.

Maximum restraint in the use of nuclear forces, absolute political control over decision-making, and an attempt to evolve an effective interface between civilian and military leaders in the administration of its nuclear arsenal have emerged as the basic tenets of India's nuclear weapons policy. The declaration of its nuclear doctrine and the NCA by India marked a significant step in India's plan to develop an effective and robust command and control and indications-and-warning systems and infrastructure for its strategic nuclear forces commensurate with India's strategic requirements.

India declared a moratorium on further nuclear tests and simultaneously indicated that it would convert this de facto commitment to a de jure status. India's accession to the CTBT had been one of the main issues that were being negotiated in the Indo-US talks (also referred to as Jaswant Singh–Strobe Talbott talks). The Indian Prime Minister also in his address to the UN General Assembly in 1999 had indicated that India was prepared to bring the discussions on the CTBT to a successful conclusion.

This apparent turnaround by India on the CTBT was, on the one hand, welcomed both in India and abroad but, on the other hand, it raised serious questions that could not be overlooked. Supporters of India's accession to the CTBT have made a case that after May 1998 India is a NWS and that its central security concerns have been addressed by these tests. India is believed to have collected sufficient data to conduct sub-critical tests and computer simulations and acquired the technical capability to miniaturize weapons. Moreover, it has been argued that India could strike a bargain with the United States, whereby the economic sanctions and ban on dual-use technology transfers to India should be removed in exchange for India's accession to the CTBT.[18] India had clearly shown its willingness to limit its nuclear weapons program by joining international arms control treaties. Although many issues remained to be finessed, the elements of broad nuclear understanding between India and the United States and the larger international community seemed to be in place.

The US–India nuclear pact

It was this broader understanding that led the George W. Bush administration to declare its ambition to achieve full civil nuclear energy cooperation with India as part of its broader goals of promoting nuclear power and achieving nuclear security during the visit of the Indian Prime Minister to the United States in July 2005. In pursuit of this objective, the Bush administration agreed to "seek agreement from Congress to adjust U.S. laws and policies" and to "work with friends and allies to adjust international regimes to enable full civil nuclear energy cooperation and trade with India, including but not limited to expeditious consideration of fuel supplies for safeguarded nuclear reactors at Tarapur." India, for its part, promised "to assume the same responsibilities and practices and acquire the same benefits and advantages of other leading countries with advanced nuclear technology."[19] The Bush administration's decision to engage India as a rising global power meant that it was essential that the deadlock over the nuclear question was broken. Toward this end, the political leaderships in Washington and New Delhi had to expend voluminous political capital in the face of strong opposition from various quarters, and had to bridge the gap between the United States' entrenched non-proliferation policy and India's insistence on insurance against any future negative turn.

The Indo-US nuclear pact has rewritten the rules of the global nuclear regime by underlining India's credentials as a responsible nuclear state that should be integrated into the global nuclear order. The nuclear agreement creates a major exception to the US prohibition of nuclear assistance to any country that does not accept international monitoring of all its nuclear facilities. The passage of the nuclear deal, however, was not an easy one either in the United States or in India as both sides had to reckon with a long, largely negative historical memory as well as entrenched interests on both sides that resisted the US–Indian nuclear rapprochement.[20] But the fundamental difficulty in negotiating the US–India nuclear pact was due to the struggle between the two competing imperatives of the US foreign policy: great power politics versus nuclear non-proliferation. Whereas the Bush administration viewed the pact primarily as a means to build a strategic partnership with India, many in the US Congress would support it only to the extent it contributed to the non-proliferation objectives.[21] Similarly, while the Indian government also viewed the nuclear deal as a means to reorient its foreign policy priorities and enter the global nuclear mainstream, its political critics viewed it as ploy by the United States to constrain India's nuclear options.

Since the signing of the Indo-US agreement and special dispensation granted to India by the IAEA and the NSG, India has signed civilian nuclear energy pacts with states as diverse as Britain, France, Russia, and Canada on the one hand, and Argentina, Kazakhstan, Namibia, and Mongolia on the other. The start of negotiations with Japan on a civilian nuclear energy pact is also part of a long line of such agreements. China announced its own civil nuclear pact with Pakistan in 2010, though it has yet to receive a waiver from the NSG for selling technology to a country not a member of the NPT.

Behind seemingly innocuous agreements of civilian nuclear cooperation, India, Japan, China, and Pakistan engage in a strategic balancing game that could draw in other countries, complicate the global non-proliferation agenda and raise serious security concerns about Pakistan as a Wal-Mart of illicit nuclear technology. The unspoken context of the US–India nuclear agreement, however, was American concern about China's rapid ascendance in the Asia-Pacific. Both India and the United States realized that, to prevent China from dominating the Asia-Pacific, a close partnership between the world's two largest democracies was essential. The nuclear deal became the most potent symbol of US–India rapprochement.

But the deal was not merely between India and the United States. Successful approval by the NSG allowed India to engage other nuclear powers in civilian nuclear trade and provided new market opportunities to major nuclear powers. Even Japan, a strong critic of India's nuclear policy, has decided to fast-track negotiations for a civilian nuclear deal with India – if it materializes, this will be the first such agreement between Japan and a country that isn't a signatory to the NPT.

Though Indian–Japanese ties have blossomed in recent years on a range of issues, the nuclear issue has been a major irritant in the relationship. The new understanding between the two nations underscores Tokyo's attempts to come to terms with India's new nuclear status. Japanese nuclear companies are eager for a share of the Indian market. Given the involvement of Japanese firms such as Toshiba Corp, Hitachi Ltd, and Mitsubishi in US and French nuclear industries, an Indo-Japanese pact is essential for US and French civilian nuclear cooperation with India.

Beyond the commercial dimensions of the deal, political symbolism is even more critical. Such a deal would underline Japan's determination to put Indo-Japanese ties in high gear. The rise of China is a major factor in the evolution of Indo-Japanese ties, as is the US attempt to build India into a major balancer in the region. Both India and Japan chafe at China's not-so-subtle attempts at preventing their rise. An Indian–Japanese civil nuclear pact would signal an Asian partnership to bring stability to the region at a time when China goes all out to dispense civilian nuclear reactors to Pakistan, putting the entire non-proliferation regime in jeopardy. Given the domestic sensitivities on nuclear issues in Japan and especially after the nuclear crisis at the Fukushima Daiichi nuclear power plant, it will be some time before Japan and India will be able to come to some sort of an understanding on this critical issue.

The Sino-Pakistan nuclear relationship has been the major factor wrecking the foundations of the nuclear non-proliferation regime. China's nuclear test in 1964 propelled India's nuclear weaponization culminating in India's "peaceful nuclear explosion" in 1974. Sino-Pakistan nuclear cooperation – involving the sharing of weapon design and missile technology in the 1990s – forced India to go overtly nuclear in 1998.

When the United States announced its civilian nuclear energy cooperation pact with India in 2005, China indicated displeasure by asking India to sign the NPT and dismantle its nuclear weapons. Beijing promptly moved to make that prophecy self-fulfilling by declaring its intention to sell nuclear reactors to Pakistan. The not-so-subtle message was, if Washington decided to play favorites, China would do the same, confirming that China continues to view Pakistan as an asset in countering India. The Chinese decision to supply new nuclear reactors to Pakistan is in clear violation of the NSG guidelines that forbid nuclear transfers to countries not signatories to the NPT or not adhering to comprehensive international safeguards on their nuclear program.

China's decision to supply new nuclear reactors to Pakistan in 2010 can only destabilize the non-proliferation regime further. The IAEA has agreed to Pakistan's request to safeguard the two new reactors planned for Chashma, allowing the agency to help ensure nuclear material from the reactors is secure and not diverted into weapons-related programs. The United States and several other states want China to seek approval for the planned reactors from the NSG like the United States did for its nuclear pact with India. However, with or without the NSG approval, nuclear cooperation between China and Pakistan will only intensify in the coming years as China becomes more assertive in pursuing its interests. China is concerned about deepening Indo-US relations and India's attempts to cultivate ties with states in China's periphery. The resulting priority of the Sino-Pakistani relationship is evident in Chinese polices toward South Asia.

Moreover, there's a sense in Beijing that the Obama administration would be reluctant to challenge the deal as it needs China's help on issues ranging from Iran and North Korea to the global economy. The United States no longer seems to have the willingness and clout to enforce the rules requiring credible safeguards before civilian nuclear technology can be exported.

China is not only active in Pakistan. Iran has emerged as the second largest customer of China's defense industry after Pakistan, receiving critical defense technology from China, including some that violate the stated Chinese policy of adhering to the norms of the non-proliferation regime.[22] As China becomes more assured of its rising global profile, it challenges US foreign-policy priorities, and the non-proliferation regime fast becomes the first casualty of the emerging great power politics.

At the 2010 NPT Review Conference, the non-nuclear states also expressed their displeasure at the Bush administration's decision to sell civilian nuclear technology to India without signing the NPT. Egypt's UN ambassador, Maged Abdel Aziz, who led the 118-member non-aligned group, argued: "If you say countries outside the treaty are going to get ... even more benefits than countries inside the treaty, then what is the benefit for me to bind myself with more [non-proliferation] restrictions."[23]

Conclusion

It was only during the visit of the US President Barack Obama to India in January 2015 that the nuclear deal which had been held up for six years amid concerns over the liability for any nuclear accident could finally be operationalized. With Obama using his executive powers to roll back the condition that US authorities be allowed to monitor use of nuclear material purchased by India even from third countries and the United States agreeing to India's proposal to build a risk-management insurance pool of around US$24 million to provide cover to suppliers who shunned the civil nuclear agreement because it made them liable to pay compensation in the event of a nuclear accident, a great leap forward has been made.[24]

Whatever the final shape of the US–India nuclear relationship, India has managed to find its way into the global nuclear order on its own terms. It is one of the most significant accomplishments of Indian foreign policy that a country which was considered a nuclear pariah until 1998 has forced the NWS to refashion a nuclear order which incorporates some of its long-standing concerns. It remains to be seen if after years of being a revisionist nuclear state, India can now come to terms with the global nuclear status quo.

Notes

1 For a historical overview of India's relationship with the test ban debate, see Harsh V. Pant, "India and Nuclear Arms Control: A Study of the CTBT," *Comparative Strategy*, Vol. 21, No. 2 (April 2002), pp. 91–105.

2 See George Perkovich, *India's Nuclear Bomb: The Impact on Global Proliferation* (New York: Oxford University Press, 1999) for a detailed enunciation of this argument.

3 For a detailed explication of this viewpoint, see Amitabh Mattoo, "India's Nuclear Status Quo," *Survival* (Autumn 1996), pp. 41–57.

4 Rajiv Gandhi, "A World Free of Nuclear Weapons: An Action Plan," proposal presented at the United Nations General Assembly Third Special Session on Disarmament, New York, June 9, 1988.

5 On India's concerns regarding the CTBT not being linked to the goal of global nuclear disarmament, see the statement by Ambassador Arundhati Ghose, Conference on Disarmament Plenary, Document CD/PV.740, Geneva, June 20, 1996.

6 On India's concerns with regard to the scope of the CTBT, see Arundhati Ghose, "Negotiating the CTBT," *Journal of International Affairs*, Vol. 51, No. 1 (1997), pp. 252–3.

7 See the statement by Ambassador Prakash Shah, 50th Session of the UN General Assembly New York, September 9, 1996, p. 5.

8 For India's criticism of Article XIV, see *ibid.*, pp. 256–8.

9 For an explication of India's objections with regard to National Technical Means (NTMs), see Arundhati Ghose, "The CTBT as a Control Mechanism," *The Times of India*, February 26, 1999.

10 For details, see "Suo Moto Statement by Prime Minister Atal Bihari Vajpayee in the Indian Parliament on May 27, 1998," *India News*, May 16–June 15, 1998, pp. 1–2. Also see, "Paper Laid on the Table of the House on Evolution of India's Nuclear Policy," *India News*, May 16–June 15, 1998, pp. 3–6.

11 For an overview of these negotiations, see Pant, "India and Nuclear Arms Control," pp. 99–102.

12 C. Raja Mohan, "Fernandes Unveils 'Limited War' Doctrine," *The Hindu*, January 24, 2000.

13 V.K. Sood and Pravin Sawhney, *Operation Parakram: The War Unfinished* (New Delhi: Sage, 2003), pp. 65–77.

14 Gen. V.P. Malik, "Indo-Pak Security Relations: Kargil and After," *Indian Express*, June 21, 2002.

15 A detailed explication of this viewpoint can be found in Sood and Sawhney, *Operation Parakram*, pp. 118–44.

16 B. Murlidhar Reddy, "Musharraf Had Warned of N-War," *The Hindu*, December 31, 2002.

17 A detailed examination of India's nuclear doctrine can be found at Harsh V. Pant, "India's Nuclear Doctrine and Command Structure: Implications

for India and the World," *Comparative Strategy*, Vol. 24, No. 3 (July 2005), pp. 277–93.

18 For some of the arguments of the supporters of India's accession to the CTBT, see C. Raja Mohan, "Towards a CTBT Consensus," *The Hindu*, November 9, 1999; Kanti Bajpai, "The Great Indian Nuclear Debate," *The Hindu*, November 12, 1999; Kanti Bajpai, "Policy on CTBT," *The Hindustan Times*, December 16, 1999.

19 The details of the joint statement between US President George W Bush and the Indian Prime Minister Manmohan Singh, signed on July 18, 2005, can be found at www.whitehouse.gov/news/releases/2005/07/20050718-6.html.

20 A detailed assessment of the US–India nuclear deal can be found in Harsh V. Pant, *The US-India Nuclear Pct: Policy, Process, and Great Power Politics* (Oxford: Oxford University Press, 2011).

21 Ashley Tellis interview, "US Domestic Laws Define The Boundaries Of The N-Deal," *Outlook*, October 13, 2008.

22 John W. Garver, *China and Iran: Ancient Partners in a Post-Imperial World* (Seattle: University of Washington Press, 2006).

23 Mary Beth Sheridan, "At Nuclear Conference, US Expects Little, Gains Little," *Washington Post*, May 31, 2010.

24 "Obama, Modi Achieve Breakthrough in Civil Nuclear Over One-on-One Talks," *Indian Express*, January 25, 2015.

16

India and multilateralism: from the periphery to the center

Ever since independence, India has continued to underscore its internationalism – its desire to work with other states to fashion mutually advantageous outcomes – particularly within the ambit of international institutions. Like most other states, India has tried to strike a balance between advancing its own interests and the collective interest, between unilateral and multilateral approaches. While domestic critics suggest that India is not mindful of its own interests and that it is ineffective in international institutions, critical outsiders often conclude virtually the opposite: that under the guise of cosmopolitanism India seeks to advance its own interests and that it is frequently a rather effective naysayer. In actuality, India is probably no more altruistic than other states and no more selfish. It can be constructive in international settings, and it can also be a stubborn naysayer. Sometimes it achieves what it wants and sometimes it fails to do so.

India's centrality to the global multilateral framework has grown with the rise of India as a major economic power. It is now part of a more or less elite club within which a consensus position on trade issues is sought to be hammered out – this is the case on the issue of climate change as well. India, along with Brazil and China, has come to represent the developing countries, and yet there is a section of the developing world that has raised questions about the decisions these countries have taken on behalf of the poorer countries. In effect, there is a growing feeling that India, Brazil, and China may be special cases and need to be differentiated from the others.

India has been an active member of the international community, participating in a range of global organizations, and its engagement with other states has played out as part of India's membership in some of the oldest and largest institutions such as the United Nations (UN) to the emerging and more circumscribed ones like BIMSTEC and the Mekong-Ganga Cooperation Initiative.

The United Nations

As one of the original members of the UN, signing the Declaration by United Nations at Washington in 1942 and participating in the UN Conference of International Organisation at San Francisco in 1945, India has taken its membership in the UN very seriously and played an active role on its deliberations. During the Cold War years, India used the platform of the UN to champion the causes of the developing world by focusing on anti-colonialism, global disarmament, and demanding a more equitable global economic order. The internationalist outlook of India's first Prime Minister, Jawaharlal Nehru, was reflected in India's proactive role in the UN from the very beginning. There was a natural synergy between the goals of the Indian foreign policy in the early years after independence and the principles on which the UN was founded.

It has been suggested that working in, and through, international organizations like the UN serves not only the interests of India but also of the larger international community.[1] India viewed the UN as the central instrument for maintaining peace and security during the tense days of Cold War between the two superpowers. India led the way in demanding that China be allowed to join the UN as well as tried to play the role of a mediator in various Cold War conflicts such as the 1950 Korean War. India was a co-sponsor of the landmark 1960 UN Declaration on the Granting of Independence to Colonial Countries and Peoples that called for a speedy and unconditional end to colonialism in all its forms. India even referred the Kashmir question to the UNSC in 1948. During the 1970s and 1980s, India shifted its focus to challenging the Western-led regional and global order by focusing on issues like nuclear disarmament, the Indian Ocean as a zone of peace, and establishment of a New International Economic Order. India used the UN to put its vision of a nuclear weapons free world before the international community. The most significant of Indian initiatives has been the "Action Plan for Ushering in a Nuclear-Weapon Free and Non-Violent World Order" proposed by then Prime Minister, Rajiv Gandhi, to the Third Special Session on Disarmament of the General Assembly in 1988.[2] The action plan called for a global, universal, and non-discriminatory nuclear disarmament to be accomplished by 2010 in three stages.

India has also provided development resources to the UN, being one of the largest contributors to the UNDP and a major contributor to UNFPSA and UNICEF. India has contributed US$100,000 to the UNCTAD Trust Fund for least developed countries and has been contributing US$50,000 annually to the ITC Global Trust Fund since 1996. India is one of the leading contributors to the UN peacekeeping, having contributed nearly 100,000 troops in more than forty missions. India has served as non-permanent member of the Security Council for seven terms from 1950–52, 1965–67, 1970–72, 1976–78, 1983–85, 1990–92, and 2011–13.

Since the end of the Cold War, though India's engagement with the UN has continued, India's focus has been on a different set of issues. Most significantly, India has been spearheading a move for reforms at the UN to make the world body more representative of the changing global realities while enhancing its credibility and effectiveness. The problems related to peace and international security have become more complex. Uncertainty is the defining feature of the international security environment in the twenty-first century, with a variety of new threats, risks, and more challenges. The challenges and threats facing the international community include terrorism, proliferation of weapons of mass destruction, regional conflicts often exacerbated by the forces of globalization, state failures with concomitant problems of migration, poverty, and organized crime. These are often less visible, unpredictable, and asymmetric. The UN has had a difficult time in effectively dealing with a number of these issues and New Delhi has engaged with the UN on the basis of its changing foreign policy priorities.

India's burgeoning relationship with the United States, for example, has shaped Indian responses to issues like Iraq, Somalia, Afghanistan, Libya, and Iran.[3] Washington's open support for India as a permanent member of an expanded UNSC is viewed as a significant endorsement of India's growing economic power and global aspirations.[4] Though it is highly unlikely that the Security Council will be reformed in the near future, India continues to expend its precious diplomatic capital on pursuing the permanent membership of the Security Council. It is viewed as a foreign policy priority as India has continued to view it as an almost indispensable factor in global politics that needs substantial Indian diplomatic investment.

This view has come under scrutiny, however, with some questioning the need for India's obsession with a seat on the Security Council. The critics argue that India's experience with the UN has historically been underwhelming. Indian national interests have suffered whenever the nation has looked to the UN for support. As the Nehruvian idealism has gradually been replaced by a more confident assertion of Indian national interests, the argument goes, it is time for India to make a more forceful dissociation from the perfunctory modalities of the UN.

Notwithstanding this criticism, the UN continues to be taken seriously and policy elites in New Delhi desire to make it "a platform for establishing India's place in the world."[5] One of the most significant issues in this context involves decisions on where and when to deploy its military assets. Indian policy-makers have been playing safe by making foreign deployments of Indian military contingent on being part of a UN mission. This was perhaps tenable when Indian interests were limited in scope. This policy is under attack as it gives the government a shield from allegations of abdication of its primary responsibility of protecting Indian interests. There continues to remain uncertainty under what conditions India would be willing to use force in defending its interests. Ruling out sending troops to Afghanistan, then Indian Army Chief had suggested that "India takes part only in UN approved/sanctioned military operations and the UN has not mandated this action in Afghanistan so there is no question of India participating in it."[6]

India continues to be one of the largest contributors to these peacekeeping contingents. Indian forces working for the UN have suffered more casualties than any other nation. Indian policy-makers argue that this is being done not for any strategic gain but in the service of global ideals – "strengthening the world-body, and international peace and security."[7]

There was always a calculation that being a leader in UN peacekeeping would help India in its drive toward permanent membership of the Security Council. India remains one of the top sources of peacekeeping contributions though there is a growing concern about the dangers of the changing context of peacekeeping operations as peace enforcement and peacemaking have started gaining salience. It has also become increasingly apparent that the UN by its very nature is inherently militarily incapable of mounting large-scale operations. It is capable only of limited actions such as monitoring or observation and small traditional peacekeeping missions. Yet, despite the ambition of its founders and with the exception of a brief period in the early 1990s, the UN has never professed a military capability or indeed a desire to develop one. The UN is political by nature and cannot be separated from those political characteristics that constrain and restrict the development of the ability to manage a military force.

The post-Cold War international acceptance of the UN's questionable "right to intervene" where it believed it to be necessary allowed the UN to act with little debate.[8] As a result, the nature of the military operations increased both in number and complexity over an extremely short timescale. Additionally, the UN peacekeepers were deployed to environments in which the belligerent parties where not entirely consensual and seriously threatened the safety of the troops under the UN flag. The danger of such a rapid transformation from traditional UN missions to these new operations has been acknowledged widely as the UN's "diplomatic and bureaucratic structures are inimical to initiating and overseeing military efforts when serious fighting rages, and where coercion rather than consent is the norm."[9]

Yet, the activities and interventionist behavior of the international community that flourished in the early years after the Cold War indicated a new appetite for proactive global peace. The Responsibility to Protect report adopted by world leaders at the 2005 World Summit in many ways is a literal articulation of the shift in international mindset from one of where "if it isn't on your doorstep it isn't your problem" to one where a failure to act to save human life is regarded internationally as morally abhorrent. However, member states wishing to intervene for humanitarian reasons are not supported by the legal framework of international society. Since the cessation of the Cold War there have been attempts to reform the international legal system to reflect the rights of the individual over and above those of the state, but these attempts have met resistance. The non-Western world, including India, remains skeptical of these attempts at reforms, believing that any such reforms would afford the privileged few, with the means to intervene, the moral justification to do so.

There is recognition of India's credentials as a major global power. But India still needs to convince the world that it has a legitimate claim to a permanent seat on the Security Council. As a rising global power, India now finds itself in the spotlight and its actions on critical global issues including Iran, Israel-Palestine, Sudan, North Korea, and Myanmar are being scrutinized closely and critically. As a consequence, India will be forced to jettison its old foreign policy assumptions and will have to create a new balance between the pursuit of its narrow national interest and its responsibility as a rising power to maintain global peace and stability.

Global trade and environmental challenges

In recent years, India has coordinated its efforts with other emerging powers, in particular China, on issues as wide-ranging as climate change, trade negotiations, energy security, and the global financial crisis. Both nations favor more democratic international economic regimes. As discussed in Chapter 3, the forces of globalization have led to a certain convergence of Sino-Indian interests in the economic realm, as the two nations become even more deeply engaged in the international trading economy and more integrated in global financial networks. The two have strongly resisted efforts by the United States and other developed nations to link global trade to labor and environmental standards, realizing clearly that this would put them at a huge disadvantage in relation to the developed world, thereby hampering their drive toward economic development, their number one priority. Both have committed themselves to crafting joint Sino-Indian positions in the WTO and global trade negotiations in the hope that this might provide them greater negotiating leverage over other developed states. They would like to see further liberalization of agricultural trade in the developed countries, tightening of the rules on anti-dumping measures and ensuring that non-trade-related issues such as labor and environment are not allowed to come to the WTO. They have fought carbon emission caps proposed by the industrialized world and have resisted Western pressure to open their agricultural markets.

It has been suggested that India is schizophrenic in its negotiating postures: on nuclear issues, particularly after the deal with the United States in 2006, it has shown a proclivity to look after its own interests and not worry too much about its older stand, namely, that the non-proliferation regime was discriminatory and unequal; on trade, however, it has largely stuck to the older ideological position of standing with the developing countries and arguing for justice.[10]

India was one of the founding Contracting Parties to the General Agreement on Tariffs and Trade (GATT) that was concluded in 1947. The eighth GATT round, known as the Uruguay Round, launched in 1986, established the WTO in 1995 to help trade flow smoothly and freely around the world. The Doha Development Round commenced in 2001, committing all nations to negotiations opening agricultural and manufacturing markets, as well as trade-in-services negotiations and expanded intellectual property regulation, but talks have stalled since 2008 primarily because of significant differences between developed nations and major developing nations led mainly by India, Brazil, and China. India was a closed economy until the early 1990s but since then trade reforms managed to push the Indian economy to among the fastest growing in the world. The Doha talks had collapsed in 2008 after coming very close to an agreement primarily because of differences between Washington and emerging economies, led by India, over proposals to help farmers in poor nations. China teamed up with India to scuttle the Doha Round. Because of their much greater economic power compared to the past, states like China and India now have much greater bargaining power. The West has serious differences with the developing countries on the level of protection that can be given to farmers as and when the global market for farm products is opened up. India was blamed for the failure of these talks as the Indian Commerce Minister made it clear that he would not risk the livelihood of millions of farmers.

The United States has suggested that developing nations such as India need to provide greater market access for the talks to advance. India and China argue that they cannot compromise on food security and livelihood concerns even as the United States and the EU remain resistant to scaling down agricultural subsidies for fear of offending their domestic farm lobbies.

After prolonged negotiations, a Bali package was agreed upon in December 2013 which addressed some contentious issues, primarily focused on trade facilitation. Two decades after the establishment of the WTO, 150 states reached a TFA in December 2013 in Bali, Indonesia which was intended to give a fresh lease of life to global trade talks.[11] India agreed to this package after some tough negotiations whereby final decisions on the status of state-supported food programs were postponed until 2017. But New Delhi then did a U-turn in July 2014 by rejecting the TFA, demanding immediate talks on the unresolved issues and rendering moot the entire trade facilitation effort. India threatened to block the signing of the TFA agreed at the Bali Ministerial in 2013 if it did not receive WTO assurance on its policy of stockpiling subsidized grain.[12] The Indian government would have committed political suicide if it had accepted the TFA without being able to show that it had secured the interests of the nation's farmers and safeguarded food security for its poor consumers. Though India received the support of only a handful of nations, including Cuba, Venezuela, and Bolivia, its decision ended up not only jeopardizing multilateral negotiations but also putting the future of the global trade body at risk in its present form.

With the United States, EU, and China more focused on supra-regional trade pacts, many in India have suggested that it will be up to countries like India to put in the extra effort to save and resuscitate the WTO.[13] India has also signed trade pacts with its neighbors and is seeking new ones with countries in East and Southeast Asia as well as the United States. Some of the most significant trade agreements that India has signed include the India-Sri Lanka FTA; trade agreements with Bangladesh, Bhutan, Sri Lanka, the Maldives, China, and South Korea; the India-Nepal trade pact; the Comprehensive Economic Cooperation Agreement with Singapore; framework agreements with the ASEAN; and preferential trade agreements with Afghanistan and Mercosur. India's veto of the TFA was viewed as the beginning of the end for the WTO, potentially leading to a fragmented world of separate trade blocs.

India, however, did not want to be seen as merely an obstructionist power. So after rejecting the TFA, it signed a pact with the United States on the sidelines of the East Asia Summit in Nay Pyi Daw in November 2014 which indefinitely extends the so-called "peace clause" in the TFA. India's food procurement and subsidy program cannot now be challenged in any fora until a conclusive deal on the subject is finalized on the issue.[14] India was also able to reassure the United States that it was not opposed to trade facilitation and in fact was on course to implement it. This India–US understanding is expected to pave the way for the implementation of the TFA, which is meant to simplify customs procedures, facilitate the speedy release of goods from ports, and cut transaction costs.

To understand India's negotiating posture on trade, according to some, one has to comprehend that it tailors its approach to the nature of the issue area and the regime governing that area. Thus, in trade, India has increasingly tended to work with "hybrid coalitions" of countries (coalitions built around a specific issue area such as, say, agriculture, but consisting largely of developing countries); adopted a "distributive," demandeur, naysaying strategy (and tolerated "free riding" by weaker countries in the group); and used "framing" devices based on notions of fairness – fairness conceived of as "legitimacy of process" or as "equity of outcomes."[15] India has sometimes benefited from this negotiating posture and sometimes lost. For instance, its hard stand on the Doha Round has arguably hurt it and others from the developing world, but it has stood firm, playing for the longer term, perhaps with an eye to a bargaining game beyond trade. It has been argued that while India holds ideologically to the importance of solidarity with the developing world, it also sees a larger strategic advantage in doing so: New Delhi's bargaining hand in relation to the developed countries is strengthened if it stands at the head of a bigger coalition of developing countries;

and it is able to deepen relations with countries in Africa, Asia, and Latin America.[16]

What is clear, however, is that as India's role in the global trade negotiations becomes more prominent, there are new pressures on New Delhi to move merely beyond obstruction. It is now more willing than ever before to provide solutions, as has been evident in India's attempt to seek a modus vivendi on the TFA.

Another crucial issue in multilateral diplomacy for India is climate change. India is one of the most vulnerable countries in respect of the effects of climate change and therefore has an enormous stake in a global accord. India was one of the earliest to draw attention to the relationship between environmental protection and development, arguing that economic development for the vast mass of humanity was vital if the environment was to be protected and that the industrial powers had historically been the greatest cause of environmental distress.

International climate change negotiations under the United Nations Framework Convention on Climate Change (UNFCCC) have been taking place against the backdrop of continuing growth in global greenhouse gas emissions and the dangers of rapidly transforming environmental landscape. Over the two decades, following its adoption in 1992 at the first Rio Conference on Environment and Development, while the UNFCCC has achieved important progress toward tackling the climate change challenge, serious differences remain among member states on the best strategy to move forward. The key challenge to the UNFCCC's legitimacy is its perceived lack of effectiveness in producing meaningful progress on climate change mitigation. Its global and consensus-based decision-making is widely perceived as not conducive for reaching agreement on an effective climate treaty.[17] It is being argued that over the last two decades, multilateral negotiations on climate change have become "ossified," "gridlocked," and otherwise unlikely to produce meaningful results in the near future.[18]

The Montreal Protocol came out of lengthy negotiations which unofficially began in 1976 with the UN Environment Programme's call for an international response to ozone depletion and culminated in 1987 with the signing of the treaty. The discovery of the ozone hole on 1985 prompted swift action from states, resulting in the comprehensive Montreal Protocol banning chlorofluorocarbons, which caused much of the damage. After that, however, progress has been tardy. The UNFCCC came into force in 1994 and now boasts of 196 states which are parties to the convention. They have met annually since 1995 in Conferences of the Parties to assess progress in dealing with climate change. The Kyoto Protocol was finalized in 1997, which established legally binding obligations for developed states to reduce their greenhouse gas emissions.

India is a party to the UNFCCC and its Kyoto Protocol as part of which it had voluntarily pledged to reduce its carbon emission by 20 to 25 percent over the 2005 levels, by the year 2020. India has consistently argued that it is unfair to ask developing countries that have played a minor part thus far in creating the problem, to take on greenhouse gas reduction commitments. But India and China are together responsible for a fifth of world's emissions and with their economic growth trajectories, their energy use is on the rise. In 1990 their combined emissions accounted for 13 percent of the world's total; in 2030 the proportion is expected to reach 34 percent, of which China will account for 29 percent. Climate change will critically impair India's economic growth and its ability to meet its developmental goals.

During the 2009 Copenhagen negotiations, India, along with the United States, China, Brazil, and South Africa, brokered a deal in a private meeting, making many developing countries furious who were not willing to adopt a document that had been negotiated in secret.[19] It was during this conference that India joined hands with Brazil, China, and South Africa to form the BASIC group. This group worked out the controversial Copenhagen accord with the United States which called for voluntary reductions in greenhouse gas emissions rather than the mandatory reductions that many other participants favored. India, as part of the BASIC group, is viewed as a country that can play a veto-wielding role in global negotiations and rule-making even though it doesn't seem to have a positive agenda.[20] Despite being the poorest of the four BASIC states, India has tried to make a case of financing its own green agenda by suggesting that "green technology is an area where India can be a world leader" and a country like India "should be able to stand on its own feet and say we will do what we have to do on our own." In recent years, India tried to evolve a more flexible negotiating position which proposed voluntarily cutting Indian emissions through a US$20 billion investment in solar energy, a plan to return a third of its area to forest, and many energy-efficiency measures. Such emission-curbing steps, according to some estimates, could reduce the carbon intensity of India's economy by around 25 percent by 2020 compared with 2005 levels.[21] But these measures did not receive domestic political support after Copenhagen and Cancun and New Delhi reverted back to arguing that a poor country like India could not be expected to take on the economic development costs of solving the climate change problem.[22]

In the climate change debate, Sandeep Sengupta suggests that India has been quite successful.[23] Early on, it chalked out a position consistent with the stance it took in the 1972 Stockholm conference on the human environment, namely, the responsibility of the industrial, chiefly Western, powers in creating environmental problems. Since then, in successive conferences on climate change, India has defended the position that there must be differentiated responsibilities in controlling carbon emissions, that those who created the problem must commit themselves to verifiable reductions in emissions, and that the rich must also provide technology and funding for the poorer countries if the latter are to reduce their carbon dependence. Sengupta concludes that India has succeeded in deeply embedding these norms in the climate change debate and while New Delhi in more recent conferences has had to show some flexibility, it has worked astutely with others in the developing world, including most importantly China, as well as with non-governmental organizations in the developed world to defend those norms.[24]

It remains to be seen of course if this continues to be the case. As things stand, there is growing pressure on India and the larger developing countries such as Brazil and China to commit to some verifiable limits on their carbon emissions. The United States in particular has insisted that it will not sign a climate deal that does not have countries such as India and China committing to limits. There is pressure also from a set of developing countries who argue that India and China should be considered separately: India's argument on differentiation is in effect being turned against it. New Delhi has shown some inclination to move away from its pristine position without giving up the core of its stand. It has also outlined a national energy and environmental plan that will try to reduce its dependence on hydrocarbons. The pressures on India could grow. As a country that will be massively affected by climate change, it needs a deal that will slow down, if not reverse, carbon emissions. Conversely, most developed countries, given their location in more temperate climes, will be less affected – and will be in a position to adapt better given their economic strength. This puts India in a weak bargaining position. In such a situation, perhaps the only realistic way ahead for India is to focus far more than it has in the past on adaptation and to put in place physical and social systems that will help Indians cope with the effects of climate change in the decades ahead. The risks of such a strategy of course are that the richer countries will continue to pollute the atmosphere in the expectation that adaptation, not mitigation, is the only real possibility.

The Modi government that came to power in May 2014 has reiterated its commitment to reduce emissions though its preference remains clear: India cannot address the challenges of climate change unless it eradicates poverty through economic growth.[25] India seems to be hardening its stance in so far as the role of the developed world is concerned toward their larger responsibility to not only cut down emissions but also help out poor nations in taking various mitigation and adaption measures. The negotiations through the UNFCCC are now centered on hammering out a new international agreement to limit global greenhouse gas emissions. There is a growing perception that India is supplanting China as the developing world's chief climate agitator, thereby doing damage to stall progress on international climate negotiations in recent years.[26]

Conclusion

As India becomes a more important player internationally, its engagements with its global interlocutors will come under ever more scrutiny. Indian negotiating positions on key issues of global governance such as trade and environment as well as in multilateral institutions such as the UN will have implications not only for India but also for the larger international system. It remains to be seen if India can leverage its growing heft into balancing its national interest with the requirements of global governance.

Notes

1 C.S.R. Murthy, "Assessing India at the United Nations in the Changing Context," *International Studies*, Vol. 47, No. 2. (2010), p. 26.
2 Details at www.nti.org/media/pdfs/Gandhi_1988.pdf.
3 Teresita C. Schaffer, *India and the United States in the 21st Century: Reinventing Partnership* (Washington, DC: Center for Strategic and International Studies, 2009), pp. 75–8.
4 Scott Wilson and Emily Wax, "Obama Endorses India for UN Security Council Seat," *Washington Post*, November 8, 2010.
5 Shashi Tharoor, "The Capacity to Engage," available at http://tharoor.in/press/the-capacity-to-engage/.
6 "No Indian Troops for Afghanistan, Says Army Chief," *Indian Express*, August 6, 2008.
7 Tharoor, "The Capacity to Engage."
8 Alex J. Bellamy, *Responsibility to Protect: The Global Effort to End Mass Atrocities* (Cambridge and Malden, MA: Polity, 2009).
9 Thomas G. Weiss, *Humanitarian Intervention: Ideas in Action, War and Conflict in the Modern World* (Cambridge: Polity Press, 2007), pp. 24–30.
10 Amrita Narlikar, "India and the World Trade Organization," in Kanti Bajpai and Harsh V. Pant (eds.), *India's Foreign Policy: A Reader* (Oxford: Oxford University Press, 2013), pp. 415–37.
11 Larry Elliott, "Bali Trade Agreement: WTO Set the Bar High But Has Achieved Little," *Guardian*, December 6, 2013.
12 Alyssa Ayers, "India: Tough Talk and the Bali Trade Facilitation Agreement," *Forbes*, July 30, 2014.
13 Rajiv Kumar, "India is Not the Bad Guy, But It Can Do Better," *East Asia Forum*, August 14, 2014.
14 Remya Nair, "India, US Resolve WTO Food Security Row," *Livemint*, November 13, 2014.
15 Narlikar, "India and the World Trade Organization."
16 *Ibid.*

17 Rafael Leal-Arcas, "Top-Down versus Bottom-Up Approaches for Climate Change Negotiations: An Analysis," *IUP Journal of Governance and Public Policy*, Vol. 6, No. 4 (2011).

18 Kathryn Ann Hochstetler, "The G-77, BASIC, and Global Climate Governance: A New Era in Multilateral Environmental Negotiations," *Revista Brasileira De Politica Internacional*, Vol. 55 (2012), p. 53.

19 P. Meilstrup, "The Runaway Summit: The Background Story of the Danish Presidency of COP15, the UN Climate Change Conference," *Danish Foreign Policy Yearbook 2010* (Copenhagen: Danish Institute for International Studies, 2010), pp. 113–35.

20 Andrew Hurrell and Sandeep Sengupta, "Emerging Powers, North-South Relations and Global Climate Politics," *International Affairs*, Vol. 88, No. 3 (2012), pp. 463–84.

21 "Back to Basics," *The Economist*, December 3, 2009.

22 Hochstetler, "The G-77, BASIC, and Global Climate Governance," p. 64.

23 Sandeep Sengupta, "Defending 'Differentiation': India's Foreign Policy on Climate Change from Rio to Copenhagen," in Kanti Bajpai and Harsh V. Pant (eds.), *India's Foreign Policy: A Reader* (Oxford: Oxford University Press, 2013), pp. 389–414.

24 *Ibid.*

25 Vishwa Mohan, "India Invokes 'Right to Grow' to Tell Rich Nations of its Stand on Future Climate Change Negotiations," *Times of India*, June 17, 2014.

26 John Upton, "The India Problem," *Slate*, November 27, 2013, available at www.slate.com/articles/health_and_science/energy_around_the_world/2013/11/india_blocking_climate_talks_warsaw_bangkok_and_kyoto_negotiations.html.

Snapshot 5: India's tryst with terrorism

India's response to a terrorist event follows a predictable pattern: the government pledges to bring the perpetrators to justice while the opposition denounces the government's counter-terrorism policy without offering any constructive solutions. Media coverage surges for a few days but soon reverts back to other more interesting topics.

India faces a structural problem given its location in one of the world's most dangerous neighborhoods – South Asia – which is now the epicenter of Islamist radicalism. India's neighbors harbor terrorist networks and use them as instruments of state policy. The tribal areas along the Pakistan–Afghanistan border, which have long been outside the realm of effective control, have become a breeding ground for Islamist radicals.

India began dealing with the threat of terrorism long before it reached Western shores. The terror saga in the Indian state of Jammu and Kashmir is more than three decades old. But until 9/11, the West viewed the Kashmir problem through the lens of India's inability to improve its human rights record. The threat spiked in the early 1990s; Mumbai witnessed multiple terror strikes in 1993, and then in November 2008, jihadists, aided and abetted by Pakistan's military-intelligence complex, openly confronted the might of the Indian state in full glare of the global media.

Internally, the Indian state is witnessing a gradual collapse of its authority. From left-wing extremism to right-wing religious fundamentalism, it is facing multiple challenges that threaten to derail the story of a rising India. India remains – in the words of Fareed Zakaria – a strong society with a weak state, unable to harness its national power for national purpose. A remarkable degree of uncertainty has gripped Indian internal security, leading to a situation where a band of thugs can force the state to its knees. Violence is becoming the currency of political and social discourse in a modernizing, economically galloping India. Those who seek to challenge the authority of the state feel emboldened enough to take advantage of the disaggregated decision-making processes in New Delhi. Maladministration, dithering, and incompetence are making India ungovernable, with a growing loss of respect for all major state institutions.

There has been a governance deficit in the country in recent years which is affecting every sphere of society – and internal security is no exception. Across the political spectrum, no consensus exists on how best to fight terrorism and extremism. The BJP has been more interested in making terrorism a primarily Muslim issue to generate Hindu votes. The Congress Party, on the other hand, has not allowed open discourse on Islamist extremism to take place for fear of offending Muslim sensibilities. Such vote-bank politics have created an environment in which political and religious polarization has been so complete as to render effective action against terrorism impossible.

India had long claimed to be detached from Al Qaeda or any international terror plot – even though it has the second largest Muslim population in the world. This of course has turned out to be false: every major Islamist urban terror cell in the country since 1993 has seen a preponderance of Indian nationals. India is fast emerging both as a target and a recruitment base for organizations like Al Qaeda and the Islamic State, and attacks are being carried out with impunity by home-grown jihadist groups, trained and aided by organizations in neighboring Pakistan and Bangladesh. Abu Bakr Al Bagdadi, the leader of the Islamic State, has claimed that India, along with neighboring regions in South Asia, belongs to the global Caliphate his group is fighting – and killing – for. Ever since it emerged in mid-2014 that four young men from Mumbai had joined a group of Shia pilgrims and gone to Iraq to fight with the Islamic State, evidence has been mounting of radicalized Indians, including women, trying to make their way to West Asia to join the terror group's ranks. Much like Al Qaeda, the most prominent terrorist group in India today – the Indian Mujahideen – is a loose coalition of jihadists bound together by ideological affiliation and personal linkages, with its infrastructure and top leadership scattered across India. Though India has had experience of dealing with threats from Pakistan-based terror groups like Lashkar-e-Toiba and Jaish-e-Mohammed for more than two decades, a whole new approach and new methods will be needed to cope with organizations like the Islamic State, which banks heavily on social media and the Internet to spread its message

Institutionally, India remains a poor performer with no lessons learned despite numerous tragedies. India's intelligence coordination and assessment apparatus is not suited to the changing nature of the terrorist threat facing the nation. Despite the horrendous attacks on Mumbai in November 2008, it took the government nearly three years to approve the proposal for a National Intelligence Grid, a facility to improve coordination among government agencies to fight terrorism. The other major proposal – to create a National Center for Counterterrorism (NCTC) – is yet to move forward. The government did set up the National Investigation Agency (NIA) to improve intelligence-gathering and sharing but it remains underfunded. Despite the creation of the NIA, modeled on the US FBI, none of the terror investigations in recent years have yet reached their logical conclusion.

Rather than improving grassroots capabilities to effectively counter terrorism, the government has gone for grand initiatives such as the NIA and the NCTC. Police modernization is lagging; the police forces, the frontline agencies in dealing with the threat of terrorism, remain underfunded and ill-trained.

Terrorist organizations appear to be able to strike at will, demoralizing an entire nation even as the government continues to rely on symbolism to deal with terrorism. In this day and age, no government can provide its citizens with a foolproof guarantee against terrorism. But in India, citizens continue to suffer around 700 terror attacks every year without any accountability. Indian policymakers will have to find a way to change this if their ambitions of making India front-ranking global power are to be realized.

Index